COLD ★ WAR
MONTANA

KEN ROBISON

CAPTAIN, UNITED STATES NAVY (RET)

THE
History
PRESS

Published by The History Press
Charleston, SC
www.historypress.com

Front cover: Colonel Fred V. Cherry (*upper left*), first and highest-ranking Black officer among Vietnam POWs, bravely withstood all attempts by his captors to make race in the United States a propaganda issue. *U.S. Department of Defense*; LGM-30 Minuteman II U.S. solid fuel, land-based ICBM (*center*) fired in a missile test launch. *U.S. Air Force*; Colonel Einar Malmstrom (*right*) earned the respect and love of all around him. His impact on the community was so great that local leaders appealed to the U.S. Air Force to change the name Great Falls to Malmstrom Air Force Base. Colonel Malmstrom's painting graces the entrance to the Malmstrom Museum. *Author's photo*; President John F. Kennedy (*lower*) receives a model of PT Boat 109 from young Luke Flaherty as he meets the overflow crowd at Great Falls High School Memorial Stadium in September 1963. *JFK Presidential Library and Museum, ST-C310-117.*

Back cover: Lend-Lease P-39 Airacobra (*upper*), with Soviet Red Star, ready to leave Great Falls to fight Germans on the Eastern Front. Russian Senior Sergeant Andrei Vinogradsky (*right*), who Major Jordon believed "kept tabs" on Colonel Kotikov, stands with Sergeant Bronislava Caplan (*middle*), U.S. WAC interpreter, and Major George Jordon (*left*) on the snow-covered field. *U.S. Army Air Corps*; President Reagan (*lower*) meeting Soviet General Secretary Gorbachev at Höfdi House during the Reykjavik Summit, Iceland, October 11, 1986. *Ronald Reagan Presidential Library, C37406-14.*

First published 2021

Manufactured in the United States

ISBN 9781467149273

Library of Congress Control Number: 2021943563

To Americans who lived through the dangers of the Cold War and supported our strong national defense.

To fellow Cold Warriors, military and civilian, around the world for our successful fight for freedom against Soviet Communism.

To the great American POW heroes we met at Operation Homecoming as we welcomed them back to freedom—Stockdale, Knutson, Cherry, Guenther…and all.

To my family of Cold Warriors—dear Michele, Karin and Mark—as we moved around the world helping our United States Navy confront the "Evil Empire."

CONTENTS

Introduction   7

1. World War II Sets the Stage: An Airlift for Stolen Secrets   15
2. The Iron Curtain Descends: A Cold War Begins   35
3. Proxy War Korea: Montana's Military Power   56
4. The Race for Space: Cuban Missile Crisis and
    the "Ace in the Hole"   108
5. Proxy War Vietnam: Protests and POWs   142
6. The Wall Falls: An End to the Cold War   173

Notes   197
Bibliography   205
Index   213
About the Author   223

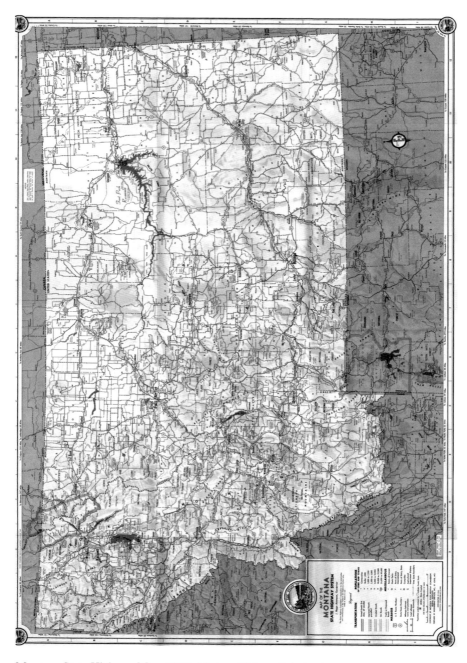

Montana State Highway Map, 1956. *Montana Highway Department.*

INTRODUCTION

What was the Cold War? What did it mean to Americans? Why did the Big Sky Country of Montana play such a significant role in it?

For those of us who lived through those Cold War years filled with danger, we likely know the answers. For new generations, I urge you to learn the Cold War story and pray that in your lifetime we do not have to repeat it.

World War II ended with victory over Nazi Germany and Imperial Japan in the summer of 1945, and Montanans joined in as Americans celebrated in anticipation of many years of peace and prosperity. Thousands of Montana's men and women received their honorable discharges and began planning their futures, attending college, buying homes and raising families. The United States seemed supreme among the victorious Allies—the sole power to possess the atom bomb.

Yet less than one year later, an Iron Curtain was descending on Eastern Europe as wartime smiling Soviet dictator "Uncle Joe" Stalin began to show his paranoia and use his powerful army to occupy the homelands of so many Montana immigrants and their sons and daughters and make strategic moves to spread international Communism. With the Iron Curtain and the series of actions taken by the United States and our allies to contain the spread of Communism, in the four decades that followed, the world teetered on the brink of a third world war, one with no protecting oceans. In the terms of scientists, the world faced an atomic "clock" just minutes and seconds from nuclear holocaust. A protracted Cold War began with both the nuclear-armed United States and its North Atlantic Treaty Organization (NATO) allies facing off against a nuclear-armed Union of Soviet Socialist Republics (Soviet Union) and its puppet Warsaw Pact allies.

Although few understood it at the time, the Cold War began during the depths of World War II. Nazi Germany dominated western Europe and engaged in a desperate struggle on the plains of eastern Europe against the Soviet army and air force. Our Soviet ally of desperation faced seemingly insurmountable odds as it traded blood and land for time. We were building an army, far from ready to open a second front to ease German pressure on the Soviet Union. How could the U.S. "Arsenal for Democracy" help keep our totalitarian communist Soviet ally in the fight until we were armed and ready to begin to roll back the victorious Imperial Japanese in the Pacific and invade Nazi-occupied Europe? Our options centered on just one: arming the Soviets with vital weapons and combat aircraft through the Lend-Lease program.

In this mighty contest, one man had a preview of Soviet intentions. That man was U.S. Army Air Corps Major George Racey Jordan, administering the Lend-Lease program at Gore Field and the newly constructed Great Falls Army Air Base (AAB), where the plains meet the mountains in Montana. Within this Lend-Lease pipeline rested a preview of the Cold War to follow. Major Jordan held the ringside seat as he watched the massive scale of Soviet espionage steal our nuclear and industrial secrets, load them in diplomatic pouches and ferry them through the Lend-Lease pipeline that sent eight thousand aircraft and massive supplies from Great Falls, Montana, to the Soviet Union via Fairbanks, Alaska. The two Great Falls air bases were in reality Red Army Air Bases. Russians were present in numbers in downtown Great Falls and Alaska throughout the war.

Every Montanan—man, woman and child—lived through and participated in the Cold War from 1945 to 1991, whether practicing civil defense drills in school, building radiation fallout shelters or serving our nation in the military or other governmental agencies. And Montana played a most surprising role. Although far distant from Moscow and Washington, D.C., the state's Big Sky broad spaces and thin population made Montana a vital part of the country's Cold War strategy.

During and after World War II, Great Falls served the nation as a great aerial gateway through which passed tremendous military air traffic to and from the Arctic and Alaska. In the early years of the Cold War, Great

Falls Air Base trained pilots and aircrews bound for the Berlin Airlift as Operation Vittles saved that strategic German city from Russian domination. Throughout the 1950s, Great Falls and Glasgow air bases in northern Montana played vital roles in our air defense network, with an innovative Ground Observer Corps mobilized throughout the state until radar sites could be constructed to guide fighter aircraft to intercept Soviet bombers carrying nuclear weapons to attack the northern United States.

In the critical race to field operational Intercontinental Ballistic Missiles (ICBMs), central Montana became the largest missile network in the U.S. arsenal, centered on the renamed Malmstrom Air Force Base at Great Falls. The first U.S. Minuteman ICBMs in Alpha Flight became operational at the height of the Cuban Missile Crisis, providing President John F. Kennedy an "ace in the hole" in forcing the Soviets to back down and remove their missiles from Cuba.

In 1963, less than two months before his tragic assassination, President Kennedy visited Great Falls, paying tribute to its importance in our nation's defense as well as adding a personal touch by visiting the boyhood home of powerful U.S. Senator Mike Mansfield before appearing before a massive crowd at Great Falls High School's Memorial Stadium. Senator Mansfield went on to become the longest-serving, and highly effective, senate majority leader from 1961 to 1977 through many of the years of the Cold War. In his speech in Great Falls that day, President Kennedy proclaimed:

> *Montana is a long way from Washington, and it is a long way from the Soviet Union, and it is 10,000 miles from Laos. But this particular State, because it has, among other reasons, concentrated within its borders some of the most powerful nuclear missile systems in the world, must be conscious of every danger and must be conscious of how close Montana lives to the firing line which divides the Communist world. We are many thousands of miles from the Soviet Union, but this State, in a very real sense, is only 30 minutes away.*[1]

Over the next quarter century to the end of the Cold War, Malmstrom Air Force Base served as a vital component in our nuclear arsenal, and Montana continues in that role today in our post–Cold War world. The Cuban Missile Crisis and the little-known Able Archer Crisis of 1983 brought the United States (and our NATO allies) and the Soviet Union (and its Warsaw Pact allies) to the brink of war. That a catastrophic World War III did not happen is a tribute to both power and luck—the sobering power of the atom and the essential components of good judgment and luck along the way.

As the 1970s progressed, signs of cracks began to appear in the Iron Curtain with events like the Hungarian Revolution, the mutiny on the destroyer *Storozhevoy* and the defection of Lieutenant Viktor Belenko with his Foxbat aircraft. The 1980s brought a series of new leaders to the global stage, and they began performing with one another and the world: John Paul II the Polish pope, Prime Minister Maggie Thatcher in Great Britain, President Ronald Reagan and the new generational Soviet leader Mikael Gorbachev. Their fascinating and vital interaction brought the fall of the Berlin Wall and at last the collapse of the Soviet Union. The Cold War ended in the dramatic year of 1991. The Wall had fallen…Mutual Assured Destruction had ended…the mortal enemy had disintegrated…the Cold War was over. Every Montanan rejoiced, man, woman and child. After all, every Montanan had fought in the Cold War.

Montanans pay tribute to the Cold War and its "proxy wars" in Korea and Vietnam in many ways. Memorials include the Montana State Veterans Memorial in Great Falls; the State Korean War Memorial in Missoula; the Korean War Memorial in Butte; and others. Three major military museums present many aspects of the Cold War. The Malmstrom Museum and Air Park, located on Malmstrom AFB, under Director Rob Turnbow, presents exhibits and history of Great Falls air bases from World War II throughout the Cold War, with an emphasis on the mission and role of Minutemen ICBMs.

The Montana Military Museum at Fort William Henry Harrison in Helena, under Director Ray Read, operates under a memorandum of agreement between the Department of Military Affairs, the State of Montana, the Montana National Guard Museum Activity and the Fort William Henry Harrison Museum Foundation. The museum's displays honor brave Montanans who served Montana and the nation and follow the military in Montana from the arrival of the Lewis and Clark army expedition in 1805 through the Frontier Wars, the Spanish-American War, World Wars I and II, the Korean Conflict, the Vietnam War, Desert Storm and peacekeeping operations.

The Rocky Mountain Museum of Military History, located at Fort Missoula, under Director Tate Jones, presents exhibits and programs covering U.S. military history from the Revolutionary War to the present War on Terror, with an emphasis on the interwar U.S. Army (1920–41). By special arrangement with the Montana National Guard, the museum's

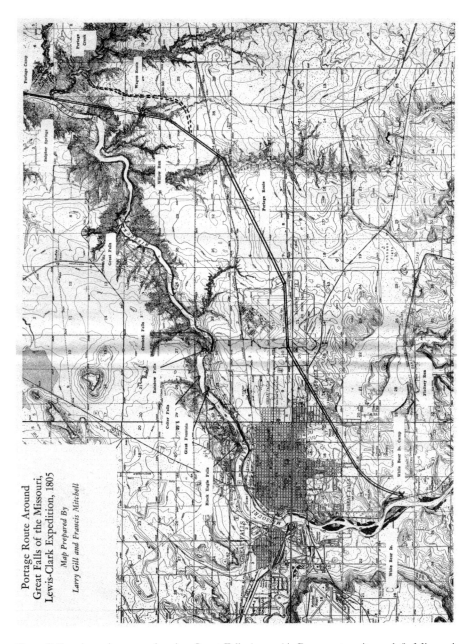

Great Falls orientation map showing Great Falls Army Air Base center, city on left, Missouri River and 1805 Lewis and Clark Portage from southwest to northeast. The portage ran through the center of the air base and just east and south of the city. *Map by Larry Gill and Francis Mitchell; Great Falls Tribune, August 15, 1965.*

I was one who served throughout much of the Cold War. In April 1960, I graduated from the University of Montana and left Montana to begin my U.S. Navy career on the sunny beaches of Pensacola, Florida, at the Naval Aviation School of Pre-Flight. For more than twenty-eight years, my career in Naval Intelligence would keep me intimately involved in our global campaign to maintain peace through strength during those dangerous years that spanned the Cold War. This Montanan was on the frontlines often during these Cold War years, and my commentary will appear throughout this story in sidebars as *Montana in the Cold War* unfolds.

main exhibit building is located in Building T-316, Fort Missoula—the former headquarters for the Fort Missoula District of the U.S. Civilian Conservation Corps.

In addition, many county museums and archives, like The History Museum in Great Falls, hold important materials and photographs of the Cold War. Finally, the immensely important Montana Historical Society holds a treasure-trove of material from throughout Montana's history.

Many have helped assemble this tribute to Montana in the Cold War, including the military museums and directors. My special thanks extend to Troy Hallsell, 341st Missile Wing historian; Megan Sanford, The History Museum; Benjamin Donnelly, University of Providence; Kim Briggeman; Kristen Inbody; Kevin Kooilstra, Western Heritage Center; Rich Aarstad, Montana Historical Society; and Paul Wylie. A very special thanks to Warren Kukay, my Wednesday preservation lunch partner, for our many discussions about his years in the Montana Air National Guard, his time as a security guard for the new Minuteman missiles and his father's World War II years loading Lend-Lease aircraft at Great Falls Army Air Base.

This book is the story of the Cold War, the profound impact it had on Montana and the broad range of ways Montanans participated at home and abroad. You'll meet Montana smokejumpers recruited by the Central Intelligence Agency; those who served as "sky watchers" in the Ground Observer Corps; Montana's men and women who served in the "proxy wars" of Korea and Vietnam, including brave prisoners of war (POWs); those murdered or captured in international incidents around the globe;

Malmstrom Museum and Air Park, located just inside the main gate at Malmstrom Air Force Base. *Author's photo*.

and a sampling of military men and women who served their country knowing that one miscalculation, on either adversarial side, could trigger a nuclear holocaust.

> *Know Your Enemy—Knowledge Is Power*
> If you know the enemy and know yourself, you need not fear the result of a hundred battles. If you know yourself, but not the enemy, for every victory gained you will also suffer a defeat. If you know neither the enemy nor yourself, you will succumb in every battle.
>
> —The Art of War, *Sun Tzu*[2]

Aerial view of Gore Field, home of Seventh Ferrying Group Lend-Lease operations during World War II. Gore Field served as the civil airport and, since 1947, the home of the Montana Air National Guard. *The History Museum, 1991.027.0026.*

CHAPTER 1

WORLD WAR II SETS THE STAGE

AN AIRLIFT FOR STOLEN SECRETS

Great Falls: A Wartime Aviation Center

A little Christmas magic never hurts, and magic is what the delegation from Great Falls needed just after Christmas 1941, as it arrived in wartime Washington, D.C. After a decade of hard work by the chamber of commerce and several favorable army surveys, Great Falls appeared poised for selection for a coveted army air base in the rapid buildup following Pearl Harbor. Yet the delegation, led by Mayor Ed Shields, touched down in D.C. to receive confirmation that the Great Fall base had been tossed in the army's "dead file"—a morgue for plans.

Undaunted, the delegation pressed on to seek a touch of magic. General Henry H. (Hap) Arnold, chief of U.S. Army Air Forces, granted an interview to the men from Great Falls, listened intently to their story and in their presence ordered that the proposed base be reconsidered, raising it from the grave.

Months passed. Wartime secrecy prevailed concerning army plans, until at last, the first word came on April 18, 1942, that an air base would be constructed at Great Falls. Consulting engineer Bill Killgreen, of Ellerbe & Company of St. Paul, arrived with news that work would begin that summer.

Soon, more great news arrived. On June 18, Great Falls was notified that Gore Field, the municipal airport, would host the Northwest Ferrying Command—one of six such bases in the nation. Finally, on July 1, the army announced that a subdepot installation would come to handle supplies for the two big Great Falls air bases and for satellite air bases planned for Glasgow, Lewistown and Cut Bank.

With these dramatic developments, Great Falls and Montana were destined to play leading roles throughout World War II, with prospects that extended into a key role during the Cold War.[3]

LAUNCHING THE SEVENTH FERRYING GROUP

On January 18, 1942, Long Beach Ferrying Group, Air Transport Command (ATC), opened a Northwest Division at the municipal airport at Seattle, Washington. This unit, with Major Leroy Ponton de Arce in command, would ferry B-17 "Flying Fortresses" from the nearby Boeing factory to Alaska for delivery to the Union of Soviet Socialist Republics (USSR).

In May, Colonel William H. Tunner, commanding the ATC Ferrying Division, directed that a survey be made of Spokane, Washington, and Great Falls to relocate the Northwest Division Headquarters away from the West Coast. At that time, aircraft were being ferried north to Alaska by the way of Spokane, but this was proving unsatisfactory. Within a few days, newly promoted Lieutenant Colonel de Arce and staff flew to Spokane, and then to Great Falls, to conduct the survey—and Great Falls was selected.

On June 12, Colonel Tunner directed Colonel de Arce to move his command to Great Falls and execute this mission: "You will take necessary action to organize and operate a ferrying route between Great Falls, Montana and Fairbanks, Alaska, through Lethbridge, Calgary, Edmonton, Fort St. John, Fort Nelson, Watson Lake and Whitehorse, Canada and through Northway and Big Delta, Alaska."

Arrangements fell quickly into place, renting the Civil Center for barracks, opening a mess and setting up bunks and all other needs so that when the soldiers arrived, they had only to fall into bed. Nine days later, Colonel de Arce and his staff left by plane for Great Falls. The move was made "in such fast time that it seemed as though there was no move."

Relocated to Great Falls, the command increased so rapidly that it was nearly impossible to track the many new faces. Operating from Gore Field, the Army Air Corps arrived, soon to be known as the Seventh Ferrying Group. Enlisted men were quartered at the Civic Center and officers at local hotels. The Fine Arts Building at North Montana State Fairgrounds became the group's administration building, while spare aircraft engines filled the Mercantile Building.

Secrecy prevailed in wartime, but the mission of the new army base soon became clear. That mission centered on climate and geography. Great Falls has three hundred days of clear flying weather a year, and it is the southern terminus of the shortest route between the United States and the Soviet Union through Alaska and Siberia. Great Falls was perfect as the southern hub to fly massive numbers of combat aircraft under the Lend-Lease program to the Soviet Union in its desperate struggle against the Wehrmacht on the Eastern Front.[4]

LIKELY A DECISIVE CONTRIBUTION TO THE SOVIET WAR EFFORT

Until the Anglo-American invasion of Normandy in June 1944, the Soviet Union fought the Germans alone in Europe except for the United States– United Kingdom (U.S.-U.K.) strategic bombing campaign. Keeping the Soviets in the war became essential to President Franklin D. Roosevelt's strategy—the United States could provide massive Lend-Lease aid, and the Soviets critically needed it and believed that they were earning it at Leningrad and Stalingrad and all along the brutal Eastern Front.

From the arrival of the first Lend-Lease aircraft at Ladd Army Airfield, Fairbanks, Alaska, on September 3, 1942, after a two-day flight from Great Falls, the Alaska-Siberia (ALSIB) operation was underway. Before it ended, some 8,057 aircraft left U.S. factories for delivery to the USSR via Great Falls over the 8,700-mile ALSIB route. Just 175 aircraft were lost en route, a 98 percent delivery success rate, with 74 lost in the United States, 59 in Canada and 42 in the Soviet Union.

Overall, more than fourteen thousand combat aircraft were delivered under the Lend-Lease program, with almost 60 percent via the ALSIB route. This constituted a critical 12 percent of the wartime Red Air Force strength. American Lend-Lease aircraft made a significant, likely a decisive, contribution to the Soviet war effort.

ATC ferry pilots delivered Bell P-39 Airacobra and Bell P-63 Kingcobra fighters, multi-engine North American B-25 Mitchell and Douglas A-20 Havoc bombers and Douglas C-47 Skytrain transports from U.S. factories to Great Falls. About 1,100 of the ferry pilots were women, civil service

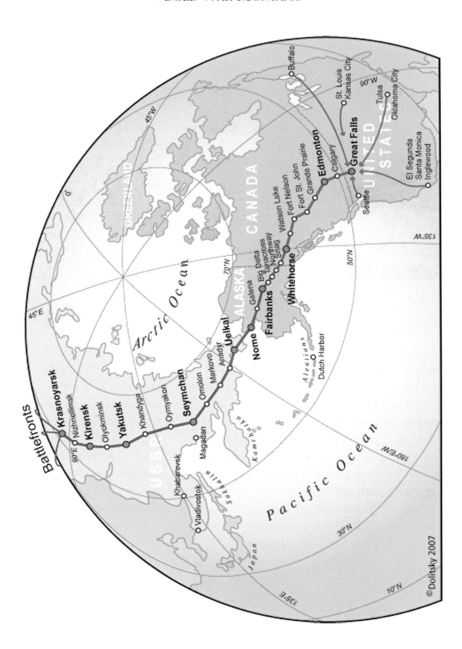

Alaska-Siberia (ALSIB) Lend-Lease route was established in 1943, a year after President Roosevelt extended the Lend-Lease program to the Soviet Union. *ADASRC.*

On July 4, 1944, a wagon and carriage flying an American flag stand next to Lend-Lease B-25 and T-6 aircraft with American markings—soon be changed to Soviet markings and depart for the Soviet Union. *The History Museum, 2008.31.2.*

employees and members of the Women Airforce Service Pilots (WASP) attached to the Army Air Forces—freeing up male pilots for combat duty. From Great Falls to Ladd, army pilots flew the Lend-Lease aircraft, with Soviet red star markings; on the final leg from Alaska to the Soviet-German killing fields, Soviet pilots manned the cockpit.

The ALSIB route via Great Falls also provided a diplomatic route between Washington, D.C., and Moscow, for a wartime safe (though still dangerous) path for officials like Wendell Willkie, Vice President Henry A. Wallace, Soviet Foreign Minister Vyacheslav Molotov and Ambassador Andrei Gromyko.[5]

More than Aircraft:
Stolen Secrets Launched for Russia

Far more than aircraft departed Great Falls for the Soviet Union, for these planes were loaded with almost 4 million tons of military and civilian goods—and buried within these massive shipments was a wide range of stolen secrets.

The U.S. Army officer in charge of expediting deliveries from Great Falls was Major George Racey Jordan, a tough veteran of Eddie Rickenbacker's First Pursuit Group during World War I and a peacetime businessman. Heading the Soviet mission at Great Falls was Colonel Anatoli M. Kotikov, a Soviet hero. The interplay between Jordan and Kotikov became legend, as Major Jordan revealed the extent of Soviet spying through his detailed diaries. Jordan provided evidence that during the Lend-Lease operation, hundreds of undocumented Soviets arrived and spread out across the United States with no accountability. In turn, huge numbers of suitcases under diplomatic seal departed, most uninspected but some opened to reveal classified documents, as well as quantities of uranium and heavy water related to development of the atomic bomb. Major Jordan's attempt to stop this flow of stolen secrets was thwarted directly by powerful White House advisor Harry Hopkins. Clearly, President Roosevelt was willing to pay a heavy price affecting the future of national security of the United States to keep the USSR in the war.

In his diary in March 1943, Major Jordan recorded his impression of the flow of Soviet "visitors":

> After my return to Great Falls I began to realize an important fact: while we were a pipeline to Russia, Russia was also a pipeline to us. One really disturbing fact which brought this home to me was that the entry of Soviet personnel into the United States was completely uncontrolled. Planes were arriving regularly from Moscow with unidentified Russians aboard. I would see them jump off planes, hop over fences, and run for taxicabs. They seemed to know in advance exactly where they were headed, and how to get there. It was an ideal set-up for planting spies in this country, with false identities, for use during and after the war.[6]

To historian Benjamin Donnelly, Great Falls "became a hotbed of Russian spying" during the Lend-Lease program. Donnelly wrote of this espionage activity in the *Great Falls Tribune*:

> The commander of the Soviet side of the Lend-Lease arrangements arrived in early 1943. Col. A.M. Kotikov already was well-known in aviation circles as a pilot and parachutist; he had pioneered the "Great Circle" route over the North Pole, now commonplace for airliners.
>
> He and his wife stayed at the downtown Pennsylvania Apartments. The Russians were generally well-liked, though the officers acquired a reputation for not paying their bar tabs.

Above: Douglas A-20 Havoc Lend-Lease bomber at Gore Field, painted with Soviet Red Star marking and ready for the long journey to the Eastern Front. *The History Museum, 2008.031.0027.*

Right: Colonel Anatoli M. Kotikov (*left*), head of Soviet mission at Great Falls, pins new promotion rank on Major George Racey Jordan, U.S. Lend-Lease liaison officer. *U.S. Army Air Corps Photo.*

…As Lend-Lease went into full swing, [Gore Field] *became one of the busiest airfields in the Northwest. Aircraft either would be flown in, usually by Women's Air Service Pilots (WASPs), or brought in on railroad flatcars.*

Once at the base, aircraft would be assembled if necessary and prepared for cold-weather duties. The planes then would have their temporary American insignia replaced with the red star of the Soviet Union.

Though officially belonging to the USSR, American pilots would fly the aircraft to Alaska, where Soviet pilots would take over for the 8,700-mile journey to the Russian Front.

More than 7,600 aircraft would make the long trip, including P-39 Airacobra fighters, A-20 Havoc light bombers, T-6 Texan trainers and C-47 Skytrain transports. The Russians liked the P-39 the best, referring to them as cobrastochkas*—"brave little cobras."*

Aircraft were not the only thing the Russians took home. [Gore Field] *became a hub for Soviet spies.…On one occasion, Maj. George Jordan…opened some of the sealed Russian cargo, expecting to find smuggled morphine capsules.…Instead he found American industrial data, railroad timetables and data on the top-secret atomic research plant at Oak Ridge, Tenn., the home of the Manhattan Project. Some of the documents were signed by Alger Hiss, a spy exposed in a sensational 1950s trial.*

It is also estimated that several tons of enriched uranium was shipped… to Russia, and became the foundation for the Soviet nuclear program.[7]

Great Falls Army Air Base

On April 18, 1942, engineer Bill Killgreen and a survey team selected an area more than three and a half square miles near the Green Mill Dance Hall and Rainbow Dam Road, about six miles east of Great Falls—along the portage route made famous by explorers Lewis and Clark. The popular Green Mill hosted Louis Armstrong's jazz band shortly before the dance hall fell victim to wartime need. Construction on the new air base began on May 9, with prime contractors for the airfield Birch-McLaughlin of Great Falls beginning work one month later to prepare runways and other facilities.

Over the summer, contractors and workers transformed this stretch of bare Montana prairie at breakneck speed into the bustling community

A Boeing B-17E Flying Fortress four-engine heavy bomber flying a training mission out of Great Falls. *Author's collection.*

Sign commemorating the Lewistown satellite bomber training base, including 358th Bomb Group–548th Bomb Squadron (*top center*) at Great Ashfield England circa late June 1943, shortly after leaving Lewistown, and airmen from 2nd Bomb Group–49th Bomb Squadron (*bottom center*). *Author's photo.*

of Great Falls Army Air Base (AAB), known informally as "East Base," ahead of schedule. East Base was activated on August 20, when 352nd Headquarters Squadron moved in from Pendleton Field, Oregon.

By November 27, the runways, taxiways and parking aprons had been paved, and the base was ready for its initial mission: heavy bomber training under the Second Air Force, preparing B-17 aircrews for combat operations in Europe and the Pacific. Ranges were set up for high-altitude bombing and strafing practice, and by the end of 1942, Great Falls AAB and its satellites were in operation. The first B-17 Flying Fortress landed on November 30, and over the next eleven months, four bombardment groups—the 2nd, 385th, 390th and 401st—trained for war at Great Falls and satellite bases Glasgow, Lewistown and Cut Bank.

The four-engine B-17s would take off at set times, form up in squadron formations and, later, over central Montana, join up in group formations. More than 2,200 bomber crews were trained in Montana for about four months in their final phase of training. These bombardment groups then went on to participate in critical bombing campaigns from bases in North Africa, Italy and England.

The winter of 1942–43 was extremely severe, and when spring thaws came, runways began to settle and crack; as the concrete weakened, the runways could not support heavy bomber operations. The high cost of runway repairs caused B-17 training to end in October 1943, and the satellite fields closed as well.[8]

The 34th Subdepot in Operation

The Air Service Command's 34th Subdepot assumed command on October 16, 1942, relocating its operations to the air base from the fairgrounds. Under the command of Major Alexander Cohn, the subdepot formed at Great Falls in July 1942, using temporary quarters at the Cascade County shops building, east of the fairgrounds. A staff of eight officers built up a civilian workforce of four hundred, recruited locally with many World War I veterans and young women, avoiding draft-aged men. The subdepot was one of several scattered around the nation to serve as the vital supply organization for the army air arm, designed to function as a tremendous "garage" for repair and a "filling station" for planes, with a huge parts and supply department in a giant supply and maintenance center.

The feminine touch is applied to a motor "tune-up" at the Great Falls Air Service Command Subdepot. Beth Gross, *left*, from Walla Walla, Washington, and Isabell Harwood, from Great Falls, trained aircraft mechanics, were two local women filling roles to free men for combat duty. *From the* Great Falls Tribune, *October 5, 1942.*

The subdepot had three major functions: administrative, supply and engineering. Put together, this combination consisted of extensive records keeping, large-scale warehouse storage and maintenance, repair and refueling—all in support of army air operations at Great Falls and the three satellite bases.[9]

LEND-LEASE OPERATING AT BOTH AIR BASES

Jurisdiction of Great Falls AAB passed to the Air Transport Command on January 1, 1944, and the Lend-Lease program began operations at both bases. As one measure of the pace of Lend-Lease operations at its height, during the first four months of 1944, 2,200 aircraft went to the Soviet front lines over this ALSIB route—almost 20 aircraft per day. To maintain this rate, ferry aircraft were received from factories, inspected and had any necessary repairs made; winterized; had Soviet markings implanted, including the prominent red star; had cargo loaded, both legal and contraband; were refueled; and were launched on their way to the Soviet Eastern Front. This all required a herculean effort sustained throughout the thirty-one-month life of the program.

AIR FORCE ANTHEM

Off we go into the wild blue yonder.
—a Seventh Ferrying Group entertainer

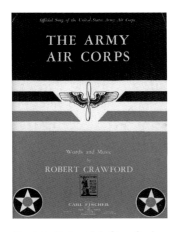

Captain Robert M. Crawford created the Army Air Corps anthem, which served during World War II and became the U.S. Air Force anthem. Captain Crawford and his family lived in Great Falls from 1944 to 1945 while serving the Seventh Ferrying Group. *Author's collection.*

These words begin the famed "Army Air Corps March," composed by Captain Robert M. Crawford, who was stationed in Great Falls during 1944–45 with the Seventh Ferrying Group. Born in Dawson City, Yukon, in 1899, Crawford tried to enlist in the Army Air Service in World War I but was dismissed when his age was discovered. After the war, he graduated from Princeton University and then studied and taught music at the Juilliard School. He learned how to fly airplanes and flew around the United States to concerts, performing as "The Flying Baritone." In 1938, *Liberty* magazine sponsored a musical composition contest for a song that would become the official song of the U.S. Army Air Corps. Out of hundreds of submissions, Crawford's was selected as the winner. The song was officially previewed at the Cleveland Air Races on September 2, 1939, where Crawford first sang it in public.

During World War II, Captain Crawford flew as a ferrying pilot for the Seventh Ferrying Group, stationed in Great Falls with his wife and four sons. In a talk to the local Kiwanis, Captain Crawford said, "Gore Field is ranked highest among the ferry command stations by ferry pilots and crews." While ferrying bombers, he actively performed his compositions at benefits around the West, adding another composition, "Born to the Sky," as a tribute to the Air Transport Command. Today, as you sing the U.S. Air Force song, remember Captain Robert Crawford, the composer, as he ferried and entertained in support of the war.[10]

FIGHTING FOR TWO COUNTRIES: GALLANT HAZEL YING LEE

Hazel Ying Lee died from a fiery crash of her P-63 fighter aircraft at Great Falls AAB on November 25, 1944. Her P-63 was one Lend-Lease aircraft that would not see action against the Germans on the Eastern Front. Hazel was the first Chinese American woman to fly for the U.S. military and the last of 38 women to die flying for the WASP program. A shortage of male pilots in World War II led to creation of the WASP program, made up of some 1,100 female pilots serving under military command.

Born in 1912 into an ethnically Chinese family in Portland, Oregon, Hazel fell in love with flying after her first flight in 1932. Within months, she earned a pilot's license, and the next year, she traveled to China to join the Chinese Air Force. Turned away because of gender, she served as a pilot for a private airline in southern China. When war with Japan began in 1937, she tried again to join the Chinese Air Force but again was rejected. In 1938, Hazel fled advancing Japanese troops and spent most of a year as a refugee in Hong Kong before returning to the United States.

In 1943, Hazel Lee was among the first to enroll in the WASP program and complete the grueling six-month training program. Based in Romulus, Michigan, she ferried aircraft from factories to military bases, primarily Great Falls. In September 1944, she attended Pursuit School at Brownsville, Texas, one of 132 women pilots to qualify to fly P-51, F-47 and P-63 fighter aircraft. While ferrying a P-63 Kingcobra fighter from Niagara Falls, New York, to Great Falls, in the early afternoon on November 23, she collided with another P-63 aircraft with an inoperable radio while landing at Great Falls AAB.[11]

For decades, members of the WASP and their supporters attempted to secure military status for these brave women pilots who flew more than five thousand aircraft to Great Falls for delivery to the Soviet Union. Finally,

Hazel Ying Lee, *left*, Women Airforce Service Pilot, ferried Lend-Lease aircraft from factories to Great Falls. She was the first Chinese American woman to fly for the U.S. military and tragically died in a midair collision at Great Falls AAB. Private First Class Emma Jane "Windy" Windham Burrows, *right*, served at Great Falls AAB, becoming the first crew chief and aerial engineer in the Women's Auxiliary Army Corps. Windy died in a fatal crash in England when her B-17 was struck by a C-47. *U.S. Air Force.*

in March 1977, following U.S. Congressional approval of Public Law 95-202, the efforts of the WASP were recognized and military status granted. In 2004, Hazel Lee was inducted into Oregon's Aviation Hall of Honor for native Oregonians who made historic contributions to aviation. Hazel Ying Lee left a remarkable legacy of inclusion and bravery in service of her country.[12]

FIRST SPECIAL SERVICE FORCE: THE DEVIL'S BRIGADE

Early in World War II, a most unconventional fighting force formed in secrecy in the mountains of Montana, and all U.S. Special Forces and Canadian Special Operations Regiments that have followed are direct descendants. The First Special Service Force (FSSF) was formed with three elite light infantry regiments composed of Canadians and Americans. Organized and trained in the summer of 1942 at Fort William Henry Harrison in the Helena Valley, they specialized in high alpine combat, covert amphibious landings, parachuting and nonconventional tactics. Their mission was to slip behind German lines to create chaos while targeting and sabotaging enemy military and industrial installations.

Born in the fertile mind of Englishman Geoffrey Pyke, on the staff of Lord Louis Mountbatten, chief of combined operations, and promoted by Prime Minister Winston Churchill, the Force formed and prepared over eight months of rigorous training. The only joint U.S.-Canadian unit during the war, the FSSF never failed a mission and suffered 2,314 casualties (134 percent of original combat strength) in conducting key raids against the German First Panzer Paratroop Division and capturing Rome.

Earning the nickname the "Devil's Brigade" for their painted faces, nighttime combat raids and stealth tactics, this 1,800-man force—composed of 900 Americans and 900 Canadians—accounted for 12,000

Sergeant Del J. Stonehouse, 5th Company, 2nd Battalion, First Special Service Force, from Forest, Ontario, Canada, standing in center. Signed by Sergeant Stonehouse. *Author's collection.*

German casualties, while capturing 7,000 prisoners during the war. In 2015, this pioneer special forces regiment received the Congressional Gold Medal, the highest civilian honor awarded by Congress. In the words of Speaker John Boehner, "For every man they lost, they killed 25. For every man captured, they took 235. The force was so fearless, that the enemy dubbed them 'the Devil's.'"[13]

THE ALASKA HIGHWAY: THE "ROAD TO CIVIL RIGHTS"

Another major project with tentacles reaching Great Falls was the Alaska Highway, built through 1,700 miles of rugged wilderness from Dawson Creek, British Columbia, Canada, to Delta Junction, Alaska, in just six months during 1942. Great Falls was considered the jumping-off point for that land route, extending 2,300 miles to Fairbanks, important militarily in the event the Japanese navy cut off sea access to Alaska.

Soldiers of the U.S. Army Corps of Engineers Corporal Refines Sims Jr., *left*, and Private Alfred Jalufkamet meet in the middle after completing construction of the Alaska Highway. *U.S. Army Corps of Engineers.*

As it was one of the most difficult construction projects ever completed by the U.S. Army Corps of Engineers, eleven thousand men were required, including about one-third African Americans from four regiments: the 93rd, 95th and 97th Engineer General Service Regiments and the 388th Engineer Battalion. Their greatest accomplishment was constructing Sikanni Chief River Bridge over a fast-moving river three hundred feet wide, built without heavy equipment. The success of these Black engineers on the Alaska Highway provided impetus to the postwar desegregation of the military, and this important wartime highway has been called the "Road to Civil Rights." At a cost of $138 million, the Alaska Highway, completed on October 28, 1942, was the most expensive U.S. World War II construction project.[14]

THE WORLD WAR ENDED
AT THE DAWN OF THE ATOMIC AGE

After the United States dropped atomic bombs first on Hiroshima and then Nagasaki, the end of World War II unfolded slowly like a Kabuki dance. Finally, on September 2, 1945, the formal surrender ceremony was held onboard USS *Missouri* in Tokyo Bay. A bloodbath invasion of the Japanese homeland was averted by the dawn of the atomic age. The United States emerged from the war as the world's sole atomic power, and a Montanan had played a key role in developing that weapon of new dimensions: Dr. Harold C. Urey.

Dr. Harold C. Urey and the Manhattan Project

On February 18, 1946, Dr. Harold C. Urey returned to Missoula, Montana, to deliver the 53rd Charter Day address at the University of Montana.[15] His speech, "ATOMIC ENERGY: Master or Servant?," was masterful, considering just who Dr. Urey was and his timing, just seven months after the first atomic bombs had been dropped on Japan—just as the Cold War was dawning.

Harold Urey graduated from the University of Montana in 1917 with a Bachelor of Science in chemistry and then taught there for two years. He worked as a physical chemist whose pioneering work on isotopes, isolating heavy hydrogen, earned him the Nobel Prize in chemistry in 1934. Urey

Members of the Emergency Committee of Atomic Scientists meeting to plan an educational campaign on atomic energy. *From left to right, seated*: Harold C. Urey, Albert Einstein and Selig Hecht. *From left to right, standing*: Victor F. Weisskopf, Leo S. Szilard, Hans A. Bethe, Thorfin R. Hogness and Philip M. Morse. *From the* St. Louis Post-Dispatch, *November 18, 1946.*

went on to play a significant role in the development of the atom bomb as a key member of the Manhattan Project.

Dr. Urey spoke that day in Missoula about the power of the atom and its potential path in the future, in peace and war:

> *On December 2, 1942, under the West Stand of Stagg Field at the University of Chicago, there occurred an event which marks a turning point of first magnitude in history. This was the generation of heat at a constant, steady level from atomic reactions. This was a first miniature power unit, a prototype of the power units which may be developed in the years to come and which may have enormous industrial importance.*
>
> *On July 16, 1945, in the deserts of New Mexico, occurred another event in which atomic energy was liberated in the form of an explosive chain reaction. This event also marks a transition from the past in the use of atomic energy for destructive purposes. These events will influence our*

lives for years to come, and in fact, will influence all of history in the future. If the former of these is predominant in the future, we may expect increased well-being for men; while if the latter becomes predominant in the future, we may expect that civilization as we know it today may be destroyed, never to rise again. In view of these spectacular events of the last years, it is well for thoughtful people to consider carefully what the future may bring, and to exercise if possible some choice in regard to future events.

…These discoveries of nature's laws and the inventions based upon them are not in themselves evil for it is only the use which men make of these things that leads to constructive or destructive results.

…The problem of the atom bomb is not primarily the problem of that instrument of warfare but the problem of war itself.

…It is of interest to consider what could possibly be the future development in a possible Third World War. Such a war may start with atomic bombs, or it may start with other mass destruction weapons and finish with atomic bombs.

…Had the development of atomic energy occurred in peacetime, the development of peacetime uses would have been predominant, and the development of the atomic bomb might have been delayed until later.

…There is no defense against the atomic bomb, and there never will be any defense. It is well to remember this in thinking of the possible solution of the problems of modern war.

…Accepting these statements—and so far as I know, all the informed atomic scientists on the entire Manhattan Project accept without question— it is necessary to review other methods for the defense of a country such as the United States.

…The greatest accomplishment of the Manhattan Project was neither the production of the atomic bomb, which is wholly evil, or the possible peacetime industrial use of atomic energy. The greatest accomplishment, in which all scientists who worked on this project take great pride, was the unlocking of nature's secrets and the production of events which never took place anywhere else in all the universes of the heavens. Nuclear chain reactions of the controlled kind or of the explosive kind are probably novelties of this earth and do not occur anywhere in the billions of stars of our milky way unless some other particle of dust such as our earth is inhabited by intelligent beings such as ourselves. Science, literature, art and all the intellectual pursuits of man are particularly those of our species. It is these of which we are all proud. It is the contribution to these things of which scientists of the atomic bomb project are proud. We ask your help

and offer ours to you for a united effort toward making this a safe and secure world in which man's constructive genius in all lines of human endeavor may expand. We ask your help and offer ours to the end that the destructive uses of science shall not destroy its constructive uses and all else of value in this civilization.[16]

CHAPTER 2

THE IRON CURTAIN DESCENDS

A COLD WAR BEGINS

Smiling Joe Stalin, leader of our wartime ally the USSR, was smiling no more—just a pose for wartime propaganda posters. Joseph Vissarionovich Stalin, general secretary of the Communist Party and chairman of the Council of Ministers of the Soviet Union, ruled supreme—and he knew it. Of his wartime allies, President Franklin D. Roosevelt was dead, and Prime Minister Winston Churchill of the United Kingdom was voted out of office. Stalin's postwar agenda centered on *security*—security for Joe Stalin, security for his Communist Party, security for the Soviet Union and security for the Communist international movement. Britain retained pretense but weakened power, while the United States faced the reality of superpowerdom brought with victory in the war and its awesome atomic power—delicately balanced by its unaccustomed role as world leader.

The myth of "free elections" in Eastern Europe evaporated under Soviet jackboots as the Baltic States, Poland, Romania and part of Finland were swept up, with others soon to follow. Even Western Europe wavered under the weight of Communist moral authority, earned by leading partisan warfare against the Germans during the war.[17]

"Wartime Big Three." *From left to right*: Joseph Stalin, Franklin D. Roosevelt and Winston Churchill on portico of the Russian embassy during the Tehran Conference in December 1943. *Library of Congress.*

CHURCHILL'S IRON CURTAIN SPEECH: AN IRON CURTAIN DESCENDS

On a warm spring day, March 5, 1946, in a small college town in Missouri, former British Prime Minister Winston Churchill spoke words that became the clarion call beginning the Cold War. Accompanied and introduced by President Harry Truman, Churchill accused Soviet Russia of seeking "indefinite expansion" of its power. As he spoke, the great wartime leader of Britain urged an Anglo-American alliance to police a postwar world in which an "iron curtain" descends on Europe:

> *A shadow has fallen upon the scenes so lately lighted by the Allied victory. Nobody knows what the Soviet Russia and its Communist international organisation intends to do in the immediate future, or what are the limits, if any, to their expansive and proselytising tendencies....*

> *From Stettin in the Baltic to Trieste in the Adriatic, an iron curtain has descended across the Continent. Behind that line lie all the capitals of the ancient states of Central and Eastern Europe. Warsaw, Berlin, Prague, Vienna, Budapest, Belgrade, Bucharest and Sofia, all these famous cities and the populations around them lie in what I must call the Soviet sphere, and all are subject in one form or another, not only to Soviet influence but to a very high and, in many cases, increasing measure of control from Moscow....The Communist parties, which were very small in all these Eastern States of Europe, have been raised to pre-eminence and power far beyond their numbers and are seeking everywhere to obtain totalitarian control. Police governments are prevailing in nearly every case, and so far, except in Czechoslovakia, there is no true democracy.*[18]

Montana's Reaction

The morning after Churchill's dramatic "Iron Curtain" speech, the *Billings Gazette* reported:

> *Briton Urges U.S. Pact*
> *If Winston Churchill had not scaled heroic heights as Britain's doughty wartime prime Minister, history might have recorded him as the tragic figure who tried vainly and virtually alone to rouse his country and the world to the seeds of World War II sprouting in Germany.*
>
> *Britain's distinguished elder statesman...raised a warning voice as he had a score of years ago. He spoke in a little college town, Fulton, Mo., and this time the whole world listened.*[19]

While Congressional response to Churchill's speech varied, Montana's senior senator, Burton Wheeler (Democrat), said that he found Churchill's address confirmed fears that he, Wheeler, had expressed before the United States became involved in World War II. Senator Wheeler declared, "Instead of making Europe safe for democracy, we seem to have succeeded in making it safe for communism."[20]

Senator Burton Wheeler had become an institution in national and Montana politics since he first entered the Senate in 1923. He broke party ranks with President Franklin Roosevelt over Supreme Court packing and became a leader in the isolationist movement prior to Pearl Harbor.

Yet Senator Wheeler would be defeated narrowly just three months after Churchill's speech in the Democratic Party primary by internationalist Leif Erickson for many reasons, not least because Wheeler had lost, at last, his strong support from Montana's urban, labor counties. Erickson, in turn, would lose in the general election of 1946 to conservative Republican Zales Ecton.[21]

UNITED NATIONS FIRST GENERAL ASSEMBLY: THE EXPLOSIVE COLD WAR ISSUE OF DISPLACED PERSONS

President Truman asked Eleanor Roosevelt, widow of President Roosevelt, to serve on the U.S. delegation at the first meeting of the United Nations (UN) General Assembly in London in January 1946. Roosevelt was assigned to the Human, Social and Cultural Committee, and there she took on the Soviet Union over the explosive issue of displaced persons (DPs). In postwar Germany, about 1 million Eastern and Central Europeans resided in refugee camps. The Soviet Union wanted them returned to their home countries, now under Soviet domination behind the rapidly descending Iron Curtain. The refugees, DPs, were a mix of anti-Communists, Catholics and Jews, all fearful that death awaited them if they were sent home.

Eleanor Roosevelt took up their cause, arguing that they were not "fascists" or traitors as the Russians claimed. The powerful Andrei Vishinski—Stalin's legal mastermind behind the Soviet Great Purges of the 1930s—led the Soviet delegation. In dueling speeches, Eleanor Roosevelt took on Vishinski in the General Assembly, clearly and forcefully presenting the case for the DPs to have resettlement freedom, based on the rights of man. She infuriated Vishinski but prevailed. The DPs, saved from sure death, were resettled in Western countries, including the United States.[22]

MONTANA'S DISPLACED PERSONS

The Christian Rural Overseas Program (CROP) was organized in the United States, and Montana state director Dr. H.G. Klemme, of Bozeman, toured the state, promoting this program designed to bring relief to millions in the war-torn countries. Rural Chouteau County chairman Bill

Johnstone joined Dr. Klemme in October 1948 to promote CROP at Fort Benton. Dr. Klemme spoke:

> *We are bringing some needy people to your door. Some of them are hungry—some are near starvation. Some of them are ill. All of them are undernourished or suffering from malnutrition. Most of them are homeless, and many are hopeless. Millions of them are children orphaned by war's mad upheaval. Thousands of these children have rickets or tuberculosis. Hundreds were maimed by bombs or shell fire.*
>
> *We are bringing to your door thousands of displaced persons who have no home, no work, no future. They merely roam from place waiting for whatever tomorrow may hold....*
>
> *We bring them to your doors—you people whose homes have not known the blight of bombers or the destroying fury of artillery fire. To you, whose crops this year have set an all-time record high. To you, whose children, well-fed and well-clothed, go to school without fears or terrors. To you, who can so easily give out of your great prosperity the money and the food to keep life and hope alive for millions of our destitute fellowmen....*
>
> *Your county committee has organized to solicit food and money. As state director for Montana, I urge your cooperation with them and plead for your generosity.*[23]

Montanans responded both with money for camps and by sponsoring DPs to move to their communities. At least 351 DPs settled around Montana, with Reverend Russell Scheidler of Fairfield and the National Catholic Welfare Conference playing leading roles. Holy Rosary Hospital in Miles City became home for seventeen displaced persons, while Billings welcomed many.[24]

Fort Benton greeted Mr. and Mrs. Andreas Wenhardt and their twin eight-month-old sons. Andreas Wenhardt, of German descent from Yugoslavia, had been held for forced labor in Serbia and Russia before escaping to Austria. There he met and married his wife. Reverend Roger Robison, Frank Morger and dozens of other Fort Benton residents contributed funds to enable the Wenhardts to open the Benton Bakery.[25]

Farmer Elmer Dostal, just returned from combat action with the Marine Corps in the Pacific, and his family welcomed teenage Miloslav Vanasek to work on their farm on Square Butte Bench. St. Margaret's Parish in Geraldine sponsored Vanasek, who was born in 1930 in Czechoslovakia.[26]

THE IRON CURTAIN DESCENDS

Throughout 1946, the Soviet Union worked to translate its military presence in Eastern Europe into political power. Montana, with its large immigrant population from Central and Eastern Europe, followed developments closely as the Soviets forged their buffer-bloc that in time would become the Warsaw Pact. The *Great Falls Tribune* carried news of keen interest to the ethnic workers at the Anaconda Copper Mining Company's copper and zinc refineries:

> *SOVIETS DRIVING TO SOLIDIFY CONTROL IN EASTERN EUROPE*
> *Washington, Aug. 11 (AP)—American officials are studying current Communist moves to smash political opposition in Romania…with the aid of its local Communist leaders, appeared to be making a desperate drive—concurrent with Paris peace treaty drafting—to solidify control through eastern Europe.*
>
> *The state department is expected to make a formal statement of its views on the situation Monday. Meanwhile authorities were privately describing events in Romania, involving the detention of Romanian citizens employed by the American government there, as part of a general pattern by which an effort is being made to sweep away political opponents of the Red regimes before the peace treaties can become effective.*
>
> *It is expected here that imposition of the peace treaties will considerably curtail Russia's action in some areas, notably Romania, Bulgaria and Hungary, although so long as they manage to keep Russian army forces in any of those countries they will have effective local control.*[27]

The same issue of the *Great Falls Tribune* carried more ominous international news in two editorials about the civil war in China and the Paris Peace Conference. In China, General George C. Marshall was just admitting the complete breakdown of his arbitration efforts between Chiang Kai-shek's Kuomintang nationalist government and Mao Zedong's Communists. In Paris, the five peace treaties under consideration with the former Axis partners were far from finished, and attempts by the Big Four (United States, United Kingdom, France and the Soviet Union) to make peace with Germany and Austria were hopelessly deadlocked. The "Iron Curtain" of Soviet expansion in Churchill's warning to America was happening.[28]

An Airshow Tragedy:
The 1946 Great Falls Fair Air Collision

It was early August harvest time in Montana, and that meant the North Montana State Fair in Great Falls, which was still glowing in the aftermath of the great victory over fascism. Servicemen were being discharged daily and coming home to resume their hard-earned lives, with many taking advantage of the G.I. Bill to attend college in Bozeman or Missoula or to buy homes. Unlike many army installations, Great Falls AAB was not to be abandoned as the nation rapidly downsized its massive military. Rather, the base was designated to become a permanent installation as a gateway to Alaska and the Arctic. With its wartime growth in military and industry, Great Falls was fast becoming Montana's largest city.

Fair time in Great Falls always brought huge crowds from all across northern Montana. Yet this was a special fair, resuming the North Montana State Fair after its wartime cancelation in 1945—people were coming for a blowout celebration of peace and prosperity. More than fifty-three thousand flocked through the gates during the first two days to visit the Midway, agricultural exhibits and historic Old Town, as well as to attend the horse races, rodeo and night shows. Both civilians and former soldiers visited a popular army exhibit featuring captured enemy weapons.[29]

The "Shoots the Works" Tragedy

On Wednesday, August 7, the Army Air Corps put on an aerial demonstration for a near-record crowd in the grandstands. Billed as "just a preview" of the big Army Air Show planned for Friday, this thirty-minute event thrilled spectators with a jet P-80 Shooting Star and other combat aircraft performing aerial acrobatics at low level and close range. Various types of army aircraft demonstrated speed, aerobatics and precision flying, with the Shooting Star stealing the show by blazing before the grandstand at more than six hundred miles per hour.

Pilots demonstrated techniques of strafing following the half-mile racetrack and other tactics used in World War II aerial warfare, and all this was billed as just a preview of what could be expected on Friday.

Friday morning, August 9, arrived, with *Tribune* readers greeted by the headline, "Army to 'Shoot the Works' at Fair Air Show Today."

My mother, sister and I, age seven, were among the crowd in the grandstands that tragic day. Seated forward of the center of the stands, we watched the A-26s approach from the south. Just as they began to pass at low level in front of the stands, we began to see material falling from the aircraft. My first thought was that they were dropping chaff as part of the show. But just then, one of the aircraft burst into flames and began falling from the sky. All the while, the public affairs announcer called for calm and an orderly exit, and we began to be moved with the crowd toward the exit stairs on the south side of the stands. I didn't want to leave—I didn't understand what was happening, but it was all so fascinating that I wanted to stay and watch.

With a capacity crowd of twenty thousand in the grandstands cheering on rodeo events commencing early in the afternoon at 1:45 p.m. and the first of seven horse races, the air show was slated to begin at 2:05 p.m.[30]

The opening event of the air show featured three Douglas A-26 Invaders, uniquely used in three wars—World War II, Korea and Vietnam. The fifty-foot-long aircraft had a seventy-foot wingspan and two two-thousand-horsepower engines, making it the fastest bomber in World War II. On that summery Friday afternoon, the three A-26s, from an experienced demonstration team home based at Lake Charles, Louisiana, roared from the south into the view of an excited capacity grandstand crowd, flying low level in a tight V-formation. Just as the A-26s neared the rodeo grounds in front of the grandstands, disaster struck. A midair collision of the three bombers led to a tragic aftermath that stunned the crowd as death and destruction reigned at the scene.

Douglas A-26 Invader, a twin-engine light bomber and ground attack aircraft that served in three wars: World War II, Korea and Vietnam. *Author's collection.*

Scene in aftermath of collision of three A-26s over the North Montana Fairgrounds on August 9, 1946. This tragic A-26 crash destroyed the horse barn, taking the lives of four people and nineteen horses. A second Invader, in the circle above the flames, returned to GFAAB to crash land. The third Invader, not visible, crashed to the north, killing its crew. *Photo by Wallace Ruetter, Cut Bank;* Great Falls Tribune, *August 10, 1946.*

Death and Destruction

What was happening was a tragedy, as reported the next morning in the *Tribune*:

> SIX DIE IN DOUBLE AIR CRASH AT FAIR
> *Bomber's Plunge Into Barn Seen by 20,000 Horrified Spectators in Grandstand*
> *4 Army Fliers, 2 Civilians, 19 Horses Perish as Aerial Show Ends in Disaster*
>
> *Tragedy struck in the first minute of the air show before the eyes of a capacity crowd, spreading death and destruction in its wake. The planes collided immediately after springing into view of the crowd and wreckage from the ill-fated craft spraying the infield in front of the grandstand as the tangled bombers, flying in a formation of three, swept past at nearly 400 miles an hour.*
>
> *The lead plane, its tail sheared, crashed at the north end of the race track, plunged into a horse barn and hurtled across the grounds more than 900 feet, leaving a mass of burning debris. The second plane, its wing destroyed, veered dizzily out of view and crashed in the hills five miles north of the fairgrounds. The third plane, its tail damaged, returned safely to the east base to make a crash landing.*
>
> *Killed were four army fliers in the two aircraft and at least two civilians who perished in the flames that engulfed the horse barn following the explosion of the first plane. Fuel from the stricken bomber sprayed the barn, turning it into a raging inferno.[31]*
>
> *The tragedy ended the holiday spirit for the largest fair crowd of the week and forced cancellation of the races that afternoon. The night show and other entertainment continued in the evening, and full operations resumed the next day.*
>
> *Three of the Army aviators who died were stationed at Lake Charles, Louisiana: Capt. Howard C. McElroy, 28; Lt. George F. Osgood, 27, Lt. George B. Cowell Jr., 25; and Lt. Arthur Pelletier, from Great Falls Air Base. The two flyers who landed safely were identified as Lt. Branston R. Redmon and Lt. Ralston Bennett, also from Lake Charles. The two civilians who died in the horse barn were: Dorothy Szabo, of Belt, student, and Andy Seman, of Great Falls, smelter worker. In addition, twenty-five people were injured or burned. Seventeen race horses worth more than $50,000 were killed. The barn, valued at $10,000, was completely destroyed, and eight automobiles or trucks were destroyed.[32]*

The Aftermath

The rodeo events went on as scheduled, after cancelation of the races. The grandstand crowd determinedly turned their heads away from the fire and aided the arena stars who carried on the show. But as the embers died down and the crowd thinned out, and as the army moved in, there still were anxious faces along the fence and murmurs of impressions and rumors. Being an eyewitness to this tragedy was a disturbing experience. Sensations of fear, excitement and thrill carry a crowd for a while, but they burn out—only sadness, grief and awe remain.[33]

An army investigation began almost immediately, with General Carl Spaatz, Army Air Forces commander, ordering an inquiry and sending Major General Junious Jones, inspector general, to Great Falls to oversee the work. While army investigators gathered information and talked to witnesses, no findings were shared.

When finally declassified in 1954, the report concluded the obvious: the planes were too close together and flew too low, both violations of procedure. The rules required the aircraft to stay at least a distance of half the wingspan apart. While investigators never determined how low the planes flew that day, they were likely half the authorized altitude of one thousand feet.[34]

THE TRUMAN DOCTRINE AND THE MARSHALL PLAN

On January 12, 1946, George F. Kennan, a junior Foreign Service officer in the U.S. embassy in Moscow, sent a hastily written telegram to the State Department. Kennan's remarkable "long-telegram" identified the problem: internal Soviet paranoia required hostility toward its capitalist enemies. In turn, Kennan offered the solution that became the pillar for U.S. strategy toward the Soviet Union for the duration of the Cold War: consistent "containment" of Soviet expansionism.

Shortly after Germany surrendered, Greece descended into civil war between the Greek government, backed by Great Britain, and a Communist army rising from wartime partisans. Britain's postwar financial weakness forced its withdrawal, and on March 12, 1947, President Truman outlined a plan for U.S. military and economic assistance to both the Greek government and Turkey, also under pressure from the Soviet Union. The president announced what would become known as the Truman Doctrine: "[It] must be the policy of the United States to support free peoples who are resisting attempted subjugation by armed minorities or by outside pressures....[W]e must assist free peoples to work out their own destinies in their own way."[35]

Saving Austria from Soviet Domination

Few Montanans have influenced the fate of a nation the way Hal Ekern did in postwar Austria. From army major to State Department officer, Ekern worked tirelessly to keep Austria free from Soviet domination, while signing a treaty and forming a democratic government.

Born on March 31, 1917, in Lewistown, Montana, Halvor Olaf Ekern worked as a trapper, logger and dam construction foreman before graduating from the University of Montana in 1941, just before the United States entered World War II. Commissioned as a second lieutenant, Ekern joined the 87th Mountain Infantry Regiment, 10th Mountain Division, at Fort Drum, New York, and assisted in organizing the ski troops of the 10th. Late in the war, the 87th Mountain Infantry fought around Lake Garda, Italy. Major Ekern, with several other men from the 87th, captured the northern Italian villa of dictator Benito Mussolini in May 1945, when Italian partisans seized Mussolini.

At war's end, Major Ekern transferred to headquarters of U.S. Forces Austria, where he was assigned as quadripartite adviser to the commanding general and U.S. high commissioner General Mark Clark. Promoted to lieutenant colonel, in 1947 Ekern served on the delegation of Secretary of State George Marshall to the Council of Foreign Ministers.

In an interview, Ekern spoke of those chaotic early postwar days in Austria:

> *Well, you may remember that Germany was a conquered country, but the four allies decided that Austria was a liberated country. In Germany they had the nonfraternization policy, a very stern attitude, but in Austria we were free to make friends. The city [Vienna] was devastated, having been bombed very badly. The Russians got in there first. The Allied Authority in London had decided where the demarcation lines between the four zones were, as well as the four portions of the city, to be divided among the British, French, Russians and US. We were supposed to move in, but the Russians weren't quite finished looting the place and they stalled. Mark Clark was our High Commissioner and Commanding General. The Russians*

wanted to come in, but he said not until they sign the agreements on access, something they didn't bother to do in Berlin [leading to the Berlin crisis of 1948]. *Al Gruenther was the Deputy High Commissioner and went in and talked to the Russians and said that his Commissioner was not coming in until they sign the agreements for access by rail, air and road. A smart decision. So we got there in August.*

The city was totally demoralized, looted and violated. They had really sacked that place. It was a terrible chapter that had been sort of passed over. We got the High Commission operating by September 1 [1945].[36]

Major Ekern served as an assistant to General Clark in Allied Commission meetings. General Clark was "a grandstander," but the Austrians saw him as their "deliverer." When the U.S. State Department assumed responsibility from the army, the goal remained the same: to get a treaty to enable the Austrians to establish a democratic government. Yet the Russians had no intention of leaving, stalling the treaty until at last a breakthrough came. Soviet dictator Joseph Stalin died on March 5, 1953, and some things began to change.

Meanwhile in 1950, Hal Ekern joined the U.S. Foreign Service, overnight changing from army lieutenant colonel to State Department FSO-3 and remaining at the U.S. embassy in Austria as quadripartite director. He was respected and feared by the Soviets for his card file "memory," the most complete files in existence on Austrian treaty negotiations. During conferences, many pairs of Soviet eyes would focus warily on Ekern whenever Soviet Ambassador I.I. Ilyichev made a point. When Ekern quickly scribbled and handed a note to the American ambassador, the Soviets would hurriedly whisper among themselves and then brace for a telling counterblow to their proposal. For instance, Ekern's note might outline, from memory, eight cases that proved the Soviets wrong.

Stalin's death and West Germany's entry into NATO led the Soviets to finally agree to a treaty in 1955 that made Austria neutral. Ekern stayed on and helped the transition, transferring in early 1956 back to Washington, D.C. There, he served as special assistant to the secretary of state for atomic affairs, with a primary duty to establish the International Atomic Energy Agency. While Hal Ekern went on to other important State Department assignments during his long career, nothing would top the key role he played in keeping Austria from Soviet domination.[37]

Saving Berlin with a Song of Freedom:
Operation Vittles

The first dramatic showdown of the Cold War, the Berlin Blockade, occurred when the Soviet Union closed all road, rail and canal travel between West Germany and West Berlin. The United States and Britain vowed not to abandon West Berliners to the Soviet blockade. On June 25, 1948, Operation Vittles was initiated, a massive airlift of supplies to Berlin's 2 million residents. Great Falls AFB played a critical role in ensuring the success of this vital operation. Officials selected Great Falls as the only replacement aircrew training site for Berlin Airlift–bound C-54s, officially activating the 517th Air Transport Wing. Using radio beacons, Great Falls AFB was transformed to resemble Tempelhof Airport in Berlin. Hundreds of pilots and flight engineers, many just recalled to active duty, were qualified on the C-54 aircraft and on flight procedures to and from Berlin by practicing on ground mock-ups and flying simulated airlift missions here.[38]

The Soviet plan for the Berlin Blockade was framed in the postwar occupation of Nazi Germany. The Soviet Union held the eastern third, while the British and Americans divided the western two-thirds, with the Americans in the south and the British in the north. Later, a fourth zone was carved for the French from portions of the American and British zones. The zones were characterized as "the Russians received the agriculture, the British the heavy industry and the Americans the scenery."[39] Similarly, the Allies agreed to divide Berlin, located one hundred miles inside the Soviet zone, into four sectors.

In the spring of 1948, Joseph Stalin conspired with East German leader Wilhelm Frick to force the western allies out of Berlin. While the western allies had failed to secure Soviet agreement guaranteeing surface transportation to Berlin, deep, mutual concern for air safety had led to a written guarantee with the Soviets that provided for air corridors in and out of Berlin. Thus, the stage was set for the first showdown of the Cold War. Stalin gambled that a land blockade of Berlin would force the withdrawal of the western allies from that strategically important city. While the historic German capital was a shell of its former glory, it still had 2.5 million residents, most in the Allied sectors. Food and fuel in immense quantities were essential, and this is what the Soviets targeted.

On June 24, 1948, the Berlin Blockade began. Soviet authorities announced that the Autobahn highway connecting western Germany to Berlin would be closed indefinitely "for repairs." Then the Soviets halted all railroad traffic from west to east and barred all canal barges from entering West Berlin. Berlin was cut off from surface transportation.

The western allies faced a crisis, and options were few: evacuate West Berliners; negotiate from a position of weakness; abandon Berlin entirely; or determine how to resupply Berlin by air. They judged quickly that withdrawal from the city was not an option. American military commanders concluded that the surrender of Berlin would endanger the American position in all of western Europe. President Truman decisively pronounced, "We shall stay, period." Yet he was not willing to risk turning the Cold War into a nuclear war by forcing land entry. Finding another way to resupply Berlin proved the only response.

Quickly, an airlift was implemented, and Operation Vittles began. The Allies would supply their sectors by air using the open-air corridors over the Soviet zone to deliver food, fuel and other supplies. Intended as a short-term measure, as the months passed, and the Soviets refused to lift the blockade, the Allies settled in for the long haul. Month after month, hundreds of American, British and French cargo planes ferried provisions from western Europe to Tempelhof (American sector), Gatow (British sector) and Tegel (French sector) airfields in West Berlin. From a beginning with some 5,000 tons of supplies to West Berlin each day, the capacity rose to about 8,000 tons per day. Over the eleven-month duration, the Allies carried about 2.3 million tons of cargo to save free Berlin.

By the spring of 1949, it had become clear that the Soviet blockade of West Berlin had failed. Despite many hardships, West Berliners did not reject their allies in the West, and Western Germany formed a unified state with the creation of the Federal Republic of Germany in May 1949. On May 12, the Soviet Union lifted the blockade, reopening roads, canals and railway routes into West Berlin. The airlift continued until September, as the Allies wanted to stockpile supplies in Berlin in case the Soviets reinstated their blockade. The results of Stalin's miscalculation were profound: the USSR showed Europe and the world its cruelty; the creation of West Germany was hastened; the Cold War threat of Communist expansion proved real; and this motivated the formation of the North Atlantic Treaty Organization (NATO).[40]

So, how had the United States managed on short notice to mount the massive air transportation operation essential to sustain Operation Vittles for so many months? This happened despite the rapid drawdown of U.S. forces in Europe in the immediate postwar period. Three key factors were excellent transport aircraft (C-47s and C-54s), many hundreds of well-trained transport crews and exceptional leadership. The leadership came in large part when Major General William H. Tunner touched down at Wiesbaden, West Germany, on July 28, 1948. General Tunner was a brilliant leader and the U.S. Air Force's preeminent authority on air transport. He had led creation and operation of the Ferrying Command early in World War II, including the Seventh Ferrying Command at the Great Falls air bases.

Air Force Europe Commander Curtis LeMay called General Tunner "the transport expert to end transport experts." When the Air Transport Command combined with Naval Transport Command to form the Military Air Transport Service (MATS) in mid-1948, General Tunner became deputy commander for operations under Major General Lawrence S. Kuter. Now, General Tunner was on scene, establishing his headquarters the next day as the 7499th Air Command and within two days activating the Airlift Task Force (Provisional) in charge of airlift operations. Despite many complexities in relations with the British and within U.S. Air Force Europe, General Tunner "managed the airlift as if the three air corridors were conveyor belts constantly moving to and from Berlin."[41]

VITAL AIRCREW TRAINING

As the months passed, the need for additional pilots and aircrews for C-54s became clear. To meet this critical need, the U.S. Air Force transferred the MATS training school from California to Great Falls AFB in September 1948.

Great Falls proved an ideal location for crew replacement training. The magnetic course at Great Falls matched that on the approach to Berlin, and aircraft had to land on the first part of the runway just as they would have to do on the short runway at Tempelhof. The C-54 Skymasters were heavily loaded with sandbags to provide experience in handling fully loaded aircraft—each crew had to complete three landings at seventy thousand pounds gross weight before graduating. Over the three-week course, all crew members received preflight and flight training, supplementary ground training for pilots and training for flight engineers. Most trainees were former bomber airmen recalled to active duty, few had flown in the past three years and even fewer had flown Skymasters, so this training was critical.

Some irate residents complained about the noise and air traffic over the city. But the reason for the increased traffic over Great Falls went back to the construction of the runways at Great Falls AAB early in World War II.

For Operation Vittles, during Berlin Blockade in 1948, GFAFB was selected to train pilots and aircrews bound for the Berlin Airlift. Shown is a Douglas C-54 Skymaster coming low over a Ground-Controlled Approach radar van at GFAFB. *Author's collection.*

It was then necessary to construct runways and other facilities more with speed than durability, and now these runways were gradually becoming unserviceable for the faster and heavier C-54 aircraft. As a safety factor, the decision was made to use Gore Field for nighttime operations, thus increasing the traffic over the town. The current training had just one purpose: to train crews to fly the Berlin airlift. This meant following a route laid out for the airlift as a narrow corridor simulated at Great Falls, according to the *Tribune*: "The constant droning of these ships overhead threatens the mental tranquility of a whole city of people. By this time the importance of the Berlin airlift has waned in the mind of the average citizen....Low flying airplanes are noisy and uncomfortable but even so it is a small price to pay for the security. To the people of Berlin, the beat of the C-54 engines is a song of freedom."[42]

Replacement crew training in Great Falls had a major impact on the success of Operation Vittles. As the monthly quota of one hundred crews completed training and reported to their European duty stations, they replaced exhausted crews. This began a welcomed and crucial rotation of crews after they served ninety-mission tours in the hectic-paced environment.

During Operation Vittles, this trainer allowed student pilots to use a flight simulator for navigation training. The relief map of the Berlin corridor is tracked as the radar antenna moves slowly over it. The student pilots *(from left to right)* are First Lieutenants Robert Pfegl, Frank Simms, Lowell Wheaton, Leonard Rush, Earl Miller and Joseph Schreiner. *Author's collection.*

As the replacement program closed down in early August 1949, more than two thousand airmen had been trained for service. With the closing of Operation Vittles training, Great Falls AAB continued on as a training center for MATS pilots, engineers, mechanics and traffic personnel.[43]

A Cold War Incident: A Shoot Down in the Baltic

Throughout the Cold War, an open, democratic society and its allies faced off against a paranoid, closed totalitarian state leading an international movement. How could our open society "know the enemy" and its military capabilities in preparing for a "hot" war? How could our open society keep Stalin's Soviet Union from knowing us and our military capabilities? World War II's Lend-Lease experience provided a preview of the aggressive espionage operations being waged by the Soviet Union.

Electronic, signals and imaging reconnaissance—first by aircraft and then, as technology advanced during the 1960s, by satellites—provided a major source of our knowledge of the Soviet Union and its allies. Throughout the 1950s, U.S. Air Force and U.S. Navy reconnaissance aircraft and ships patrolled international waters off the coasts of the Soviet Union, Communist China and North Korea. Long-range reconnaissance aircraft, seldom escorted by fighter aircraft, became inviting targets all too often to our enemies. By the mid-1970s, some twenty U.S. military aircraft had been fired on and all too often shot down in Cold War incidents.

An early incident occurred in the Baltic Sea on April 8, 1950, when a U.S. Navy PB4Y-2 Privateer electronic and signals reconnaissance aircraft was shot down by Russian fighters on a flight from Wiesbaden Air Base, West Germany, to Denmark. Onboard were pilot Lieutenant John Fette of Connellsville, Pennsylvania; copilot LT Howard W. Seeschaf of Fairlington, Virginia; and a crew of eight, including Aviation Machinist Mate (AD)1 Joseph H. Danens Jr. from Cut Bank, Montana, with his wife, Ruth, living in Passiac, New Jersey. The PB4Y-2 was a navy patrol aircraft derived from the Consolidated B-24 Liberator.[44]

The Privateer's disappearance touched off a diplomatic row between the United States and the USSR. The Soviets announced that an American plane had penetrated Soviet airspace by flying over Latvia, a Baltic state under Russian control. They claimed that the aircraft had exchanged fire with a Russian squadron before flying off over the sea.

A PB4Y-2 Privateer, a U.S. Navy reconnaissance aircraft, was shot down by Soviet fighters in international waters in the Baltic Sea. *U.S. Navy.*

The United States maintained that the navy aircraft was unarmed and on a routine training flight and that the four-engine Privateer would have had to veer four hundred miles off course to reach Latvian airspace. The Russians never responded to American charges that they had shot down an unarmed aircraft.

It was clear that on April 8, Soviet fighters shot down the unarmed PB4Y-2 over the Baltic Sea, off the coast of Latvia. While the full story never came out, one year after the shootdown, the U.S. Navy declared the ten crewmen legally dead. Were they dead, or did life rafts found during U.S. Navy search and rescue operations in the Baltic reveal that the crew survived the crash, had been captured and were being held by the Soviets? Were these Americans held in the Soviet Gulag?[45]

Post–Cold War investigation with some Russian cooperation provided the best insight into this Cold War incident, the full details of which will likely never be known. A report by Lieutenant Colonel Jim Caswell, U.S. Army, may be the final word:

On April 8, 1950, Soviet Lavochkin La-11 fighters shot down a US Navy PB4Y-2 Privateer (BuNo 59645) over the Baltic Sea, off the coast of Liepāja, Latvia.....Named the Turbulent Turtle, *the aircraft was assigned to Patrol Squadron 26 (VP-26), Detachment A. In addition to other types of missions, Privateers were used by the US Navy for signals intelligence (SIGINT) flights off of the coast of the Soviet Union and the People's Republic of China. The crew was reported missing in action on April 9, 1950 in the Baltic Sea, 80 miles southeast of Libau, Latvia....Each of the crew members were posthumously awarded the Distinguished Flying Cross.*

...It is the official position of the United States that aircrew members of flight 59645 were captured and held in Soviet Gulag until their death.... Although the search and rescue effort was unsuccessful, two unmanned life rafts from the aircraft were eventually recovered, as well as some wreckage (found by commercial fishing vessels). None of the ten crew members were recovered, dead or alive.[46]

CHAPTER 3

PROXY WAR KOREA

MONTANA'S MILITARY POWER

Dramatic Military Advances: Unity and Integration

On Saturday, May 21, 1950, Great Falls celebrated the first Armed Forces Day in the aftermath of two dramatic national military events: the National Security Act of 1947 and Executive Order 9981.

Experiences from World War II led to the National Security Act of 1947, unifying the Departments of the Army and Navy into a Defense Department and initiating a trend toward unification of the U.S. armed forces that would continue beyond the end of the Cold War. In addition, over the strong objection of the navy, the act created the Department of the Air Force, effective September 18, 1947, when the first secretary of the air force, Stuart Symington, assumed office.

On July 26, 1948, President Harry S Truman signed Executive Order 9981, which ordered "that there shall be equality of treatment and opportunity for all persons in the armed services without regard to race, color, religion or national origin." With the stroke of his pen, this president from a Missouri family with historic ties to the Confederacy set in motion the greatest political act since Reconstruction ended in 1875. Implementation would not come quickly or easily, and it would take six more years until the army's last segregated "colored" units were disbanded. Several more decades would pass before the navy and other services would come to grips fully with discrimination. Yet Executive Order 9981 established a most important breakthrough in racial relations.

Major General Laurence S. Kuter, commander of the MATC, was the principal speaker at the Armed Forces Day observance in Great Falls. General Kuter's speech about the recent dramatic reforms in the military resonated with the times and the crowd, as reported in the *Tribune*:

KUTER SAYS FREEDOM THREATENED

"This is the atomic age—and today our freedom is threatened by the false promises of communism—our native land itself is exposed to a danger that it never knew before," Maj. Gen. Laurence S. Kuter, said in a keynote address at the Armed Forces day observance here.

…He discussed unification of the armed forces, explaining its accomplishment and declared: "Unification and integration of our armed forces, together with integration of civilian agencies to aid and advise our military and civilian leaders, is one of the most progressive steps taken in the military history of our country."

Kuter opened his address with a review of the role of the Great Falls Air Force Base in the last war, describing it as "the great aerial gateway through which passed our tremendous military air traffic to and from our Arctic and Alaskan activities." He said "this requirement in no way has diminished in importance in peacetime.

"Our forces in Alaska are becoming geared to the tempo of air movement. Your city still remains the gateway that makes that tempo possible. It is a focal point in our global air route system."

…Kuter said that "no longer can civilians dissociate themselves from war as they did in the days of Genghis Khan, Napoleon, and even in World wars 1 and 2.

…"We are threatened, as never before, with the possibility of sudden attack on our cities and homes….We have no alternative, therefore, except to prepare against attack, should it come, and to maintain the nucleus of an armed force strong enough to carry the counter attack to the enemy.

…"Today, we know cold war and hot war—still the continuation of national policy by unpeaceful means still aimed at overcoming the enemy's will and ability to resist an intruding policy. Time and distance have been telescoped. Mountains and oceans are neither barriers nor assets. An army alone, a navy alone, or an air force alone is no barrier nor guarantee to security. Companies no longer are pitted against companies, ships against ships, squadrons against squadrons. This is the atomic

age—an age synonymous with complete, all-out war. And in order to insure maximum security and insure ultimate victory at a cost within our resources, it is imperative that members of our armed forces should be in fact United for Security."[47]

Our First Proxy War: Korea

Just one month after General Kuter's speech, on June 25, ten North Korean People's Army (NKPA) divisions smashed across the 38th parallel in a massive invasion of South Korea. Overnight, the United States became engaged in this Korean "conflict"—a war by any other name and our first proxy war with the Soviet Union and its Communist allies.

The stage had been set by the surrender of Japanese forces on the Korean Peninsula to Soviet and American forces in August 1945 with an agreed division along the 38th parallel. Two years later, on November 14, 1947, the United Nations passed a resolution calling for withdrawal of foreign soldiers from Korea, free elections in both the U.S. and Soviet administrations and the creation of a UN commission dedicated to the unification of the peninsula. This led to the withdrawal of Soviet and American occupying forces. The following year, Syngman Rhee was voted president of the Republic of Korea, while in September 1948, the Soviet Union declared the Democratic People's Republic of Korea the legitimate government of all Korea, with Kim Il-sung as prime minister, with no election. In January 1950, Stalin, in secrecy, reversed his previous policy of restraint on North Korea and gave the green light, with Kim's assurance, that the North Korean attack would be so swift that the invasion would be over in just three days.[48]

The North Korean invasion across the 38th parallel surprised and shook the U.S. government to its core. In turn, Stalin, who expected American acquiescence, just as they had failed to support the Nationalists from Communist domination of China, was surprised when, within hours, President Truman decided that the United States had to act. The president proclaimed, "We can't let the UN down." After all, for the United States to fail to lead the UN now would harken back to the catastrophic failures of the League of Nations to act against Italian and German aggression.[49]

With decisive United States leadership, the UN Security Council immediately condemned the invasion and voted to intervene to defend

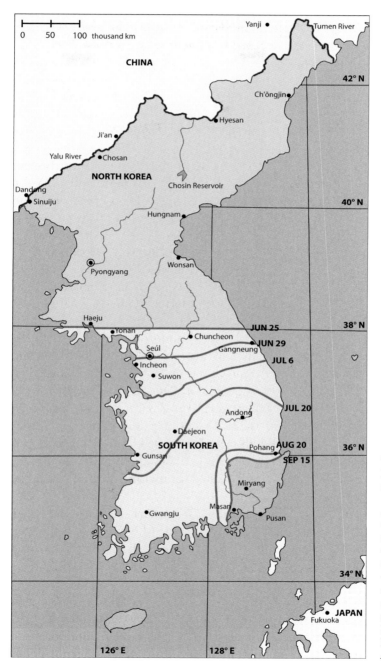

The surprise North Korean invasion in June 1950 swept southward until U.S./UN reinforcements were rushed to South Korea, where in desperate fighting a fragile line held at the Pusan Perimeter, shown lower right. *Author's collection.*

59

South Korea. This dramatic action happened without Soviet veto in the Security Council because at that time the Soviets were boycotting over the issue of admission of the People's Republic of China.

The international community began to act within days, helped greatly by the presence of U.S. occupying military forces across the Korean Strait in nearby Japan. On June 30, General Douglas MacArthur ordered the immediate movement of the 24th Infantry Division to Korea from Kyushu Island. Commanding General William F. Dean was ordered to send one battalion and division headquarters by air to the nearby South Korean port of Pusan, with the remainder of the sixteen-thousand-man division to follow by sea. The mission of the 24th was to "take the initial shock" of the North Korean assault and then try to slow its advance until more U.S. divisions and UN forces could arrive.

Task Force Smith was underway—and the desperate combat action that followed over the next three months came to the brink of catastrophe. South Korean soldiers were underequipped and overwhelmed by the magnitude of the North Korean attack, led by columns and columns of Soviet-built T-34 tanks. Within three days, South Korea's capital, Seoul, was captured, and the attack drove on south.

Task Force Smith, named for its commander, Lieutenant Colonel Charles Smith, dug into positions north of Osan on July 4 and prepared to block advancing NKPA forces. The next day, the 540 men of the Task Force engaged 5,000 NKPA forces led by columns of tanks. The ensuing Battle of Osan became a rout as the Task Force's light arms and lack of anti-tank weapons were no match for the oncoming T-34s, outnumbered ten to one. At the cost of 30 percent casualties, the Task Force succeeded in delaying the enemy advance for seven hours before the soldiers were forced to fall back southward, toward the hastily formed Pusan Perimeter. Dozens of American soldiers were captured, with some executed on the spot, while others were taken to Pyongyang, where they apparently were murdered later—affording a preview of the brutality of this proxy war.[50]

On July 3, the 24th Division's 34th Infantry Regiment arrived at Pusan, with 1,800 men organized into the 1st and 3rd Battalions. The 34th Infantry was commanded by Montanan Colonel Jay B. Lovless. A native of Texas, Lovless graduated from the University of Montana. During World War II, Lovless served in three regiments of the 2nd Division and commanded two of them. For twenty-one months, Colonel Lovless served with the 2nd Division, which landed in Normandy on June 7, 1944; aided in capturing Brest; held the north breakthrough in the Battle of the Bulge; took

Gottingen and Leipzig; and ended the war in Czechoslovakia. Colonel Lovless skillfully and courageously commanded the 23rd Infantry Regiment during the operations and at other times commanded the 38th and 9th Regiments. In June 1945, he served as assistant 2nd Division commander.

Colonel Lovless was awarded the Distinguished Service Cross, Silver Star with one cluster, Legion of Merit, Bronze Star with medal, Combat Infantry Badge, the French Legion of Honor and Croix de Guerre with palm, the Czechoslovakia Cross for Bravery and the Russian Order of Suvorov. At war's end, Colonel Lovless returned to the University of Montana with his wife to join their two daughters, who made their homes in Missoula. There, he served as professor of military science and tactics and chairman of the ROTC department.[51]

Colonel Lovless left Missoula to assume command of the 34th Infantry Regiment, occupying Kyushu, Japan. The 34th served in the African American 24th Infantry Division, a part of the army not yet integrated. One year later, Colonel Lovless and his understrength peacetime regiment went to war, as he sent his two battalions into their near-suicidal mission to delay the overwhelming strength and armor of the NKPA army. In these early chaotic days of the war, the 25th and 34th Regiments fought with little artillery, heavy mortar or air support. The NKPA forces easily flanked them and threatened their encirclement within hours of contact.

The 34th Infantry arrived in Korea with 1,898 officers and enlisted men. The 1st Battalion numbered just over 600 men, and the 3rd (there was no 2nd) had about 640, well below the normal army battalion strength of 900 men. On July 5, veteran Lieutenant Colonel Harold "Red" Ayres took command of the 1st Battalion, 34th (1/34th). Major General William F. Dean, 24th Division commander, ordered Ayres's battalion to a blocking position near Pyongtaek and Asan Bay on South Korea's west coast and Lieutenant Colonel David H. Smith's 3rd Battalion to a similar position at Ansong, about ten miles east of Pyongtaek. Brigadier General George B. Barth, commanding 24th Division artillery, informed Ayres that Task Force Smith had been defeated earlier and admonished Ayres to delay the enemy but not allow his battalion to suffer the same fate as Colonel Smith's.

The Battle of Pyongtaek was the second engagement between U.S. and NKPA forces during the war, occurring on July 6, 1950, in the village of Pyongtaek in western South Korea. This battle would bring defeat not only for Ayres's battalion but also for 34th Regimental Commander Colonel Lovless. The fight ended in a North Korean rout following unsuccessful attempts by American forces to delay the advancing North Korean units.

The North Korean 4th Infantry Division attacked the 1/34th at 5:00 a.m. on the sixth. The American battalion had no artillery support and only a few rounds remaining for its 4.2-inch mortars. Meantime, Regimental Commander Colonel Lovless directed Ayres to hold as long as possible and then fall back to a position in the vicinity of Cheonan. The battalion held for about five hours, with a loss of eighteen troops wounded and thirty-three missing. Then, as North Korean infantry flowed around his flank, Ayres withdrew.

University of Montana graduate Colonel Jay B. Lovless, a highly decorated World War II officer, became a victim of the North Korean surge south toward the Pusan Perimeter. *U.S. Army.*

Poor communication flow led to conflicting orders, causing Ayres to retreat directly to Chonan, thirteen miles in the rear, rather than falling back in successive stages. General Dean was furious when he learned that the Ayres Battalion was not fighting and delaying incrementally, causing more hours of delay for the NKPA forces—every hour bought precious time for more U.S. forces to arrive in Korea. General Dean blamed Lovless for the rapid fallback, fired him and replaced him with Colonel Robert R. Martin, who in turn was killed shortly after. Within two weeks, General Dean himself would be captured by the North Koreans. The desperate battle to establish a perimeter around the vital port of Pusan was underway, and it was not going well.

With his removal from combat, Colonel Lovless returned to Japan for another year before returning to the United States. His twilight tour in the army was as commandant of the cadets at Louisiana State University.[52]

As more U.S. units arrived and South Korean troops were reformed and stabilized—joined by British, Australian and other UN forces—a 140-mile defensive perimeter hastily formed by early August on the southeast tip of the Korean Peninsula. The major Battle of Pusan Perimeter was underway, to last from August 4 to September 18, 1950—a battle between 98,000 NKPA troops and a rapidly growing UN army that reached some 140,000 soldiers.

Just as the build-up was accelerating in the Pusan Perimeter, another Montanan arrived on scene. Major General Frank W. Milburn of Missoula arrived as interim commander of U.S. 1st Corps, assuming command of U.S., ROK and British forces.

General Frank W. Milburn had had a distinguished career in World War II. Born in Jasper, Indiana, on January 11, 1892, he graduated from the United States Military Academy and was commissioned a second lieutenant in 1914. At the academy, Milburn joined fellow cadet Dwight D. Eisenhower in the backfield of Army's football team. On July 21, 1926, Major Milburn reported for duty at the University of Montana in Missoula to serve as professor of military science and tactics. During his five-year tour, he coached Grizzly football, married Margaret Orr of Dillon and adopted Missoula as their home.

Following his departure from the university, Major Milburn served in varied assignments, and by early 1942, he had been promoted to brigadier general, with command of the 83rd Division. He was soon promoted to major general and named to command the U.S. XXI Corps. As it deployed to Europe, the XXI Corps entered combat under the U.S. 7th Army in January 1945 and fought for 116 days, starting in Alsace, crossing into southern Germany and swarming into Austria, with elements reaching into Northern Italy.

Four tank landing ships unload men and equipment on Red Beach one day after the amphibious landings on Inchon. Despite complex navigational obstacles, the Inchon Landing, ordered by General MacArthur and planned by Captain U.S. Grant Sharp from Fort Benton, proved a masterstroke allowing a breakout from the Pusan Perimeter. *U.S. Navy.*

At war's end, General Milburn remained overseas, commanding in succession the 7th Army, XXIII Corps, V Corps and the 1st Infantry Division. Promoted to lieutenant general in 1949, Milburn served as the deputy commander of U.S. Army Europe until 1950, when he was suddenly ordered to Korea.

With the Pusan Perimeter stabilized, Lieutenant General Milburn assumed command of U.S. I Corps. Three days later, on September 15, UN Supreme Commander General Douglas MacArthur conceived and the U.S. 7th Fleet landed X Corps—including the 1st Marine Division, the 7th Infantry Division and other units—in a bold and risky amphibious landing at the strategic port of Inchon, on the west coast of Korea, about one hundred miles south of the 38th parallel and just twenty-five miles from Seoul. Planning this masterstroke was complex and difficult in the face of drastic post–World War II force reductions, requiring men, supplies and landing craft that were not readily available. Captain Ulysses S. Grant Sharp Jr., planning officer on the staff of the commander, U.S. 7th Fleet, led the planning for the Inchon landing, codenamed Operation Chromite. Captain Sharp, born in Chinook, was raised in Fort Benton and graduated from Annapolis in 1927. This brilliant officer's star rose rapidly during the 1950s.[53]

FROM DEFENSE TO OFFENSE

The amphibious landing at Inchon changed the course of the war, opening a second front that began a rout of the NKPA. While X Corps hit the NKPA forces from behind, I Corps, commanded by General Milburn, broke out from the Pusan Perimeter and commenced a major offensive northward against crumbling opposition to establish contact with X Corps. Major units of the NKPA were trapped and destroyed. With the two UN Corps linked up, the offensive continued northward, capturing Seoul on September 30 and moving across the 38th parallel into North Korea. With the momentum of the attack unchecked, I Corps cracked the "iron triangle," a vital North Korean supply and communications hub, located south of the capital, Pyongyang. The race to Pyongyang ended on October 19, when elements of the ROK 1st Infantry Division and the U.S. 1st Cavalry Division captured the capital.

Just three days later, Communist China intervened with 300,000 soldiers of their People's Volunteer Army (PVA), surprising General MacArthur and the

Montana POW Sergeant Lyle Jacobson greeted a POW buddy from Izmir, Turkey, in Jacobson's hometown, Butte, Montana. The two friends were held in Chinese Communist Camp No. 5 until war's end. *From* Montana Standard, *October 1, 1955.*

Last Time They Met It Was in POW Camp

The last time that Sgt. Lyle Jacobson, right, Butte veteran of the Korean War, and Fethi Hepcakici of Izmir, Turkey, met it was in Red China's infamous Camp No. 5 in North Korea where both were held as prisoners of war. Hepcakici, in the United States to look up American friends he made in the POW camp, came to Butte to renew acquaintance with Jacobson.

＊ ＊ ＊　　　＊ ＊ ＊

Young Turk Travels to Butte to Look Up Soldier Who Was His Buddy in POW Camp

UN. While the initial Chinese incursion withdrew after initial engagements, as UN forces approached the Yalu River, China again intervened, this time with a massive 500,000-man force. The war would eventually grind into a costly stalemate along the 38th parallel until an armistice was reached two and a half years later on July 27, 1953.

Some 1.8 million Americans and an estimated 22,000 Montanans served in the Korean War, which cost 2 to 3 million Korean casualties; 33,665 U.S. military killed in action; 3,375 died of non-hostile causes; 103,284 U.S. wounded; 8,176 missing in action (MIA); and 7,000 prisoners of war (POW), 51 percent of whom died in prison camps. Montana suffered 138 killed in the war. Among American POWs returned during the prisoner exchange at the end of the war were two Montanans:

- Sergeant John T. Brockes, of Great Falls, 69th Tank Battalion; captured on March 23, 1951
- Corporal Lyle Jacobson, of Butte, 7th Cavalry Regiment, 1st Cavalry Division; captured on November 10, 1950

The remains of one Montana POW/MIA, Harold Peter Haugland, have been recovered, while twenty-seven Montana POW/MIA are unaccounted for. Army Sergeant First Class Harold P. Haugland, born in Glendive and serving with Company D, 15th Antiaircraft Artillery Battlation, 7th Infantry, was killed in action in a fierce battle with Chinese troops at the Chosin Reservoir in December 1950.[54]

POW: CORPORAL LYLE JACOBSON OF BUTTE PLAYED DEAD

After Corporal Lyle Jacobson's repatriation in 1953, he provided insight into his capture and brutal treatment. Serving with the 7th Cavalry, on November 10, 1950, just weeks after the Chinese crossed the Yalu River, Corporal Jacobson and his unit were ordered into action. Their mission was to feign an offensive to help the Marines withdraw from Chosin Reservoir.

While the diversion was a success, Corporal Jacobson's platoon was engaged by sniper fire and an attack by Korean NKPA soldiers. Corporal Jackson described his capture in the *Montana Standard*:

> *"They opened up another hail of fire, and* Boom! *I'm flying through the air, and I'm sitting there, dazed, hollering for guys to throw me their hand grenades."*
>
> *Jacobson was shot through the leg. A mortar round exploded near his head, driving chunks of shrapnel into his skull. He and other injured soldiers did their best to cover so they could escape.*
>
> *"We told them to get the hell out, to just throw us their ammo and grenades," he said. "We figured we were all dead, anyway."*
>
> *Jacobson kept yelling for more grenades as he crawled through a ditch. A North Korean soldier ran alongside, shooting to kill.*
>
> *"He was blowing clumps of mud out alongside my head," he said, "then he decided he would jump in and bayonet me, but it didn't work his way."*
>
> *Jacobson reached into his boot for a knife.*
>
> *"I cut him open like a side of beef," he said calmly.*
>
> *Jacobson slumped and played dead when a North Korean officer spotted him.*
>
> *The officer kicked him in the head, smashed his teeth out with a grenade, ordered him to stand and strip then lashed his hands together. That wire fastened around his wrists left scars that lasted for decades.*

*"It was a nightmare turned inside out, everything happened so fast,"
Jacobson said. "All I could see was my mother's face, and I said, "I'm
sorry, Mom...." I knew she would be getting a telegram stamped,
"Verified Deceased."*

*Later a North Korean soldier who was wearing Jacobson's dog tags
when he was captured, told officials the group of Americans had been
killed.*

*Back home in Butte, the notice arrived shortly before Christmas in 1950,
and bore the dreaded official stamp, "Verified Deceased."*[55]

Following his arrival at Great Falls AFB in September 1953, Corporal
Jacobson related a horrific tale of beatings, starvation diets and his captors'
attempt to indoctrinate him at Camp 5.[56] After his return to Butte, Lyle
Jacobson suffered seriously over the years. Almost fifty years after his
captivity, he described the permanent scars:

*"The [7th Cavalry] was George Custer's outfit," Jacobson mused recently,
"so that was a bad omen, too."*

*Jacobson withdrew from life, he said, and like many veterans, drank
heavily to forget his experiences. Today he admits his family also paid a price.*

*"We were just having a hell of a time adjusting," he said of the POWs.
"To this day, I don't have much feeling."*

*It wasn't until after Vietnam vets came home saddled with myriad
psychological problems that Post Traumatic Stress Disorder was widely
identified, and Jacobson finally received treatment.*

*Even after 50 years, everyday events still bring flashbacks, anxiety and
a rush of adrenaline.*

A plane overhead. A loud noise. A sudden movement.

*Sometimes in his sleep, the faces and sounds of war still haunt his
dreams, and he wakes in a panic—heart pounding. Although the dread has
lessened with the passing years, it's still there.*[57]

Sergeant Lyle Jacobson fought the Korean War every day and every night
for the rest of his long life until he passed on February 12, 2010, at age
eighty. Today, he rests at Mount Olivet Cemetery, Anaconda.

POW: Sergeant John T. Brockes, of Great Falls

Just before Christmas 1951, Mrs. Frances L. Brockes, of Great Falls, learned that her husband, Sergeant First Class John T. Brockes, was a POW in Korea. Serving with the 69th Tank Battalion, Sergeant Brockes was reported missing in action on March 23, 1951. Mrs. Brockes said:

> *"I've felt certain all along that my husband was safe, but hearing his name on that prisoner of war list was a thrill I'll never forget.*
>
> *"I feel quite hopeful now. I sat up until midnight listening to the radio. First I heard the name of my husband's buddy and then my husband's name.*
>
> *"I ran and woke up my 8-year-old John, to tell him his daddy had been heard from. I didn't waken my 4-year-old David, though."*
>
> *…In the last letter Mrs. Brockes received, dated March 22, "He had been sick and returned to duty only that day," she explained. "He was with the 69th tank battalion attached to a marine unit, which was beginning the second rush past the 38th parallel.*
>
> *"They were the last to move out when there was any turning back, he always said. But I've had a feeling all along that he was hiding out somewhere. He is a husky man, able to take care of himself in rugged country better than most men. He was a great hunter and fisherman. And he knew the Korean country and its people. He had a long tour of duty in Japan and Korea when he first re-enlisted in 1946."[58]*

Sergeant Brockes served four years in the army during World War II and remained on active duty. In May 1950, the Brockeses came to Great Falls to visit Mrs. Brockes's mother, Ida Brawner. When the North Koreans invaded, Sergeant Brockes was ordered to Korea, while his family remained in Great Falls.

Brockes was released from Prison Camp 1 in September 1953 as part Operation Big Switch. At that time, most of his army records—including his pay, promotion and decoration records—were lost in the repatriation shuffle. It took five years to untangle his records, but at last in 1958, he was promoted to master sergeant, received four years' back pay and was awarded the Silver Star and Bronze Star for valor in combat, as well as the Purple Heart with two clusters.

Sergeant Brockes was wounded five times: he was shot in the ankle, the shin and the arm; bayonetted in the back; and sustained an eardrum perforation from an explosion. Fighting with the 534th Transportation Company, he was captured when he led five men on a reconnaissance and recovery patrol into North Korean territory to retrieve much-needed truck parts.

He was herded with other prisoners to North Korea's Camp 1 in a grueling two-hundred-mile march. Of the 762 who started the march, only 267 finished, and only 60 or 70 of them lived. He was moved with the other sergeants from Camp 1 to North Korea's Camp 4 in October 1952. "The morale among the prisoners was excellent," Sergeant Brockes said. "The men never stopped bolstering each other and helping each other whenever possible." After his repatriation, Sergeant Brockes entered a hospital, and upon recovery, he was assigned as recruiting sergeant in Great Falls.[59]

REMEMBERING AMERICA'S "FORGOTTEN WAR"

The Korean War, the first major proxy war of the Cold War, is known as America's "forgotten war." Forty-three years after the end of the Korean War, on June 22, 1996, Butte dedicated a Korean War Memorial in Stodden Park. The monument stood twenty feet tall and twenty-four feet wide, with the word *Korea* spelled out in plaques representing each of Montana's fifty-six counties. The monument roof follows Korean design and features a map of Korea and a list of Montanans killed in the war.

In June 1996, Butte unveiled a Korean War Memorial, the first to honor Montanans serving in the Korean War. *Korean War Memorial.*

Above: The Montana State Korean War Memorial was dedicated on June 14, 1997, in Memorial Rose Garden in Missoula. *Author's photo.*

Opposite, inset: Lieutenant General Frank Milburn became a Montanan when he coached University of Montana Grizzly football in the 1920s and went on to a distinguished army career in combat in World War II and Korea. *From the* Great Falls Tribune, *July 4, 1965.*

The following year, on June 14, 1997, Missoula dedicated a Korean War Veterans' Memorial in Memorial Rose Garden. Two years later, Governor Marc Racicot and Montana's legislature designated this memorial as the Montana State Korean War Memorial. The memorial is a tribute so that Montanans who served and died are no longer forgotten. The names of the 138 Montanans lost in combat in the war are etched into the black academy granite slabs. The original design and artwork were donated by Missoula artist and Vietnam veteran Bruce Haegg Johnson. The memorial features a map of Korea and a soldier looking down at the helmet of a fallen comrade.[60]

GENERAL MILBURN'S RETURN TO MONTANA

FRANK W. MILBURN

During the Korean War, Major General Milburn served under Generals Douglas MacArthur and Matthew B. Ridgway. When Milburn was relieved of command of I Corps in July 1951, General Ridgway wrote, "In high-principled integrity, loyalty and devotion to duty; in personal courage, cheerfulness and steadfast coolness and composure under adversity; in professional competence, tactical skill and selfless, considerate, personal leadership, your service was superior."

Lieutenant General Milburn retired from the army on May 1, 1952, after thirty-eight years of active service and rejoined the University of Montana. There, he served one year as director of athletics coaching freshman football in 1952 and baseball in 1953. In addition, Milburn, in retirement, served as military coordinator for the university departments of military and air science during 1953–54.[61]

GENERAL MILBURN CAMPAIGNS IN MONTANA WITH IKE

Just months after General Milburn returned to Missoula, his old friend and Military Academy football teammate came to Montana to campaign for the presidency. Barnstorming through the West, Republican candidate Dwight

D. Eisenhower arrived in Montana by Northern Pacific passenger train. Making short campaign stops at Billings, Livingston, Bozeman, Whitehall, Logan and Butte, Ike's eighteen-car special train approached Missoula on Sunday, October 5, 1952. Onboard the train were Lieutenant General Frank Milburn and his wife, together with Montana Republican leaders.

The *Missoulian* estimated that a huge crowd of nine thousand turned out that Sunday evening to greet General Eisenhower and hear him speak from the rear platform of his campaign train. Adhering to his policy of avoiding politics on Sunday, General Eisenhower talked about Americanism and directed much of his speech toward the youngsters in the crowd.

On the platform as the train rolled slowly through the massive crowd was Senator Zales N. Ecton, candidate for reelection. General Milburn came from the interior of the car to present Senator Ecton to the audience. Senator Ecton in turn introduced J. Hugo Aronson, the "Galloping Swede" and GOP nominee for governor, and Wellington D. Rankin, candidate for U.S. Representative in the western district. Senator Ecton then said, "I'm now going to give you a treat—here is General Dwight D. Eisenhower, the next President of the United States."

Ike stepped from the rear door of the train to the platform, and the crowd roared in welcome to the nation's World War II hero. The general stood with both arms upraised, flashing his famous smile. After his address, as the train began moving west, he ended by saying, "Don't forget to elect Mr. Ecton and Mr. Rankin to Congress."

In November, Montanans cast almost 60 percent of their ballots for Ike over Adlai Stevenson, after the state had voted Democratic in the previous five presidential elections. The other races were all close, with Republican Aronson elected governor, Democrat Mike Mansfield elected over Senator Ecton and Democrat Lee Metcalf defeating Rankin.[62]

MONTANA ARMY NATIONAL GUARD

From guerrilla warfare in the Philippine Insurrection of 1898–99 to German machine gun nests in Argonne Forest in 1918, and on to hand-to-hand combat with the Japanese in the jungles and swamps of New Guinea and the Philippines in 1942–45, the Montana National Guard has served well in our nation's wars. Upon its return from the South Pacific, the Montana Guard was deactivated at the end of 1945.

What the *New* National Guard means to you...

A Message from the President of the United States

WE OWE our existence as a nation to the tradition of service of our citizens. It was an army of citizen soldiers which George Washington led to victory in the American Revolution. At the end of that war, the first Congress asked General Washington to give his views on what the military policy of the new nation should be. This was his answer:

"...every citizen who enjoys the protection of a free government, owes not only a proportion of his property but even of his personal services to the defense of it."

Today the new National Guard gives every man an opportunity to give that personal service to his country and at the same time to advance himself. In National Guard units all over the country thousands of veterans and other ambitious young men are finding the opportunity to study and learn the things that help them advance in their civilian jobs. They are finding the fellowship that is part and parcel of America. They are participating in a sports and recreation program that keeps them fit. And they are receiving the training that helps keep America strong.

Because of the National Guard's importance to our national defense I have proclaimed September 16th as National Guard Day and have directed that a nationwide recruiting campaign be conducted to fill its ranks.

Harry Truman

President Harry S Truman announced the New National Guard and proclaimed National Guard Day each September 16. This advertisement recruited for the New Montana National Guard. *From the* Independent-Record, *September 14, 1947.*

In the fall of 1946, the Montana National Guard was reorganized as the 163rd Regimental Combat Team. Colonel S.H. Mitchell, adjutant general, commanded the new Montana Guard, while Colonel Walter R. "Barney" Rankin commanded the Combat Team. Colonel Rankin was a decorated veteran of World War II with the 163rd Infantry, gaining fame as a battalion commander leading Rankin's Raiders in the New Guinea campaign.

While Montana's National Guardsmen anxiously awaited the call to active duty early in the Korean War, that call never came. On March 1953, the Regimental Combat Team was re-designated as the 163rd Armored Cavalry, while the artillery battalion formed the 154th Field Artillery Group and the engineer company became the 210th Engineer Battalion.[63]

National Guard units can be mobilized at any time by presidential order to supplement the regular armed forces, as well as upon declaration of a state of emergency, such as by the governor of Montana. Thousands of Montanans served in the National Guard throughout the Cold War, with emergency missions in many Montana communities. The *Billings Gazette* provided insight into the Guard's typical training program in 1953:

Guard to Train in Three States

Helena, AP—Montana's National Guard troops will attend summer field training camps in three states in June.

An encampment will be at Camp J. Hugo Aronson at Fort Harrison June 14 to 28, Brig. Gen. S.H. Mitchell, guard commander, announced Tuesday. Training at Camp Aronson will be the state headquarters 3669th Ordinance Company, the 46th Army Band, Battalion Headquarters and Service Company of the 210th Engineer Battalion and the 163rd Armored Cavalry Regiment.

The last unit which now is entirely mechanized and mobile, is successor to the 163rd Infantry, Montana's representative in world conflicts. Conversion to an armored unit was accomplished early this month.

Units which will train at Helena include those from Helena, Bozeman, Livingston, Billings, Dillon, Miles City, Glendive, Forsyth, Sidney, Culbertson, Plentywood, Poplar, Glasgow, Malta, Chinook, Havre, and Lewistown.

Mitchell will be post commander at Camp Aronson, Col. W.R. Rankin of Somers…will command the 163rd Armored Cavalry Regiment.

The 186th Fighter Interceptor Squadron, Montana Air National Guard, based at Great Falls will train at Gowen Field, Boise, Idaho June 13 through 27. This squadron recently served on active duty for 21 months at bases in Georgia and California and was deactivated at Great Falls early this year…

Troops from the 443rd Armored Field Artillery Battalion and three howitzer companies from the 163rd Armored Cavalry Regiment will go to Fort Lewis, Wash., by special train. They will encamp with the 41st Guard Division from Oregon and Washington June 13-27. Units of this battalion are located in Missoula, Kalispell, Deer Lodge, Roundup, Harlowton and Plentywood.[64]

MONTANA AIR NATIONAL GUARD

World War II ended, and the Great Falls military installation known as the 557th Army Air Forces Base Unit at Gore Field closed down. As part of a postwar Army Air Forces reorganization, each state was authorized one air unit, and an army investigating board recommended Gore Field as the best site for the Montana Air National Guard (MANG). Gore Field, the Great Falls municipal and commercial airport, had undergone extensive improvement for use by the Seventh Ferrying Command during the war, and it now met all the requirements: three seven-thousand-foot runways, one five-thousand-foot runway, a number of hangars, gasoline storage pits, barracks, storage buildings and shops—plus a city government led by Mayor Fritz Norby and the chamber of commerce fully committed to cooperation. The planned air squadron would total 350 personnel, of whom 44 would be permanently employed.[65]

Lieutenant Colonel Willard Sperry, a decorated combat pilot stationed at Great Falls AAB, began building the MANG at Gore Field. On June 27, 1947, the 186th Fighter Squadron activated and was federally recognized with three subordinate units: 227th Services Group, Detachment C; 186th Utility Flight; and 186th Weather Squadron. Within two weeks, six P-51D Mustangs arrived with support aircraft. On September 18, the U.S. Air Force and the Air National Guard officially moved from the U.S. Army to become a separate military service.[66]

On September 17, less than three months after squadron activation, tragedy struck the new squadron. En route to pick up Montana Adjutant General S.H. Mitchell in Helena, Colonel Sperry's A-26 went down in a heavy snowstorm with Sergeant Charles Glover onboard. The wreckage—high up a mountainside forty miles southeast of Helena—was not located until June the following summer. General Mitchell appointed Major Cliff Owens, a Montanan and F-51D pilot, to command the 186th.

One of the earliest state emergencies for the MANG happened during a major blizzard in February 1950, when livestock and hundreds of families on the Blackfeet Reservation were stranded, snowbound. With roads impassable, Air Guard cargo aircraft delivered more than six tons of lifesaving food and supplies.

MANG played an important role in the Korean War. With the North Korean invasion, the 186th delivered ten P-51Ds to California to help the air force respond to the emergency. The next spring, on April 1, 1951, the 186th Fighter Squadron federally activated with support units and was sent to Moody AFB, Georgia, assigned to the Strategic Air Command as fighter escorts. In November, the 186th transferred to George AFB, California, with a new mission of ground attack support under the Tactical Air Command.

Upon its return to Gore Field in late 1952, the squadron began transitioning to jet aircraft, receiving two T-33 Shooting Stars. Shortly after, the 186th became the first Air Guard unit in the nation to be equipped with F-86 Sabre Jets. By November, the 186th had five F-86As, the F-51s were leaving and the squadron was re-designated the 186th Fighter-Interceptor Squadron.

F-89H Scorpion all-weather, twin-engine long-range interceptors began arriving in 1955 to replace the F-86s, and MANG was re-designated the 120th Fighter Group (Air Defense). In early 1956, a major expansion followed, doubling the Group to an ultimate 107 officers and 796 men, with new units formed: 120th Fighter Group (Air Defense); 120th Material Squadron; 120th Air Base Squadron; and 120th Infirmary. Significantly, MANG was tied into the existing ar force air defense structure at that time; thus, the 29th Air Division at Malmstrom AFB gained direct operational control over the aircraft of the 186th Fighter-Interceptor Squadron in the event of alert, mobilization or exercise.

October 1, 1958, began the 186th Squadron's commitment to three crews in combat-ready five-minute runway alert status, fourteen hours a day, year-round—a task that would last past the end of the Cold War. Less than two years later, more powerful thrust F-89Js replaced the H version. They could be armed with the AIR2A Genie nuclear missile. With the nuclear capability, security was strengthened at Gore Field and weapons storage facilities.

While some Air Guard squadrons were federalized during the Berlin crisis in the fall of 1961, the 186th was not called up because of its integral role in the nation's air defense. Earlier, on July 1, the five-minute alert status was escalated to twenty-four hours a day to counter possible Soviet bomber attacks from the north. By the end of the Cold War, Air Guard squadrons constituted 100 percent of the nation's air defense interceptor force.

F-89J greets visitors at the front gate of the Montana Air National Guard at Gore Field. This aircraft was the only F-89 ever to have fired a Genie nuclear missile during a test conducted at Yucca Flats, Nevada. *Author's photo.*

January 25, 1962, proved the most tragic day in the history of the 120th when a C-47 Skytrain carrying Governor Donald Nutter and two other passengers, with a three-man crew, crashed into a mountainside north of Helena. Investigators determined that metal fatigue caused the right wing to fail under severe turbulence.

A study in the mid-1960s showed that MANG contributed $3.4 million annually to the Great Falls economy from 250 full-time and 550 part-time guardsmen, along with purchase of supplies, services, construction and materials. On July 1, 1968, Air National Guard units were authorized to recruit women. Jodie Lee Nichols became the first female recruit in the 120th, while Lieutenant Gwendolyn Liedmann became the first woman to hold a major managerial post when she was assigned as base communications officer.

The arrival of F-102A Delta Daggers in 1966, replacing the F-89s, ushered in the supersonic age. In 1972, the 319th Fighter Interceptor Squadron at Malmstrom was deactivated, with its air defense missions assumed by the Air Guard's 120th Fighter Group. The 120th was re-designated 120th Fighter-Interceptor Group and assigned F-106 Delta Darts, the first Air Guard unit to receive this aircraft. The F-106 was a highly complex aircraft with an

Four F-106s of the 120th Fighter Group stand on alert on the flight line at Gore Hill, ready to launch. A guardsman patrols the restricted area with a rifle slung over his back. *Author's collection.*

equally sophisticated weapons system, and it could carry both conventional and nuclear missiles. With the F-106, the 120th won its first William Tell, a biennial live-fire missile competition held at Tyndall AFB, Florida, a feat it repeated for a second successive year.

The Vietnam War's impact on the U.S. Air Force is revealed in reduction from the early 1960s of forty-five interceptor squadrons and twenty-five Air National Guard squadrons to the postwar figure of eleven and fifteen squadrons, respectively. Throughout the 1970s and 1980s, the 120th routinely earned honors in varying competitions. In 1985, the 120th won the Hughes Trophy, the ultimate honor for the best Fighter Interceptor Group, active duty or Air Guard, within the U.S. Air Force—just the second Air Guard unit ever to win that trophy.

On October 28, 1982, the 120th hosted President Ronald Reagan and provided security for Air Force One during the president's speech at nearby Charles M. Russell High School. The 120th received F-16A/B Fighting Falcons in early 1987. A few months later, British Royal Air Force Air Vice Marshal Ronald Dick—a former pilot with Fighter Command's Aerobatic Display Team (similar to the U.S. Navy's Blue Angels) and head of the British Defense Staff in Washington, D.C.—asked to visit an Air National Guard unit. He was told by the U.S. Defense Department that he might as well "see the best": the 120th Fighter Interceptor Group. During that visit, Colonel

Gary Blair, commander of the 120th, briefed Air Vice Marshal Dick and led him on a thorough tour before sending him on an hourlong flight in an F-16 piloted by Captain Mark Meyer. In a fitting tribute to the "best" National Air Guard outfit in January 1989, 120th Commander Gary Blair was appointed Montana adjutant general with promotion to brigadier general.[67]

ANTI-COMMUNISM IN MONTANA: THE SENATOR ROARS

The Cold War was all about containing the spread of Soviet Communism, and Soviet force of arms held Eastern and most of Central Europe in its iron grip. The Chinese Communists prevailed by 1949 throughout the Chinese mainland. North Korea invaded the south to unite the Korean Peninsula under Marxist-Leninism. Communism was on the march worldwide, and the voices of anti-Communism within the United States began to roar.

At home, concern for Communist influence and subversion rose in the minds of many in the late 1940s as Lend-Lease espionage was uncovered and spies like Rudolf Abel, Alger Hiss and the Rosenbergs were discovered, while others came under suspicion. Leading the "hunt" for Communists in the U.S. government were the U.S. House of Representatives Un-American Activities Committee and Senator Joseph R. McCarthy of Wisconsin, a figure who grew more controversial as the early 1950s progressed.

On October 14, 1952, Senator McCarthy came to Missoula to campaign for incumbent Montana Republican Senator Zales Ecton and against his Democratic opponent, Representative Mike Mansfield. This was a key race for control of the U.S. Senate, and both parties were pulling out all the stops. The October campaign rally jam-packed Loyola High School auditorium with an overflow crowd tuned in through an outdoor loudspeaker.

Senator McCarthy began his attack on Representative Mansfield by holding up copies of the *Daily Worker*, the Communist Party USA's organ. While emphasizing that he was not saying that Mansfield either was or had been a Communist, Senator McCarthy instead avowed that a person who so conducts himself as to win the favor of the Communist Party organ must be "either stupid or a dupe." Senator McCarthy warned that "if we blind our eyes and close our ears this nation doesn't have long to live."

Emphasizing that Americans are Americans first and Republicans or Democrats second, Senator McCarthy declared that he wasn't calling on Democrats to desert their party. Instead, he said, it's the party of Secretary of

State Dean Acheson and Alger Hiss and China scholar Owen Lattimore—in short, the "Communist Party." Senator McCarthy concluded that there had been a steady, planned, deliberate retreat from victory under the leadership of Acheson, whom he called the "Red dean of Communism."[68]

Despite Senator McCarthy's endorsement and a strenuous campaign, Mansfield defeated Ecton in the race, thus launching him to a legendary Senate career, featuring his leadership in international and Asian relations.

The Voice for Anti-Communism within Montana

Throughout the Cold War, the level of anti-Communist rhetoric in Montana was relatively mild yet persistent. Perhaps the most vocal anti-Communist in Montana during those years was Victor O. Overcash, a veteran of both world wars and Montana department commander of the American Legion. From his home base at Cut Bank, Vic Overcash assembled a vast collection of "subversive activity" literature to have the facts "to expose the Communist conspiracy for what it is." He believed that education was the best means of combatting Communism, saying, "We know what the Communists are going to do, because they have already told us. But we need to know how they plan to do it so we can take steps to prevent it."

Frequently called on to lecture on Communist infiltration and subversion, by the early 1960s Overcast had become the Montana coordinator for the John Birch Society as the best way to fight Communism.[69]

Montana House Un-American Activities Committee: A Witch Hunt that Found No Witches

In 1952, the 32nd Montana Legislature established a Montana House Un-American Activities Committee (HUAC) under Representative R.H. Weidman, a Republican from Lake County northwestern Montana. The investigating group was "broke" from the start since the legislature failed to appropriate funding.

At its first meeting in May, Chairman Weidman announced, "The Communist problem in Montana is a damn sight more serious than people think. We don't want a witch hunt in Montana—we want to feel our way along, but we do want people of this state to know which organizations have definite un-American objectives." Weidman announced that the U.S.

Supreme Court had ruled that the federal HUAC had to give hearings to organizations before branding them as subversive. He stated also that there were about eighty-seven card-carrying Communists in Montana, but many more persons have "unwittingly" joined subversive groups.

The HUAC determined that its first action would be to make a list of groups known to be carrying on subversive activities in Montana and to publish their names. The committee planned also to announce the names of Montana chapters of nationally listed groups. Weidman invited Montanans to give members of the committee any reliable information regarding subversive groups.

With no funding and very few Communists in the state, after a few meetings, the Montana HUAC quietly voted to close down—a witch hunt that found no witches![70]

A Card-Carrying Communist

One of the alleged card-carrying Communists in Montana was arrested in 1956. After a grand jury investigation, John Cyril Hellman faced charges of belonging to the U.S. Communist Party, thus violating the Anti-Communist Smith Act, a 1940 federal law forbidding persons from advocating the forcible overthrow of the government or belonging to organizations espousing that view. After a three-week trial in federal court in Butte, a jury convicted Hellman in May 1958 of being a member of the Communist Party, and he was sentenced to a five-year prison term by Judge W.D. Murray.

John Hellman had been a clerk, bookkeeper, laborer and butcher, as well as a longtime member of the Communist Party. Finding a defense attorney proved problematic, since few lawyers or prospective jury members wanted to touch the case. Judge Murray finally assigned Butte attorneys Robert A. Poore and Charles Zimmerman to represent Hellman pro bono. Poore described public reaction: "The people were quite intelligent, although at that time Communism was a real bugaboo. We had a heck of a time getting a jury."

A thorough FBI investigation provided government prosecutors with many witnesses and exhibits to prove that Hellman was active in the Communist Party and had attended many meetings and schools. One witness, Arthur W. Clowes of St. Paul, Minnesota, testified that he had been a student at the University of Montana in November 1947. Approached by Hellman,

Clowes attended three meetings, held in secrecy, with Hellman and another man, Art Bary, introduced as the Rocky Mountain district organizer for the Communist Party. At these meeting, Clowes was recruited to head a proposed campus Communist group. Clowes declined out of concern that acceptance would jeopardize his plans for becoming a teacher.

While the government proved that Hellman was active in the Communist Party, prosecutors were unable to demonstrate that he had participated in any overt act to overthrow the government, such as blowing up a building. Nonetheless, Hellman was convicted and sentenced, and Judge Murray appointed Poore counsel to handle an appeal.[71]

Attorney Poore filed the appeal, and in late December 1961, the 9th U.S. Court of Appeals reversed the conviction of John Hellman. The Appeals Court decision held that while there was testimony that Hellman was an organizer for the Communist Party in Montana and Idaho and "an exceedingly active member of the party," the government's proof failed to meet standards set up by the Supreme Court in Smith Act cases.

Recent decisions of the Supreme Court had decreed that under the Smith Act, there must be proof that the defendant has knowledge that an organization intends to overthrow the government by force and violence. The Appeals Court noted that nowhere in the evidence does it show that Hellman personally advocated violent overthrow of the government during his activities as organizer, teacher in the party's schools and distributor of party literature. The Appeals Court ordered the government to dismiss the action against Hellman.[72]

A Final Reward for Poore

Defense Attorney Poore had donated one year of pro bono time to the Hellman case and appeal. He said that no one called him a Communist to his face but that several Montana lawyers advised that they had heard him branded a Communist for defending Hellman. Defending Hellman didn't mean that Poore was a Communist or a Communist sympathizer—he most certainly was not. After all, during this same period, Poore served as state chairman of the Montana Republican Party. In 1989, the Montana State Bar chose Poore to receive the first Jameson Award for his ethical and personal conduct, commitment and activities exemplifying professionalism for his career, highlighted by his defense of Communist John Hellman.[73]

A Cold War Chicom Shootdown:
Captain Elmer Llewellyn

Combine a Montana aviator flying for the 91st Strategic Reconnaissance Squadron with a Chinese Communist shootdown over North Korea, and follow that with 935 days of captivity in Communist China, and you will be reading the Cold War saga of Captain Elmer F. "Sonny" Llewellyn, USAF.

It all began on Janury 12, 1953, at 5:20 p.m., when Captain Llewellyn and thirteen other men, aboard a B-29 Superfortress, rolled down the runway at Yokota Air Base, Japan. Their destination was North Korea, with a mission to drop propaganda leaflets on six cities south of the Yalu River.

The B-29 that Captain Llewellyn was navigating proceeded without incident until 11:16 p.m., when it transmitted a distress signal. With no further radio contact, a ground radar station reported indications that the B-29 was deep in North Korean territory and in proximity to about a dozen unidentified aircraft. These aircraft appeared to merge with the B-29, which then vanished from the radar screen. The B-29 failed to return to base, and all men aboard were listed as missing. Their long ordeal had begun.

Born in Missoula on August 19, 1925, to grocer Elmer H. and Mamie Jo Llewellyn, Sonny Llewellyn grew up loving football and flying. He attended Missoula High School, where he was selected to the All-State football team. Graduating in 1943, he joined the Army Air Corps' aviation-cadet program. After basic training at Shepard Field, Wichita Falls, Texas, he was assigned to a college training detachment at Creighton University in Omaha. Further instruction followed at Santa Ana, California, and Hondo Field, Texas. In September 1944, at age nineteen, Llewellyn was commissioned second lieutenant and called to active duty. Trained as a navigator, Lieutenant Llewellyn deployed to Europe with the 314th Troop Carrier Wing flying C-47s, towing gliders and dropping paratroopers. In August 1945, with his face disfigured from a service-related crash, he was discharged from active duty with the rank of captain.

Returning to Missoula and entering the University of Montana, he played for the Grizzlies football team. Captain Llewellyn remained active in the reserves, serving at Great Falls AFB when North Korea invaded. Recalled to active duty in early April 1951, Captain Llewellyn was assigned to the 91st Strategic Reconnaissance Wing in October and attached to the 581st Air Resupply and Communications Wing based at Yokota Air Base, Japan. This air force wing, with the innocuous name, was a collaboration between the

Eleven U.S. Air Force airmen arriving at Travis Air Force Base on August 12, 1955, after two and a half years as prisoners of the Chinese Communists. *Front row, left to right*: Colonel John Arnold Jr.; Captain Elmer Llewellyn, Missoula; Airman Second Class John Thompson; Captain John Buck; Lieutenant Wallace Brown; and Sergeant Howard W. Brown. *Standing, left to right*: Airman First Class Steven Kiba, Airman Second Class Harry H. Benjamin Jr., Airman Second Class Daniel Schmidt, Major William H. Baumer and Captain Eugene Vaadi. *From the* Houston Post, *August 13, 1955, author's collection.*

newly created CIA and the air force, providing a new Cold War weapon: an unconventional warfare group.

The night of January 12, 1953, Captain Llewellyn's B-29 had dropped propaganda leaflets at four of six scheduled targets just south of the Yalu River when they were shot down by Communist Chinese MiG fighters. Bailing out, eleven of the fourteen-man crew landed and were captured. This began their two-and-a-half-year ordeal enduring extended periods of thirty-hour-long interrogations.[74]

Finally, on August 4, 1955, Captain Llewellyn and his crew were released to the British in Hong Kong. Crewman Sergeant Steve Kiba wrote of their freedom:

> *"We arrived in Hong Kong on Aug. 4, 1955," Kiba wrote. "At 1:36 p.m. I don't think any of us ever forgot that date and time." It was 935 long days since the night they survived the shootdown of Stardust Four-Zero by Chinese MiGs and bailed out into the skies over North Korea.*
>
> *The Chinese turned the crew over to the British, and the British walked them to the American Consulate. Nine days later, on August 12, Llewellyn, Kiba and the rest of the crew landed at Travis Air Force Base in California.*[75]

The time was about 5:00 p.m. on August 12, 1955. After more than two and a half years in a Peking prison as a captive of the Communist Chinese—years during which he and ten other Americans convicted of spying became the subject of considerable national and international attention—Air Force Captain Elmer Fred Llewellyn came home to Missoula to a tumultuous homecoming.

A slender, handsome man just a week short of thirty, Sonny Llewellyn wore a new khaki uniform as he descended from the plane to the pavement. He offered a trim salute to a nearby American flag and then, overcome by emotion, broke into a run toward his family. His wife, crying, greeted him with outstretched arms, and his son danced about the couple in a frenzy. Their relatives wept openly, as did many in the huge crowd of more than one thousand at the Missoula county airport. Never in Missoula's history had there been such an outpouring of sentiment for a returning serviceman. Sonny Llewellyn was, in every sense of the term, a war hero. A motorcade and parade through downtown Missoula followed the arrival.

After thirty days' leave, in December all eleven crew members reported to Bolling Air Force Base, Washington, D.C., to learn their options for the future. One option was for the air force to pay expenses to attend a university of their choice and remain in the air force. Sonny Llewellyn returned to Missoula and entered university as a junior, majoring in political science. Newly promoted Staff Sergeant Steve Kiba opted to join Sonny at the university, where he entered in January 1956 as a freshman in French, and he continued through three quarters before moving on from Montana and beginning to write of his horrible memories of captivity in China.

A third crew member at Bolling AFB, airman Daniel C. Schmidt of Isabel, South Dakota, and Portland, Oregon, declared his intention to join Llewellyn and Kiba in Missoula and attend the university—Schmidt apparently did not follow through with this plan. His return from captivity had been dampened by news that his wife, Una, had remarried despite air force notification that her husband survived the shootdown and was a prisoner of the Chinese.[76]

While at the university in 1956, Llewellyn prepared an article for the literary magazine *Venture*. Writing on behalf of himself and the other former prisoners, Llewellyn recounted his experiences and then expressed some hopes for the future:

> *A couple of years in a communist prisoner is, of course, a horrible experience, but it does give you time to think, to wonder, and to plan ways of combating communism. We believe that students at a university such as [UM] are, or should be, a great defense army.*
>
> *First, as you study and learn and live, we hope you will grow to appreciate the freedoms you have. While still students, you have a wonderful chance to broaden your outlook and to find out not only what communism is and how it works, but to compare it with your own democracy—and see how important it is that you fight for it (democracy).*
>
> *Second, when you have learned these things, we hope you will tell others. Let people know, and support your arguments with soundness and with pride. We feel strongly about this because we believe that perhaps the greatest threat to the free world is the complacency of its people. Communists are never complacent. They plan world domination, and they've proved it in Russia, in the Soviet satellites and in China. We were told over and over again by our interrogators that someday they would put us down—that they would dominate the United States and the whole world.[77]*

AIR DEFENSE IN THE 1950s: OPERATION SKYWATCH GROUND OBSERVER CORPS

Signs that the Cold War might turn "hot" came about from Stalin's two major miscalculations: the Berlin Blockade in June 1948 and the green light for North Korea to invade the South in June 1950. Further fueling American concerns, the Soviets tested their first atomic bomb on August 29, 1949, becoming the world's second nuclear power, and their first hydrogen bomb on August 12, 1953. President Truman established the first federal civil defense organization with the passage of the Civil Defense Act of 1950. Yet early civil defense costs were left to state and local governments—and that was a problem.

With the strategic bombing of both military and civilian targets during World War II and a civil defense program called Ground Observer Corps to detect enemy air attack still fresh in mind, the primary threat in the early Cold War was perceived as Soviet long-range bombers carrying nuclear weapons. In response to the newly nuclear-armed Soviet threat, the USAF created a stopgap system to detect penetrating Soviet bombers until a radar network could become operational. This program, Operation Skywatch, used a similar Ground Observer Corps (GOC) with civilian volunteer observers reporting aircraft sightings by phone to filter centers connected to air defense bases along the northern United States.

In July 1952, President Truman promoted the program to the nation: "Our greatest hopes for peace lie in being so strong and so well prepared that our enemies will not dare attack. Every citizen who cooperates in 'Operation Skywatch' as well as in other defense activities, is helping prevent the war none of us wants to happen."[78]

Western Air Defense Force 29TH Air Division

Great Falls AFB became the northern hub of the nation's important air defense operations to protect against Russian bombers—in 1953, the Soviet Union had more than one thousand long-range bombers capable of delivering atomic bombs. The U.S. Air Force prepared to implement the new coordinated air defense and GOC Skywatch program in Montana in 1951. The headquarters of the newly formed 29th Air Division of the Western Air Defense Force was established at Great Falls AFB, with Colonel Paul E. Greiner, a native Montanan, in command.

As a component of western air defense, the 29th Air Division was charged with responsibility for detecting, identifying and intercepting all unidentified aircraft over a broad area encompassing Idaho, Montana, Wyoming, half of Nevada, Utah and Colorado, as well as portions of North Dakota, South Dakota and Nebraska.

Operation plans called for establishment of a series of radar-equipped warning stations throughout the area that, working in conjunction with

Air Defense Control Center at GFAFB became the nerve center during "Crossborder" exercises. Based on radar detections, fighter aircraft scrambled from 29th Fighter Interceptor Squadron, GFAFB; 186th Fighter Interceptor Squadron, MANG; and 403rd Fighter Squadron, Royal Canadian Air Force, Calgary. *From the* Great Falls Tribune, *October 24, 1954.*

civilian-manned GOC and filter centers, would supply aircraft detections on unidentified planes. Colonel Greiner and his staff were assigned to launch fighters to intercept these aircraft. Locations of planned radar detection stations and details of their equipment were secret.

With arrival of Colonel Greiner and his staff, personnel at the local base increased by 350 men. All operations of the division were under Major General Hugo Rush at Hamilton Field, California. Colonel Greiner, a native of Butte and a University of Montana graduate, had joined the Army Air Corps as a cadet in 1939, served as route survey pilot in various war theaters and spent three years in the Alaskan Division. His wife, the former Virginia Hall of Fort Shaw, accompanied him.[79]

Skywatch in Action

A network of GOC posts and four filter centers operated in Montana, Idaho and Wyoming. The 4773rd Ground Observer Squadron, under the 29th Air Division, served as headquarters for the scattered observer posts, with sightings reported to the nearest filter centers.

At its peak in November 1954, Montana operated 343 observation posts with about eleven thousand observers. These volunteers were equipped with Ground Observer's Guides containing photographic guides and silhouette keys for identifying U.S. and Soviet military aircraft. Montana GOC observers became experts at identifying U.S. aircraft most often seen. Many sightings were civilian aircraft off course in the broad spaces of Montana.

A GOC post could be as simple as a volunteer's backyard deck or patio, with an aircraft recognition chart, binoculars to scan the horizon, a log to record sightings and a telephone to call the filter center. Some watchtowers were also built, similar to those used in western Montana forests to watch for fires.

The posts ranged widely from observation towers to rooftops of buildings, ranch homes and others. In Missoula, a balcony of the Student Union Building at the university served until the observers moved to the rooftop of the downtown Palace Hotel. Students at Starr School on the Blackfeet Reservation operated a post. Families joined together, often from their own homes. Harold and Elizabeth Goldhahn, from their home in Geraldine, watched for their rooftop antenna to vibrate to tip them that an aircraft was passing overhead. Stepping outside, they would record the direction and altitude and call "Aircraft Flash" to the Helena filter center.

On occasion, the whole system of Skywatch and air defense was tested. One test along northern Montana's Hi-Line, the historic track of the Great Northern Railway, involved a KB-29 air refueler from Malmstrom. Flying a two-thousand-mile route between Great Falls and Fargo, North Dakota, GOC posts submitted alerts all along the aircraft's track. These timely reports enabled the launch of an interceptor jet and the successful "shoot-down" of the "bomber" before it reached its target at Fargo, North Dakota.[80]

Operation Alert 1957

In October 1953, President Eisenhower stated that the Soviet Union now possessed the capability of nuclear attack on the United States and that this capability increased as time passed. The president ordered tests of our preparedness, and annual Operation Alerts began, intended to preview substantially what would happen if the United States actually was plunged into war after a surprise attack that left millions dead or wounded and more millions homeless.

During the nationwide Operation Alert 1957, simulated nuclear bombs fell on Great Falls, Anaconda and Fort Peck Dam in a civil defense and mobilization exercise—all three were rated as prime targets of any real enemy bombers. The public took no part in the imaginary attack, except on paper. Hugh K. Potter, Montana's civil defense director, outlined the attacks and divulged the following theoretical damage.

The smelter at Anaconda was the first paper-bombing target at 11:56 a.m. There, Potter said, an atom bomb burst in the air, causing greater blast and less fallout than ground bursts. About twelve thousand residents

Glasgow, Air Force Base in Throes of Growth

Glasgow AAB closed as a satellite base after World War II. A new base was built in 1957, then closed in 1968; it was reopened in 1971 as a B-52 base and closed permanently in 1976. Shown are the twenty-six men needed to keep this supersonic F-101B "Voodoo" fighter interceptor plane flying. *From the* Great Falls Tribune, *September 6, 1959.*

theoretically were evacuated from Anaconda to Butte, Dillon and five other nearby communities. Director Potter revealed the predicted fallout pattern for radiation from the bomb at Anaconda as extending from Philipsburg to five miles southeast of Great Falls and from the center of Butte to a line ten miles east of Boulder and ten miles northwest of Stanford.

The second bombing target, Great Falls Malmstrom AFB and the Black Eagle Anaconda refineries, was struck by a mock hydrogen bomb striking the ground before exploding at 12:02 p.m. On paper, more than fifty thousand people had been evacuated from the Great Falls area before the strike to twenty-three different locations, including Havre. Malmstrom and the refineries were 90 percent destroyed and afire; 25 percent of air base personnel at Malmstrom were lost. The radiation fallout pattern extended roughly from Great Falls about 450 miles in a northeasterly direction. The northern boundary of the fallout would reach the eastern edge of Havre and continue on to Moosejaw, Saskatchewan. The southeastern boundary would be about 30 miles southeast of Fort Benton.

The third Montana target, Fort Peck Dam, was struck by a hydrogen bomb at 12:34 p.m. intended to destroy the dam to flood the Missouri River Basin and cause water damage along the length of the Mississippi River. Fort Peck residents had been evacuated to Glasgow. Communities below the dam were flooded. The radiation fallout pattern extended from Glasgow to Minot, North Dakota, as the southern boundary, with the northern boundary extending from Glasgow to Plentywood and on into Canada.[81]

ADVANCES IN LONG-RANGE DETECTION ELIMINATE GROUND OBSERVER CORPS

From its beginning, the USAF made clear that GOC Skywatch was a stopgap system until radar networks could installed along the northern border. In 1952, the air force built four Aircraft Control & Warning (AC&W) radar stations in Montana, located near Cut Bank, Opheim, Havre and Yaak. Two years later, the air force added a fifth station near Miles City. By 1958, six AC&W radar stations and eight gap filler radar stations were located in eastern Montana and near Kalispell and Eureka.

In 1956, the Air Force Semi-Automatic Ground Environment (SAGE) rapidly processed information received from the radar stations to centralized locations, which then plotted the air courses and transmitted the data to the air defense bases. This new system formed a composite scene of the air situation in real time as it developed. SAGE revolutionized air defense in the United States and Canada, ending the need for GOC.

More than SAGE was coming online, and in July 1957, the air force activated the Distant Early Warning (DEW) Line, a grid of radar installations ringing the Arctic Circle in northern Canada and Alaska. Two months later, the North American Aerospace Defense Command (NORAD) began operations.[82]

LAUNCHING THE SPACE AGE

October 1957 also brought two dramatic developments heralding the transformation of the air defense threat from bombers to Intercontinental Ballistic Missiles (ICBM). On October 1, the Strategic Air Command initiated continuous nuclear alert (24/7) in anticipation of a Soviet ICBM surprise attack capability—an alert status only terminated at the end of the Cold War in 1991. Three days later, the Soviet Union shocked America by launching the Sputnik satellite, placed into orbit by a powerful rocket. The Space Age now was underway, bringing a whole new dimension of danger.

Brigadier General Harold L. Neely, commander of the 29th Air Division, announced in late November 1958 that recent major improvements in long-range detection, coupled with developments in distant early warning of enemy aircraft, had eliminated the need to for GOC, and the volunteer corps was phased out.[83]

The GOC deactivated on January 31, 1959. Just days later, the *Billings Gazette* paid tribute to the program in an editorial:

> IMPORTANT PATRIOTIC SERVICE
> *The Ground Observer Corps joined the Minute Men in American history if not tradition with deactivation of the Billings Air Force Filter Center at midnight Jan. 31.*
>
> *It seems to be another case of the machine replacing the man because the nation's warning system against enemy attack, we are told, has now been completed and can replace the thousands of citizens who gave their time to "Operation Skywatch."*
>
> *Having turned over the skies and our safety to bulbous radomes and coldly efficient electronic brains, the nation and the community might well*

take a moment to thank those volunteers both old and young who stood ready to warn as our defenses were gradually built up.

There was nothing glamorous about the Ground Observer Corps. Its members wore no uniforms and drew no pay. They were frequently made the butt of good-natured jokes and by those who too quickly forgot the GOC counterparts of 20 years ago who dug trenches in London parks while Hitler assured the world he had made his last territorial demands in Europe.

These men and women were in effect, the eyes and the ears of the US Air Force for eight years.

Top-ranking officials of the Air Defense Command expressed their appreciation to GOC volunteers at a "farewell" banquet in Billings Thursday night.

It is now the community's turn in say thanks to these good citizens for a job well done.[84]

An Early Spy in the Sky:
91ˢᵗ Strategic Reconnaissance Squadron

In March 1955, a new reconnaissance concept arrived at Great Falls AFB. In response to Soviet and Chinese Communist threats to air force reconnaissance aircraft without fighter escort, this concept was designed to couple fighter speed and altitude with long-range reconnaissance capabilities. The first squadron of its kind married a long-range B-36 "Mother Ship" with a high-speed F-84 jet reconnaissance fighter equipped with a camera and four .50-caliber machine guns. Using an operational procedure called the Fighter-Conveyance (FICON) system, the specially designed RF-84Ks would be ferried close to the projected target location and then launched in flight to make a high-speed pass over the target area, finally to be retrieved and ferried back to their home base of operations. The pilots would enter and exit their RF-84 through the B-36's bomb bay to fly away to conduct their reconnaissance missions. In addition, the fighter jet could provide protection for the B-36.

The 91ˢᵗ SRS, commanded by Lieutenant Colonel Wante J. Bartol, was assigned to SAC's 71 Strategic Reconnaissance Wing (SRW) based at Larson AFB, Moses Lake, Washington, and attached to the 407ᵗʰ Strategic Fighter Wing at Great Falls AFB. Experimentation began in early 1955 with the first

The first-of-its-kind Experimental Reconnaissance System, the 91st Strategic Reconnaissance Squadron, married a "Mother Ship" long-range B-36 with a high-speed F-84K reconnaissance aircraft. *Polleto-Donnelly Collection.*

successful hook-up in December. By January 1956, the 91st had begun FICON missions on a regular schedule. The hook-ups were perilous, and many near-fatal accidents occurred during operations. These "strategic/tactical" reconnaissance missions were short-lived, largely due to the development of the dramatic new generation of reconnaissance aircraft: the high-altitude U-2. No longer needed, the 91st was deactivated on July 1, 1957.[85]

BIG SKY UFO SIGHTINGS

The Big Sky of Montana, so often with a clear, brilliant sky to observe the universe and stars, has been home to many UFO (Unidentified Flying Object) sightings over past decades. As the missile and space race heated up with the Soviet Union, more and more UFO sightings were reported, sometimes reaching craze proportions in the 1950s. Some led to the launch of fighters from Malmstrom Air Force Base, while a few became subject of detailed intelligence analysis.

Among the earliest episodes captured on film, and to this day remaining among the most creditable, occurred on August 15, 1950, at Great Falls. At 11:30 a.m., Nick Mariana, manager of the Great Falls Electrics baseball club, a Brooklyn Dodgers farm team, with his secretary, Virginia Raunig, looked up from the grandstand at Legion Ball Park and saw what they described as two bright, silvery flying saucers, streaking across the clear

Montana sky. Mariana observed the objects rotating while flying over Great Falls at a speed he estimated to be several hundred miles per hour. He believed that they were roughly 50 feet wide and 150 feet apart. Mariana raced to his auto outside the park, grabbed his 16mm color movie camera, ran back to the stands and panned his camera from left to right, aiming toward where he had seen the saucers and filming for sixteen seconds. Shortly after the sighting, both Mariana and Raunig saw two jet fighters streak over the baseball stadium.

Mariana showed his film and spoke about his exciting sighting to several local clubs, arousing air force interest. Malmstrom AFB intelligence officers interviewed Mariana and assisted in sending his movie film and story to Project Grudge for analysis at Wright-Patterson Air Force Base. Initially, the event was written off as reflections from two F-94 fighters, known to be flying in the vicinity at the time. Apparently, the film returned to Mariana was missing several feet of film containing the clearest coverage of the unidentified objects.

Two years later, the air force again asked Mariana for the film, and it was re-analyzed at Wright-Patterson, this time with a conclusion that the objects were not caused by F-94 reflections. Since then, the film objects remain unidentified and have been featured in documentaries, television programs and online video. The legend begun by Nick Mariana is alive today each time the Great Falls Voyagers baseball club, still performing in the Pioneer League, and its colorful mascot, Orbit, take the field on summer evenings.

Hundreds more UFO sightings were reported around Montana over the decades that followed. One such event occurred in northwestern Montana at Kalispell on September 4, 1956, when Paul Geddes, former commander of the local Civil Air Patrol, spotted a mysterious object at 9:20 p.m.; he described it as an orange-colored ball-shaped object that gave off a bright light that faded when it appeared to change direction. Geddes called the local GOC Skywatch post on Buffalo Hill, where Mrs. Gil Frandsen relayed the message to the Helena filter center.

At 10:30 p.m., Air Force Technical Sergeant Carl Clark, stationed in Kalispell, was called and ordered to investigate the object. He authenticated the Geddes report and described the object as "triangular in shape…with a bright yellow glow." Sergeant John Dalessio, on vacation from the Helena filter center, joined Sergeant Clark in observing the unidentified object.

Following the confirmation by the air force sergeants, jet aircraft were launched from Spokane with orders to shoot down any unidentified object.

Great Falls UFO reports analyzed

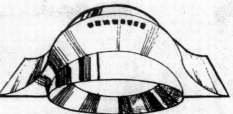

GREAT FALLS (AP) — A representative of the Mutual UFO Network is here seeking information on a reported sighting of two unidentified flying objects near Giant Springs on the Missouri River last summer.

James Leming arrived in Great Falls last month, representing the non-profit organization based in Texas.

Several witnesses reported seeing two glowing, disc-shaped objects hovering low over the Missouri River dams northeast of the city this past summer. The objects reportedly ascended at high speed and then disappeared from sight.

Leming, a free-lance artist named by the UFO network as state section director for Cascade County, said other UFO sightings were made this year near Kalispell and four cattle mutilation cases were reported within 50 miles of Great Falls.

Such mutilations throughout the West in recent years have gained national attention, with some people linking the incidents to UFO sightings.

Leming said gathering information on UFO sightings is difficult because witnesses are often "turned off" by questions about the incidents.

Witnesses should be encouraged to report their sightings, but they fear ridicule, he said. The enigma of the UFO can be dealt with only if people are allowed to express their feelings and relate their experiences without fear of reprisal, Leming said.

"There is indeed a phenomena that does exist in our skies," he added.

He recalled two earlier UFO sightings in the Great Falls area. In the 1950s, Nick Mariana, who was then manager of the local Pioneer League baseball team, captured two UFOs on 20 seconds of movie film as the objects hovered near Legion Park adjacent to the Missouri River.

Later, the U.S. Air Force borrowed the film and, according to Mariana, returned it with about 30 frames missing.

In 1978, Air Force planes chased several UFOs in the Great Falls vicinity, Leming said.

But, he added, "the natives are edgy and reluctant to discuss these events. With patience and time I am hoping they will want to know the answers more than fear reprisals."

Some of the questions Leming wants answered are whether the UFOs are extra-terrestrial, how they are propelled and where they originate.

From the 1950 sighting of two UFOs by Nick Mariana near the Great Falls baseball stadium through the 1950s spate of UFO science fiction movies, Montana has had unexplained sightings over the years. *From the* Billings Gazette, *December 3, 1982.*

All other aircraft were ordered to stay clear of the Kalispell area. The first jets arrived in the area at about 12:45 a.m. As the fighters closed in, the mysterious object faded, and as the aircraft drew away, the light again became bright. Hampered by cloud layers and mountainous terrain, the jets were unable to close in on the object.

At 5:30 a.m., Sergeant Clark and other witnesses observed that the object appeared to descend and fade from sight. When National Guard pilot Dick Rowland, with Sergeant Clark in company, took off from Kalispell airport at 6:00 a.m., they could not locate the object. One hour later, five all-weather F-94 Starfire interceptors, scrambled from Malmstrom AFB, arrived on scene but were unable to locate the mysterious object.

Observed by air force and many credible civilian witnesses, the mystery object could not be explained away as a natural phenomenon. A member of the University of Montana astronomy department commented that the object "could conceivably have been the planet Mars." Light or heavy scattered clouds in the area could have made the planet appear to fade or brighten and to move. He said that it should have been seen in the southwest and could have been bright yellow with an aurora, or light, around it. Locals were not convinced.[86]

Einar Malmstrom: World War II Ace and POW Leader—Cold War Hero and Namesake

The finest military leaders in each service earn the respect of those who serve under them, as well as those who in turn lead these great men and women. Only a very few earn both the respect and love of those around them. Einar Axel Malmstrom was one of these rare leaders.

Born in Chicago in 1907 of Swedish immigrant parents, Malmstrom enlisted as a private in the Washington State National Guard and was commissioned second lieutenant in 1932. Called to active duty in September 1940 as a lieutenant colonel, he deployed to the European theater of operations in May 1943 with the 65th Fighter Wing, where he served as assistant wing operations officer until November, when he assumed command of the 356th Fighter Group, 8th Air Force. Based in southeastern Britain at RAF Martlesham Heath and flying P-47 Thunderbolts, the 356th Group consisted of three fighter squadrons. They operated as escorts for B-17s and B-24s, attacking industrial targets, airfields and missile sites. From January 3, 1944, the 356th engaged in bombing and strafing missions targeting U-boat installations, shipyards, airfields, marshalling yards, flak towers and radar stations.

On April 24, credited with six and a half German aircraft kills and while flying his fifty-eighth combat mission, Colonel Malmstrom's P-47 was shot down over France, and he was captured by German soldiers. For thirteen months, he served as American commander of the south compound of Stalag Luft I in Barth, Germany, responsible for organizing U.S. officers for survival. Colonel Malmstrom excelled in this sensitive and difficult job, encompassing security, discipline, morale and welfare, and for this duty, he was awarded the Bronze Star medal for meritorious service. He was liberated by Soviet forces on April 30, 1945.[87]

Colonel Einar Malmstrom, deputy commander, 407th Strategic Fighter Wing, presented a collection of Swedish books to the public library. Colonel Malmstrom, *left*, is seen here with Library Director Alma Jacobs; Mayor James B. Austin; and Steve Swanberg and Harry Davison, library board members. *From the* Great Falls Tribune, *March 17, 1954.*

During his time as POW, Colonel Malmstrom enjoyed a fascinating experience when he flew a single-seat German Messerschmitt Bf-109, the fighter that, along with the Focke-Wulf Fw-190, was the backbone of the Luftwaffe's fighter force. This all came about after his Luftwaffe intelligence interrogator, Hans Scharff, learned that Colonel Malmstrom's dream was to fly the Bf-109. After Scharff arranged to make it happen, American POW Malmstrom flew the hot German fighter aircraft solo. Of course, the German ground crew made sure there was not enough fuel in the tanks to enable a flying escape. This story was revealed by newly naturalized American citizen Hans Scharff in Chicago years after the war.[88]

Returning to the United States in May 1945, Colonel Malmstrom completed several tours before arriving with his family at Great Falls AFB to serve as deputy commander of the 407th Strategic Fighter Wing under Colonel Lester S. Harris. This would prove to be a short but memorable assignment ending in tragedy. From the day he arrived, Colonel Malmstrom was out and about both on base with his airmen and in the local community. One of his first acts was to present to Director Alma Jacobs and the Great Falls Public Library a collection of four hundred books from his father's Swedish collection. Colonel Malmstrom's charismatic personality enabled him to establish close friendships throughout the Great Falls community.

A Tragic Death

On August 21, 1954, Colonel Malmstrom was killed in the crash of his T-33 shortly after takeoff from Great Falls AFB. The *Great Falls Tribune* reported the tragedy the next day:

> *Col. Einar A. Malmstrom, 47, much-decorated World War II ace and deputy commander of the 407th Strategic Fighter Wing, Great Falls AFB, was killed Saturday morning when his T-33 jet trainer crashed three miles west of Gore Field. Tragedy overtook Malmstrom at 8:40 a.m., about five minutes after his plane left...on a routine flight to 15th Air Force headquarters at Riverside, Calif. The plane was demolished, with parts scattered over a wide area. Cause of the crash is being investigated.*

In just seven short months, Colonel Malmstrom had become a loved and respected officer. An enlisted man, Airman Second Class Clifford Lee, said of him, "There wasn't a man on this base who didn't love him."[89]

Air force investigators concluded that Malmstrom's last act—to guide his stricken T-33 away from the city—probably cost him his life. His wife, Kathryn; son, James; and daughter, Barbara, survived him.

Within two weeks, the Civilian-Military Affairs committee of the chamber of commerce of Great Falls—a group consisting of civilian leaders, law enforcement officials and air force base officers—recommended that Great Falls AFB be named in honor of Colonel Einar Malmstrom. The suggestion

Colonel Einar Malmstrom earned the respect and love of all around him. His impact on the community was so great that local leaders appealed to the U.S. Air Force to change the name Great Falls to Malmstrom Air Force Base. Colonel Malmstrom's painting graces the entrance to the Malmstrom Museum. *Author's photo.*

was forwarded to Air Force Headquarters in Washington, D.C., via the 15th Air Force and the Strategic Air Command.[90]

One year later, on October 1, 1955, Great Falls AFB was renamed Malmstrom Air Force Base in Colonel Malmstrom's honor, with the formal dedication held on June 15, 1956.[91]

Cold War Brought Interstate Highways

General Dwight D. Eisenhower came to the presidency in 1953 with a plan: an American Autobahn network of highways across the nation. This was the height of the Cold War, with the Korean War ending and the Soviet Union detonating a hydrogen bomb. Thoughts in America were on civil defense, Soviet bombers coming over the horizon, fallout shelters, air raid drills and evacuation from cities. While it took several years for Congressional action, the Federal Aid Highway Act of 1956 authorized construction of a forty-one-thousand-mile network of interstate highways from coast to coast.

The Dwight D. Eisenhower National System of Interstate and Defense Highways, known as the Interstate Highway System, was a bold network of controlled-access highways intended to serve several purposes: eliminate traffic congestion; replace, where needed, slum areas; make coast-to-coast transportation more efficient; and provide easy exit from cities under threat of atomic attack.

The federal government paid 90 percent of construction costs, with money coming from increased gasoline taxes. Montana Governor J. Hugo Aronson announced that the new federal highway act would construct 1,243 miles of interstate highway in Montana, with the federal government paying 91.4 percent of the cost.[92]

By June 1957, the Montana Highway Commissioners had established five construction/maintenance districts, and the following year, the commission signed the first contract for five miles of I-15 between Monida and Lima in southwestern Montana. By 1988, when the last section of interstate was completed, Montana had 1,188 miles of interstate highways at a cost of $1.22 billion—and the highest proportion (95 percent) of rural interstate in the nation.[93]

SHOCKWAVES AROUND THE WORLD:
THE HUNGARIAN REVOLUTION AND SUEZ

Beginning as a student protest in Budapest on October 23, 1956, a revolt spread spontaneously across Hungary, and the Communist regime collapsed. A new anti-Communist government assumed power, amid signs of withdrawal of Soviet military forces. While the Eisenhower administration searched for ways to help, suddenly on October 29, Israel invaded the Egyptian Sinai. Two days later, the British and French began Operation Revise to seize control of the Suez Canal and depose Egyptian leader Gamal Abdel Nasser.

On November 4, the Soviet Politburo reversed course to send a massive Soviet invasion force into Hungary to crush the revolt. By November 10, Soviet tanks were rumbling through the streets of Budapest, and the Hungarian Revolution died in blood, costing the lives of at least 20,000 Hungarians and 1,500 Soviet soldiers. In the aftermath, more than 200,000 Hungarians fled their country, with more than 30,000 finding sanctuary in the United States. Five Montana ranchers immediately offered jobs for Hungarian refugees, while two Hungarian resistance fighters and their families, the Kovacs and Stepanecs, were greeted by the Montana legislature in January 1957. Others followed.[94]

From the beginning of this first armed national uprising against Communist oppression, students at the University of Montana responded, led by a faculty member with a most unusual background. Dr. Milton Colvin, assistant professor of anthropology and sociology, came to Montana after years fighting communism in Europe. Dr. Colvin had served as chief of Austrian operations of U.S.-sponsored Radio Free Europe. During 1953–54, he was responsible for Eastern European exile groups in Austria, and before that, he had worked for the State Department with exile groups in Germany. As a paratrooper and ranger during World War II, Dr. Colvin fought in the African and European campaigns before receiving his PhD from the University of Heidelberg in 1953.

On the University of Montana campus, when Hungary revolted Dr. Colvin organized and led a major student demonstration through the streets of Missoula supporting the revolution. In addition, he was active on campus and in the community, publicly speaking about "The Hungarian Revolt and the Problems of the Satellite Nations."[95]

As a student of Dr. Colvin, I joined in his organizing meetings and in the front line of the demonstration march, helping to carry a large banner supporting the Hungarian Revolution. We were devastated as sadness gripped the campus with the brutal Soviet suppression. A *Missoulian* editorial expressed our sentiment well:

> *Nikolai Lenin, father of the Bolshevik revolution once wrote: "The czarist government not only keeps our people in slavery but sends it to suppress other people revolting against slavery as was done in 1849, when Russian troops put down the revolution in Hungary." Lenin's successors in 1956, Bulganin and Khrushchev, have outdone the czars by drowning Hungarian freedom in blood.*[*]

---

[*] *Missoulian*, November 19, 1956.

THE BRUTAL END? OR JUST A BEGINNING?

When the Hungarian Revolution was crushed by brutal Soviet military force, it sent shockwaves throughout the Eastern European bloc and among leftist Western intellectuals. In the words of Hungarian journalist Endre Marton:

> *In the military sense, the revolt failed, but was it worthwhile? Most non-Communist authorities agree it was, and that its benefits still endure.*
>
> *The revolt broke out Oct. 23. It was not planned; it was a popular rising, and it broke out like a forest fire. It was not organized, but had to find its organization after it had begun. It assembled around no mesmeric leader. It was not made by an army, and not engineered by a class.*
>
> *Least of all could it be called an ideological revolution since it was fomented by Communists against communism. No one, at least of all those who had most to do with it foresaw the lengths to which it would go.*
>
> *The great and noble words, epitaphs in memory of those who died, have been said long ago. The House Committee on Foreign Affairs said the West's failure to help the revolutionaries constituted "the lost opportunity of our generation."*

"Russian Foreign Aid." Cartoon by John Fischetti depicting brutal Soviet troops crushing the People's Revolt in Hungary. *From the* Missoulian, *October 29, 1956.*

And Gen. Dwight D. Eisenhower, then US president, said that Budapest…"is no longer merely the name of a city: henceforth it is a new and shining symbol of man's yearning to be free."

The words were resounding. But little was done politically or diplomatically, and nothing militarily, to help.

For this inaction, historians blame, in part, the schism in the West induced by the Suez Canal crisis occurring at the same time as the Hungarian revolt.

Britain and France, joining Israel in the attack on Egypt, were unable to take a righteous position about Soviet intervention in Hungary….

The Hungarian revolution was not in vain. Notwithstanding the immediate aspect of tragic failure, it produced positive results.

The impact…worked in three directions: in Hungary itself, in the entire Eastern European area and among leftist Western intellectuals.

In Hungary, despite the period of repression and reprisal which followed 1956, the uprising laid the basis for gradual national conciliation and for political, legal, economic and social reforms.

In Eastern Europe, 1956 gave impetus to the forces of change. October 1956 in Hungary was an open and direct challenge to Soviet authority. The armed intervention by the Soviets and their suppression of the revolt could not obscure the fundamental lessons to be drawn.

In the West, scores of the intellectual elite, ranging from Jean Paul Sartre…to Howard Fast turned their backs on communism in disgust.

…Ferenc Nagy, Hungary's prime minister after the 1945 free elections, the first and only free elections in Hungary…[said] *"The intellectuals recognized that communism was not the progressive, revolutionary ideology it claimed to be, but a reactionary one."*[96]

The United Nations

Throughout the early decades of the Cold War, the United Nations emerged as an important participant. From Displaced Persons to the Korean War, Cold War drama and rhetoric dominated the UN focus. On college campuses during the 1950s, the UN garnered attention through regional Model United Nations sessions. The University of Montana represented Turkey during the West Coast Model United Nations at the University of Southern California in April 1959. Assuming their roles as Turkish diplomats, the nine members of the Montana delegation were Gary Beiswanger, Billings; David Werner,

President Eisenhower's powerful secretary of state, John Foster Dulles; Mrs. Dulles; and members of the secretary's staff paid a surprise visit to Great Falls on November 9, 1958. Their Constellation, traveling from Washington, D.C., to Seattle, was forced to make an unscheduled refueling stop after encountering strong headwinds. The secretary, *center, facing the camera*, is shown with his staff as they prepared to depart. *The History Museum, 1992.021.0025.*

Stanford; Dick Fletcher, Missoula; Suhayl Osman, Beirut, Lebanon; Tom Mongar, Missoula; Dick Josephson, Billings; John Gesell, Chinook; Teddy Roe, Billings; and Ken Robison, Great Falls.

Advisers to the delegation were Dr. Barbara Turner and Dr. Richard Garver, although much of the preparation was completed the previous year under acclaimed historian Dr. Kemal Karpat of Istanbul, Turkey. The group did extensive research on all phases of Turkey, ranging from internal political affairs to economic and military relations with the Soviet bloc. Each member had to be thoroughly versed in Turkish affairs and UN procedures for assignment to one of the five committees of the General Assembly and to protect the interests of the "parent" country.

In Dr. Karpat's opinion: "The value in the Model U.N. for the students was that it made the students try to understand things and issues in a very different way from the way they are accustomed to. It also enables them to become more objective in appraising other issues…and it's good advertisement for the University."

The "Turkish" delegation successfully won a floor fight over technical aid assistance to the Belgian Congo, with Montana delegate David Werner addressing nearly one thousand students before the General Assembly voted thirty-eight to fifteen, with twenty abstentions for the Turkish resolution.

The Model UN ended with a banquet addressed by A.C. Chagla, permanent Indian delegate to the real UN and ambassador to the United States.[97]

CHAPTER 4

THE RACE FOR SPACE

CUBAN MISSILE CRISIS AND THE "ACE IN THE HOLE"

Truth Behind the Missile Gap

The launch of Sputnik, an artificial satellite, by the Soviet Union on October 4, 1957, began the "space race," shocked Americans and stimulated a debate over the "missile gap"—a perceived superiority in numbers and power by the Soviets. One month later, the Soviets launched Sputnik 2 with dog Laika aboard. Shortly after, a special committee reported to President Eisenhower that the United States was falling far behind the Soviets in missile capabilities. Soviet leader Nikita Khrushchev chimed in, claiming that the Soviet Union had missile superiority and challenging America to a missile "shooting match" to prove his assertion. President Eisenhower knew that there was no missile gap—he could prove it by U-2 photography. Yet that secret imagery could not be released to the American public. Later, Khrushchev's son Sergei admitted, "We threatened with missiles we didn't have."

Yet the missile gap became an issue in the 1960 presidential campaign between Senator John F. Kennedy and Vice President Richard M. Nixon, with Kennedy arguing that the United States was far behind. Yet, as the new Kennedy administration took power, Secretary of Defense Robert McNamara painfully admitted the myth of the missile gap—the United States, in fact, had a substantial lead—and the solid-fuel Minuteman was just over the horizon.[98]

By the fall of 1960, development of the Minuteman missile was well underway. The Air Force Ballistic Missile Committee had just approved

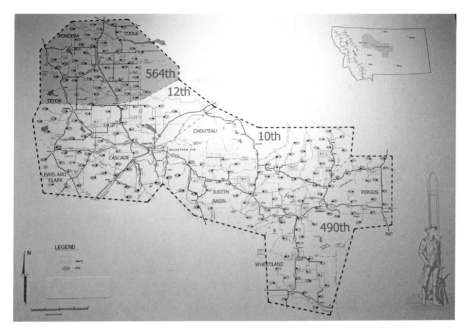

The U.S. Air Force selected Central Montana for the initial Minuteman deployment. Shown are locations for the four squadrons of the 341ˢᵗ Missile Field. The five flights of the 564ᵗʰ Missile Squadron (*upper left*) were active through the Cold War but are now deactivated and destroyed. *Display at Malmstrom Museum; author's photo.*

Malmstrom AFB to host the first Minuteman I nuclear missile silo and launch site. Colonel Harry Goldsworthy and his team were given the near-impossible task of building Minuteman missile sites up and running in just two years. Few thought they would succeed. Based in Salt Lake, reporter Murray M. Moler visited U.S. Air Force and U.S. Army Corp of Engineers officers at Malmstrom AFB and filed this report about the Minuteman story under a dramatic headline:

> *Minuteman Is Greatest Project in Magnitude Ever in Montana*
> *The Minuteman missile program is the darndest thing to hit Montana since they found copper in Butte Hill. Or maybe even in all the history of the Treasure State.*
>
> *The impact, figuratively, of the program on the state will be tremendous, economically, socially and physically.*
>
> *It will be almost as great as the impact of the slender, nuclear-headed weapons actually could have on an enemy land, should they ever be fired in anger.*

The mission of the Minuteman III, a key part of the U.S. nuclear triad, is nuclear deterrence. The missile has a range of more than eight thousand miles and a maximum speed of fifteen thousand miles per hour. *Display at Malmstrom Museum Air Park; author's photo.*

The task: To carve out, reinforce and arm 150 underground silos, holding one Minuteman each; then connect them with 15 launch control centers which in turn, will be wired in Strategic Air Command's 22nd air division headquarters here and SAC's world control center at Omaha, Neb.

The timetable. Two "flights," 10 missiles each, to be operational—ready to go—by mid-1962; all 150 cocked and aimed in their pits by around June 1, 1963....

Each of the 165 launcher and control sites will involve only about three acres of land, plus access roads and easements for a "solid" communications system.

That's a total of only about 600 acres specifically used for the nation's first, and largest, Minuteman complex.

But these sites are spread over 10,000 square miles of north-central Montana....

The sites now marked by colored ribbons attached to fence posts and survey stakes are basically in the valley basins formed by tributaries to the Sun, Missouri and Judith Rivers.

Maj. Gen. Joseph J. Preston until recently commander of the SAC bomb wing at Ramey AFB in Puerto Rico, has been designated as commander of the 22nd Air Division that will control the Minutemen in their hardened and dispersed sites in Montana....Preston moves into his headquarters at Malmstrom Air Force Base in Great Falls about Oct. 1.

...Contracts, estimated at around $50 million, for the bulk of the actual site preparation and building will be let in late November. Then the dirt will start to fly, regardless of the weather. In Montana's rugged winters, that's something.

When work starts, so will the side effects.

Engineers have estimated construction contractors will bring at least 3,600 skilled and semi-skilled workmen into the state. Boeing Airplane Co., already holder of the $247 million basic research and development contract on the missile will employ at least 1,000 in putting the "birds" in their holes and testing them.

Brig. Gen. Alvin C. Welling. Commander of the Army Corps of Engineers ballistic missile construction office, in a masterful understatement, described the program as a "unique construction job."

The task force, he added, will attempt to obtain the "explosive speed of a combat organization and yet obtain the delicate and precise work of a laboratory."

*...To farmers selling their land to Uncle Sam for the sites, construction
will mean considerable dislocation, but when the work is done, they'll have
better roads, 120 miles of improvements are already scheduled in Cascade
County alone, that are useable the year-round.*

*When the Minutemen are in place and the reinforced concrete lids to the
silos drawn into place, there will be little activity—occasional inspections
and, once in a while, replacement of the missile with a fresh "bird."*

*Each of the three operational squadrons will have about 500 men,
about 100 assigned to each of the 15 flights. All will be based in Great
Falls and commute to the sites for shifts.*

*Malmstrom's tanker and fighter tasks will remain basically undisturbed,
at least for the immediate future.*

*The total result is that Air Force expenditures, $79 million for
construction alone in Montana this year plus other millions for salaries,
goods and services will continue to be a big factor in the state's economy for
a long time.*[99]

THE CUBAN MISSILE CRISIS:
"HOW CLOSE MONTANA LIVES TO THE FIRING LINE"

The Cuban Missile Crisis of October 1962 brought the United States
and the Soviet Union closer to a nuclear exchange than any other event
throughout the Cold War. From October 16 to November 20, the world
teetered on the brink of a catastrophic and very hot war—until leadership
and luck prevailed.

One year later, just weeks before his assassination, President John
F. Kennedy visited Great Falls to pay tribute to his "ace in the hole"—
Minuteman ICBMs spread in every direction around the stadium, where
he spoke these words to an overflow crowd: "Montana [has] concentrated
within its borders some of the most powerful nuclear missile systems
in the world."[100]

The Cuban Missile Crisis unfolded through a background of escalating
tensions in the Cold War fueled by the failed Bay of Pigs invasion of
Cuba, followed six weeks later by the June 1961 summit in Vienna for
Kennedy and Soviet First Secretary Nikita Khrushchev, at which the
latter concluded that President Kennedy "is very inexperienced, even
immature"—and a weak leader.

Two months after the summit, the Soviets and East Germans erected the Berlin Wall, a direct response to the president's weakness in Vienna. Yet Premier Khrushchev misjudged the young, inexperienced American president. President Kennedy was a quick study and learned from his performance at Vienna, yet the Soviets did not know that.

The United States was deploying Jupiter medium-range ballistic missiles (MRBM) to Italy and Turkey. In response, in July 1962, Khrushchev secretly agreed to Cuba's request to place Soviet nuclear missiles on the island to deter a future U.S. invasion. Construction of missile launch facilities started later that summer, just before midterm elections in the United States.[101]

During that campaign, the president denied charges that the government was ignoring dangerous Soviet missiles just ninety miles off the U.S. coast. Yet, in mid-October, a U-2 reconnaissance aircraft captured clear photographic evidence of Soviet SS-4 and SS-5 M/IRBM facilities. President Kennedy was briefed and, with his advisors, determined that the Soviet missiles must be removed. The world was at a brink as the president weighed options ranging from military air strikes on the missile sites on down, before ordering a naval quarantine of Soviet offensive weapons on October 22 to prevent further missiles from reaching Cuba.

In a dramatic primetime televised address to the world that evening, President Kennedy announced the discovery of the offensive missiles and aircraft in Cuba: "It shall be the policy of this nation to regard any nuclear missile launched from Cuba against any nation in the Western Hemisphere as an attack by the Soviet Union on the United States, requiring a full retaliatory response upon the Soviet Union."[102]

The president declared that the United States would not permit Soviet offensive weapons to remain in Cuba, demanding that those weapons already there be dismantled and shipped back to the Soviet Union. He described his plan to halt the Soviet offensive buildup in Cuba, the commencement of a strict naval quarantine of all offensive military equipment en route to Cuba: "All ships of any kind bound for Cuba, from whatever nation or port, will, if found to contain cargoes of offensive weapons, be turned back. This quarantine will be extended, if needed, to other types of cargo and carriers. We are not at this time, however, denying the necessities of life as the Soviets attempted to do in their Berlin blockade of 1948."[103]

In the aftermath of President Kennedy's dramatic "red-line" speech, Montana's military immediately responded with "an unprecedented state of activity," according to 341st Strategic Missile Wing historian Troy A. Hallsell. Montana Governor Tim Babcock activated the National

Guard, since nearly half the state's counties did not have adequate civil defense preparations, and only Butte had a fallout shelter plan in place. The Montana National Guard established a shelter plan, communication network, warning systems and a radiological program for forecasting and detecting radioactive fallout. The air force moved fighter planes from Malmstrom AFB to Billings Airport.[104]

ALPHA FLIGHT: THE FIRST MINUTEMAN ICBM TO COME ONLINE

Historian Hallsell described the environment at Malmstrom AFB, with everyone working "at a frenetic pace over the next month":

Typically, 16-hour days were normal, weekends included. The payoff was the Missile Squadrons and Wing reaching operational readiness well ahead of schedule. The unfolding events even took the [ICBM missile] construction crews by surprise. Quality Assurance contractor Jack Gannon heard about the crisis while driving to Lewistown from Eddie's Corner. Upon arrival he told his co-workers they "Better get them wrapped up, we're going to be using them in about 20 minutes." The speed at which the Cuban Missile Crisis occurred made everyone associated with the ICBMs in Montana work to get them operational as soon as possible.

…Following Pres. Kennedy's address, SAC Commander-in-Chief Gen Thomas Power instructed Col Burton C. Andrus, Jr., the 341 SMW commander, to determine if the wing could posture all 10 Minuteman ICBMs in its Alpha flight and find a way to launch them. Engineers designed the weapon system to require launch commands from two different LCCs—the problem was that 341 SMW only had one constructed. In order to bypass the weapon system's safety procedures, Colonel Andrus had to "kluge the system." His Airmen did so by introducing "the critical part of a second launch control unit into the circuitry in Alpha's Launch Control Center so that a double crew could turn four keys simultaneously and thus launch the birds." SAC's first Minuteman went on alert at 3:07 p.m. on 27 October 1962. Colonel Andrus reported to SAC that its new weapon system had entered the war plan. Five days later all of Alpha Flight was on alert. The gravity of bringing the first flight of Minuteman ICBMs on alert was not lost on Colonel Andrus. Reflecting on the Cuban Missile

This tranquil scene masks the famed Alpha Flight Minuteman Launch Control Center and Facility site controlling the first operational Minuteman ICBMs during the Cuban Missile Crisis. The commemorative sign reads "The First Ace in the Hole Alpha-1." *Author's photo.*

An aerial view of Alpha Flight's Launch Control Center. The facility houses living quarters, a kitchen, bedrooms, a security office and other features, making it possible for men and women working there to perform their assigned duties. *Author's collection.*

Crisis, he said "If we seemed nervous it was only because we were—being not only 99% sure that you can't have an inadvertent launch is not good enough when you are looking at the possibility of starting WW III."[105]

A DANGEROUS U-2 RECONNAISSANCE PLANE INCIDENT

It is not easy today to capture the day-to-day tension on both sides as this dangerous and potentially catastrophic Cuban Missile Crisis unfolded. Two incidents occurred on October 27, just after the U.S. naval quarantine was implemented and the situation was nearing a boiling point. On that day, an air force U-2 took off from Alaska for a routine reconnaissance mission in international waters off the Soviet Siberian coast. Pilot Charles Maultsby encountered aurora borealis "northern lights" interference with his navigation, and he drifted off course, accidently crossing into Soviet airspace. Soviet air defense launched MiG fighters to intercept and destroy a potential nuclear bomber. In response, the U.S. Air Force launched F-102 fighters armed with nuclear-tipped missiles. Pilot Maultsby flew out of Soviet airspace before being intercepted, and a disaster was averted.[106]

THE B-59 SUBMARINE DANGER OF WAR

The second and even more dangerous flashpoint occurred that same day, October 27, when an incident aboard a Soviet submarine stands as likely the closest the world has ever come to nuclear war. Less than a week after the naval quarantine began, the U.S. Navy destroyer USS *Beale* acquired a submarine on sonar and began dropping practice depth charges on the nuclear-armed Soviet Foxtrot class submarine B-59, operating near the quarantine line around Cuba. B-59 was one of four Foxtrots hastily deployed to Cuban waters and had been out of radio contact with Moscow for days— knowing that war was near and wondering if it had already begun. The charges were nonlethal warning shots intended to force B-59 to the surface, but the submarine's captain, Valentin Savitsky, mistakenly took them for live explosives. Adding more fuel to the fire, a second navy destroyer arrived on scene and began dropping unauthorized hand grenades with blasting sounds like sledgehammers. Convinced that he was engaged in the opening round of war, the B-59 captain angrily ordered his men to arm his submarine's single nuclear-tipped torpedo and prepare for attack.

The misunderstanding could have resulted in disaster if not for a Soviet naval contingency measure that required all three of the submarine's senior officers to sign off on a nuclear launch. The Soviet captain ordered it, but Captain Vasily Arkhipov, not part of B-59's crew but chief of staff of the submarine brigade—and who, luck would have it, was on board B-59— refused to give his consent. After calming the captain down, Arkhipov coolly convinced his fellow officers to bring B-59 to the surface and request new orders from Moscow. The submarine eventually returned to Russia without incident, but it was more than forty years later, after the end of the Cold War, before a full account of Arkhipov's lifesaving decision finally came to light. As former Secretary of State Acheson later wrote, "In foreign affairs brains, preparation, judgment, and power are of utmost importance, but luck is essential." Captain Arkhipov's presence on board B-59 was indeed *luck*.[107]

Leadership Prevails: The Crisis Ends

During the course of several days of tense negotiations, Kennedy and Khrushchev dramatically reached an agreement. Publicly, the Soviet Union would remove its offensive missiles and aircraft in Cuba and return them to the Soviet Union, in exchange for U.S. declaration not to invade Cuba again. Secretly, the United States agreed to dismantle its Jupiter MRBMs deployed in Turkey.

When all the MRBMs and Ilyushin IL-28 Beagle bombers withdrew from Cuba, the naval quarantine formally ended on November 20. In the aftermath, Khrushchev learned that President Kennedy was a formidable leader, and both men were shocked at how close they had come to a nuclear exchange. A direct Moscow–Washington hotline was established to facilitate direct rapid communications between them. The two leaders initiated a dialogue that would lead to a series of agreements later that would reduce U.S.-Soviet tensions.

By December 11, the 341st Strategic Missile had placed its second ICBM flight on alert, and by July 1963, all 150 Minutemen at Malmstrom were operational. The Minuteman's success during and after the Cuban crisis led Secretary of Defense Robert McNamara to authorize a force of one thousand Minuteman ICBMs.[108]

During the Cuban Missile Crisis, I served at the Fleet Operations Control Center, Pacific (FOCCPAC), a new command located underground under a pineapple patch on northern Oahu, Hawaii. The facility had been built during World War II to manufacture aircraft. Mothballed after the war, the Cold War caused the site to be reactivated as a secure relocation center for the U.S. Pacific Command and its component commands. FOCCPAC was caretaker for these command centers, with peacetime missions that included development of the navy's first automated ocean surveillance program. As U.S. military readiness levels increased during the Cuban crisis, the command centers were activated in preparation for possible war throughout this very tense period.

A VISIT TO THE "FIRST ACE IN THE HOLE"

What was life like for U.S. Air Force personnel bearing the awesome responsibility on the front lines of our national defence? Reporter Doug Huigen visited the 341st Strategic Missile Wing Alpha Flight in April 1966 just east of the small town of Belt. His reports, "Newsman Visits 'First Ace in the Hole,'" provide exceptional insight into life on the front line, as in this sampling:

MINUTEMAN LAUNCH CONTROL CENTER NEAR BELT
Malmstrom AFB (AP)—The front line of what could be the ultimate war is just beyond Belt, a 27-mile drive from Great Falls. It is Alpha Flight, 10th Squadron of the 341st Strategic Missile Wing. Alpha is one of the launch control centers forming the triggers of the largest weapon ever aimed in deterrence. This weapon is the system of 800 Minuteman missiles.

Nearly four years ago this underground capsule shrouded in tons of concrete and steel was one of the first launch centers declared ready for war. It has 10 underground silo-based Minutemen deployed around it, armed with nuclear warheads.

Two of the Air Force officers who lock themselves into its vault-safe confines are the capsule commander, Capt. Carmine D. Parrella, Jr., and his deputy, Lt. Alan L. Lutsky.

They took a newsman into their front-line command post for most of their 24-hour duty, starting Thursday and ending Friday.

This is how it happened:

To write this story, an agreement had to be made to clear any information or photographs with the Air Force before use. Information in the launch control center ranges from common knowledge to "top secret."

Picture the ready room from a World War II movie. Instead of flight suits, dress the men in starched white coveralls and silk squadron scarves.

A major opens the briefing with watch synchronization. Among other preliminary remarks, he advises crews of today's war plan. The designation is "B" but the outsider knows nothing of what it means.

A lieutenant colonel briefs the men on weather for the next 24 hours. It is more than a formality. The underground missiles and launch control centers are immune to all but a direct hit and weather has practically no effect on operations. But the crews must travel by highway or helicopter to their posts.

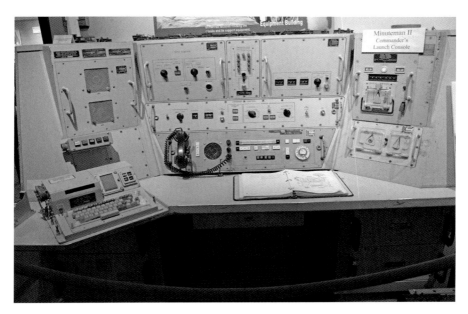

In the underground Launch Control Center, the past generation Minuteman II Commander's Launch Console allowed the commander to continually monitor the operations and security status of each of the ten missiles in the flight. *Display at Malmstrom Museum; author's photo.*

Missile Transporter/Erector (TE) arriving at Malmstrom AFB on board a Douglas C-133 Cargomaster. This sixty-five-foot TE is used to move and install Minuteman motors throughout the missile complex. *Author's collection.*

Weather could force cancellation of a flight to one of the distant launch centers, 147 miles away, making a four-hour drive. In this case, the usual changeover time is delayed until the new crew arrives.

Then come changes in technical manuals. Most crewmen post changes the previous day. At least one crewman finds in the briefing an entry he has not changed. Instead of maps and navigation charts they carry briefcases bulging with manuals explaining in detail the operation of their missiles and launch facilities.

And before the introduction of classified material—and the exit by outsiders from this fraternity—the major has other announcements. Former servicemen remembered—concurrent training, yes, even spring cleanup.

Alpha is up a dry coulee, on a prominent knoll above the highway east of Belt. It obviously is military—huge Christmas-tree antenna, cyclone fence, spic and span grounds, signs of unit designation and esprit de corps.

It's described by the site manager, M.Sgt. Fredrick Tisdell, as "sort of like a motel." He and the two cooks and six security guards see duty for three days, with three days off. Their purpose is supporting the two launch control officers 80 feet below them.

NO WELCOME MAT—Capt. Carmine Parrella Jr. opens the 8-ton door and Lt. Allan Lutsky stands in the tunnel leading to their Minuteman missile launch control center. It is buried 80 feet underground for protection from enemy attack. Levers beside Parrella operate the door lock pistons at left. It opens only from the inside and neither Malmstrom crewman may walk beyond the door when on duty.

Associated Press Photo

Left: Captain Carmine Parrella Jr. opens the eight-ton door, and Lieutenant Allan Lutsky stands in the tunnel leading to their Minuteman Launch Control Center, buried eighty feet underground. Levers beside Parrella operate the door lock pistons at left, which open only from the inside. *From the* Great Falls Tribune, *April 24, 1966.*

Below: The 341st Missile Wing has earned the Blanchard Trophy many times. The trophy goes to the best ICBM wing in the Global Strike Challenge. The trophy, first awarded in 1967, is named for General William H. Blanchard, former U.S. Air Force Vice Chief of Staff. *Display at Malmstrom Air Park; author's photo.*

HYDROGEN BOMB TESTING: DEADLY DETONATION BROUGHT RAINBOW SKIES
While I was stationed in Hawaii, the United States conducted its final high-altitude atmospheric hydrogen bomb tests. Kingfish, the penultimate test, was conducted on Thursday, November 1, 1962, high over Johnston Island in the Central Pacific. More than eight hundred miles northeast, at our vantage point in Aiea Heights, above Pearl Harbor, I observed this spectacular event. Despite the distance, I saw the immense fireball as the hydrogen bomb exploded and the fascinating rainbow of colors that followed—blood red, green, blue and yellow lights. The power of this man-made light show was stunning.

From eight hundred miles away, the immense power of a hydrogen bomb is revealed as it explodes high above Johnston Island Atoll, lighting the night sky in Hawaii. *From the* Hawaii Advertiser, *July 9, 1962.*

Environment control is the key. Pure well water is purified, filtered, chlorinated and tested every day.

Electricity comes from commercial sources but once out, emergency and auxiliary systems replace commercial service without missing a pulse. The system could rely entirely on auxiliary power.

An air conditioning system feeds the launch center massive gulps of cool, dry Montana air, re-cooled and reconditioned. Without it, high-heating equipment would fail sooner than the men.

The top sergeant and his troops could provide support for fighting men anywhere. Their job here is geared to aiding a system described in the 10th Squadron's insignia motto, "The First Ace in the Hole."[109]

PRESIDENT KENNEDY VISITS MONTANA ON A WESTERN TOUR

Less than a year after the Cuban Missile Crisis and the activation of the first Minuteman ICBMs, President John F. Kennedy visited Billings on September 25, 1963, and Great Falls the following day as part of a natural resources tour though eleven western states.

While candidate Kennedy narrowly lost Montana's four electoral votes in the 1960 presidential election, he arrived at the Yellowstone County Midland Empire Fairgrounds in Billings to the cheers of an estimated seventeen thousand people. As he began, the president spoke with measured optimism about foreign and domestic affairs to the overflow crowd. He praised Montana Senator Mike Mansfield for his leadership in getting Senate ratification of the Nuclear Test Ban Treaty through the Senate the previous day. He spoke of the 1961 Berlin crisis, the 1962 Cuban crisis and the need to reduce the threat of direct military confrontation. Speaking of all the problems that face the United States, the president concluded his remarks: "When a judgment is rendered on this generation, the generation of the 1960s, I think it will be said 'We did our best to maintain our country.'"

President John F. Kennedy delivers an address on September 25, 1963, at the Yellowstone County Fairgrounds, with the Rimrocks in the background. *JFK Presidential Library and Museum, WHP-ST-C310-57-63.*

His speech completed, the combined Billings High School bands struck up "God Bless America," and the president walked to the rear of the speaker's platform, climbed down a stairway and worked the fence line shaking hands with the enthusiastic crowd, many of them schoolchildren. The only visible dissent were a few "AuH20" (Goldwater) signs—a preview of the upcoming 1964 election.[110]

ON TO GREAT FALLS, HOME OF SENATOR MIKE MANSFIELD AND THE ACE IN THE HOLE

President Kennedy's stop in the Electric City had several goals. First, he wanted to praise his powerful Senate Majority Leader Mike Mansfield by visiting the senator's boyhood home. Second, the president intended to pay tribute to Malmstrom Air Force Base and its 341st Strategic Missile Wing for their key role in the Cuban Missile Crisis. For that reason, the president threw away his planned speech attacking Republicans for failing to back his plans for western resource development. Instead, the president delivered a memorable "Cold War" speech to the overflow crowd.

THE WHITE HOUSE
REMARKS OF THE PRESIDENT
GREAT FALLS HIGH SCHOOL MEMORIAL STADIUM
GREAT FALLS, MONTANA

Senator Mansfield, Governor, Secretary Udall, Senator Metcalf, Madam Mayor, Congressman Olson, Ladies and Gentlemen: This journey which started almost by accident has been one of the most impressive experiences of my life. We live in the city of Washington, in a rather artificial atmosphere. Washington was deliberately developed as a Government city in order to remove those who were making the laws from all the pressures of everyday life, and so we live far away.

We talk about the United States, about its problems, its powers, its people, its opportunity, its dangers, its hazards, but we are still talking about life in a somewhat removed way. But to fly…to Montana…shows anyone who makes that journey even in a short period of time what a strong, powerful and resourceful country this is.

Montana is a long way from Washington, and it is a long way from the Soviet Union, and it is 10,000 miles from Laos. But this particular State,

IT'S WONDERFUL MEETING YOU—Mutual expressions of greeting are exchanged by President John F. Kennedy and Patrick J. Mansfield, father of Sen. Mike Mansfield, the U.S. Senate majority leader, as members of the Mansfield family look on admiringly. The President visited Sen. Mansfield's parents Thursday. From left are Sen. Mansfield, President Kennedy, Kathleen (Kippy) Mansfield, 16, Pat Mansfield, 13, Patrick Mansfield and Mrs. Mansfield. Kippy and Pat are children of Mr. and Mrs. John Mansfield of Great Falls and nephews of Sen. Mansfield. Tribune photo.

President John F. Kennedy visits Patrick Mansfield, father of Montana's Senate Majority Leader Mike Mansfield, in the senator's hometown of Great Falls. *From the* Great Falls Tribune *September 27, 1963.*

because it has, among other reasons, concentrated within its borders some of the most powerful nuclear missile systems in the world, must be conscious of every danger and must be conscious of how close Montana lives to the firing line which divides the Communist world. We are many thousands of miles from the Soviet Union, but this state, in a very real sense, is only 30 minutes away.

The object of our policy, therefore, must be to protect the United States, to make sure that those over 100 Minuteman missiles which ring this city and this State remain where they are, and this is the object of the foreign policy of the United States under this Administration, under the previous Administration, and under that of President Truman. One central theme has run through the foreign policy of the United States, and that is, in this dangerous and changing world, it is essential that the 180 million people of

President John F. Kennedy speaks to an overflow crowd at Great Falls High School Memorial Stadium about the Cold War and the importance of Malmstrom's Minuteman ICBMs. *The History Museum, 2013.036.0041.*

the United States throw their weight into the balance in every struggle, in every country on the side of freedom, and so in the last years we have been intimately involved with affairs of countries of which we never heard 20 years ago, but which now affect the balance of power in the world and, therefore, the security of the United States and, therefore, the chances of war and peace.

I know that there are many of you who sit here and wonder what it is that causes the United States to go so far away, that causes you to wonder why so many of your sons should be stationed so far away from our own territory, who wonder why it is since 1945 that the United States has assisted so many countries. You must wonder when it is all going to end and when we come back home. Well, it isn't going to end, and this generation of Americans has to make up its mind for our security and for our peace, because what happens in Europe or Latin America or Africa or Asia directly affects the security of the people who live in this city, and particularly those who are coming after.

I make no apologies for the effort that we make to assist these other countries to maintain their freedom, because I know full well that every time a country, regardless of how far away it may be from our own borders— every time that country passes behind the Iron Curtain the security of the United States is thereby endangered. So, all those who suggest we withdraw, all those who suggest we should no longer ship our surplus food abroad or assist other countries, I could not disagree with them more. This country is stronger now than it has ever been. Our chances for peace are stronger than they have been in years. The nuclear test ban which was strongly led in the Senate of the United States by Mike Mansfield and Lee Metcalf is, I believe, a step toward peace and a step toward security, and gives us an additional chance that all of the weapons of Montana will never be fired. That is the object of our policy.

So, we need your support. These are complicated problems which face a citizenry. Most of us grew up in a relative period of isolation and neutrality, and unalignment which was our policy from the time of George Washington to the second world war, and suddenly, in an act almost unknown in the history of the world, we were shoved onto the center of the stage. We are the keystone in the arch of freedom. If the United States were to falter, the whole world, in my opinion, would inevitably begin to move toward the Communist bloc.

It is the United States, this country, your country, which in 15 to 18 years has almost singlehandedly protected the freedom of dozens of countries who, in turn, by being free, protect our freedom. So, when you ask why are we in Laos or VietNam, or the Congo, or why do we support the Alliance For Progress in Latin America, we do so because we believe that our freedom is tied up with theirs, and if we can develop a world in which all the countries are free, then the threat to the security of the United States is lessened. So, we have to stay at it. We must not be fatigued.

I do not believe that the test ban treaty means that the competition between the Communist system and ourselves will end. What we hope is that it will not be carried into the sphere of nuclear war. But the competition will go on. Which society is the most productive? Which society educates its children better? Which society maintains a higher rate of economic growth? Which society produces more cultural and intellectual stimulus? Which society, in other words, is the happier?

We believe that ours is, but we should not fool ourselves if the chance of war disappears to some degree.

…So I urge this generation of Americans, who are the fathers and mothers of 350 million Americans who will live in this country in the year 2000, and I want those Americans who live here in 2000 to feel that those of us who had positions of responsibility in the '60s did our part, and those of us who inherited it from Franklin Roosevelt and Theodore Roosevelt will have something to pass on to those who come, and our children, many years from now.

…This sun and this sky which shines over Montana can be, I believe, the kind of inspiration to us all to recognize what a great single country we have, 50 separate States, but one people, living here in the United States, building this country and maintaining the watch around the globe.

This is the opportunity before us as well as the responsibility.
Thank you.[111]

AN ASSASSIN STRIKES

Just eight weeks after this speech in Montana, the stunning news flashed over the wires nationally and around the globe on a November day: *President John F. Kennedy was shot and killed in Dallas!* Journalist Dick Pattison graced the next day's *Great Falls Tribune* with his thoughts:

RECENT APPEARANCE OF PRESIDENT KENNEDY HERE ADDS IMPACT TO SHOCK OVER SLAYING
Horrible Crime

Whether you are Republican or Democrat, agreed with his policies or not, you have suffered a personal loss—if nothing more you and your country are victims of a horrible crime—not a national disgrace—for a Christian nation it goes far beyond that inadequate description.

You laughed at him because he said "Cuber"—

But you wouldn't kill him.

If you knew him, you probably liked him. He was a friendly sort of person.

If you live in Great Falls, you feel as though you knew him—It was less than two months ago he was here.

Smiling, vibrant, radiating warmth.

Undoubtedly you waved to him. Perhaps you were one of those who shook his hand.

If you lived in the neighborhood of the Mansfield's he drove by your home—you felt almost as though he had visited you.

Or you and your little boy—as was the case of a man in Dallas—stood along the street. You look out to see the caravan coming.

"Wave, son," you tell your 5-year-old.

Only you were lucky.

The President's face wasn't suddenly distorted in death as you and your boy waved.

You didn't have to fall flat on the ground, bundle your son in your arms beneath your body to protect him from an assassin's bullet.

If there were tears in your eyes then, they were not from sorrow—not because you had seen your President killed.

Both of you were happy. For if he was not a great man, his was a great office. For this alone, he deserved a wave, a cheer—but not a bullet. No man deserves that…

If you knew him—

Words fail you—[112]

That fateful November 22, 1963, in the early evening, I left work at the Fleet Intelligence Center, Europe, in Kenitra, Morocco. With two navy officer friends, we drove to downtown Kenitra, where we walked along a quiet street toward a restaurant. To our surprise, two young Moroccans rushed up to us, excitedly, and told us in sadness that our young president had been killed. The tragic news indeed was flashing around the globe—this was the internet of the 1960s.

TACKLING RACIAL BARRIERS NATIONALLY AND UNDER THE BIG SKY

In 1956, Arlyne Reichert, of the McLaughlin Research Institute, invited her friend Alma Jacobs to lunch at Schell's Townhouse in downtown Great Falls. Jacobs responded sadly, "I'd love to join you, but I don't think they'll let me in." And the Schell restaurant would not! Not even the director of the Great Falls Library would be admitted to a downtown restaurant in Jim Crow–era Great Falls; after all, Jacobs was African American. This was a typical scene and problem throughout Montana during the 1950s.

And this, during the Cold War, became a key element in the propaganda campaign of the Soviet Union as it systematically attempted to publicize racial tensions in the United States.

Civil rights problems in Montana in the 1950s centered on access to jobs, union membership, public facilities and housing. Montana's population in 1960 was 650,738, with 1,467 African Americans and 21,181 Native Americans. The Black population in 1960 was the largest it had been for four decades, with Cascade County (Great Falls with Malmstrom Air Force Base) having 517 Black residents, Yellowstone (Billings) 235 and Valley (with Glasgow Air Force Base) 156. Military assignment of Black air force personnel and their families became a major factor in postwar Montana.

The United States finally began to tackle its racial problem with the passage of the Civil Rights Act of 1964, setting the stage for enforcement of Constitutional rights guaranteed after the Civil War but never enforced. Montanans played a surprisingly key role in the passage by

"A Time for Greatness" in the U.S. Senate during civil rights debates in 1963. Herblock cartoon. *From the* Great Falls Tribune, *June 28, 1963.*

the Senate of the Civil Rights Act, which outlawed discrimination in employment practices, public places and accommodations and accelerated desegregation of public schools. The Senate, under Majority Leader Mike Mansfield (D-Mont.), with a key role played by Montana's junior senator, Lee Metcalf (D-Mont.), began action on a civil rights bill (H.R. 7152) that the House of Representatives had passed.

When the Senate took up the House bill on February 26, 1964, Mansfield placed it directly on the Senate calendar, rather than assigning it to a committee chaired by a civil rights opponent. Senator Richard B. Russell (D-Ga.), the bill's opposition leader, raised objection. Critically, the Senate's presiding officer, Senator Lee Metcalf, overruled Russell's objection, and this brought the bill to the Senate floor for debate.

Senator Metcalf had been named by Mansfield to serve as acting president pro tempore to replace the aged Senator Carl Hayden. Mansfield knew that the only way to defeat southern filibuster was to outmaneuver them. And

Mansfield knew that Metcalf's mastery of Senate procedures would become critical in coming action. Senator Metcalf presided over all important Senate votes and floor debate on the Civil Rights Act in the spring of 1964.

On June 10, 1964, after seventy-five days of filibustering by opponents, Mansfield forced a vote for cloture, limiting each senator to just one more hour. Despite efforts by opponents to reject the cloture vote, Metcalf overruled them, and cloture passed the Senate by 71–29, the first time the Senate had ever invoked cloture on a civil rights bill.

A final vote came on June 19, passing 73–27. Mansfield's leadership and Metcalf's parliamentary skill successfully controlled the longest debate in Senate history. On July 2, 1964, President Lyndon B. Johnson signed into law the Civil Rights Act of 1964.

Eight years later, on June 6, 1972, Montanans ratified a new constitution. In the words of Arlyne Reichert, Great Falls delegate to the Constitutional Convention, "The time was right…the era was conducive to change." Boldly inserted among the provisions of the new Montana Constitution was Article II, a Declaration of Rights that presented a strong statement of equality. Section 4 of that declaration defined individual dignity: "The dignity of the human being is inviolable. No person shall be denied the equal protection of the laws. Neither the state nor any person, firm, corporation, or institution shall discriminate against any person in the exercise of his civil or political rights on account of race, color, sex, culture, social origin or condition, or political or religious ideas."

In 1973, just two decades after the ill-fated Reichert-Jacobs luncheon, Alma Jacobs was serving as Montana state librarian and was admitted to restaurants throughout Montana. The next year, a young air force wife, Geraldine Travis, was elected to the Montana legislature, the state's first African American legislator. Change had been slow in coming, but armed with powerful new legislation in the Civil Rights Act of 1964 and the Montana Constitution of 1972, the stage was set for progress at the local level in Montana's towns and cities. The Soviet Union's race card was being removed from its propaganda deck.[113]

North Korean Incidents: USS *Pueblo* Attack

On January 23, 1968, North Korean patrol boats fired on USS *Pueblo* (AGER-2), a navy reconnaissance ship, off the North Korean coast in

North Koreans attacked and captured the USS *Pueblo* in international waters on January 25, 1968. *U.S. Navy.*

international waters. After trying to escape and stalling for time to allow the crew to destroy classified material, the old, slow and lightly armed Banner-class *Pueblo* surrendered before most of the classified material and equipment could be destroyed. The *Pueblo* was taken to Wonsan port, where Captain Lloyd Butcher and his eighty-two-man crew (one had been killed) were tortured and held captive. President Lyndon Johnson chose not to retaliate, but rather engage in prolonged negotiations until their release on December 28, 1968.[114]

EC-121 SHOOTDOWN

North Korea struck again on April 15, 1969, when MiG-21 aircraft attacked and shot down a U.S. Navy EC-121M reconnaissance aircraft in international waters over the Sea of Japan. The EC-121M Warning Star from Fleet Air Reconnaissance Squadron One (VQ-1), flying under the Beggar Shadow signals intelligence (SIGINT) reconnaissance program,

In mid-1968, I joined CTF-77 (Commander Task Force-77/ Carrier Group Five), a small staff of forty-five officers and an equal number of enlisted men, under Vice Admiral Ralph Cousins operating in the Western Pacific. CTF-77 commanded all naval air operations off Vietnam and Laos and had contingency responsibilities for naval strike operations in Northeast Asia as Commander Task Force 71. Immediately after the EC-121 shootdown, our CTF-71 "hat" was activated, and we boarded a C-2 aircraft to fly from USS *Kitty Hawk* to cross-deck to USS *Ranger* off the southwest coast of Japan. There we commanded a rapidly assembling Task Force 71 with carriers *Ranger*, *Enterprise*, *Ticonderoga* and *Hornet* with cruiser and destroyer screens.

For a short period, we remained waiting for orders to respond to North Korea by some sort of retaliatory action, but those orders never came. We turned over our TF-71 responsibilities to another carrier group and flew back to Kitty Hawk to resume our CTF-77 Vietnam operations.

As the intelligence officer with CTF-71, each quarter I joined several others flying to the Republic of Korea for meetings with USAF Korea to coordinate Navy–Air Force Northeast Asia contingency operations. In addition, quarterly we flew to Taipei, Taiwan, to meet with key officers from 7th Air Force Headquarters at Tan Son Nhut AFB to coordinate Navy–Air Force Southeast Asia operations.

crashed ninety nautical miles off the North Korean coast, and all aboard (thirty sailors and one Marine) were murdered—the largest single aircrew loss during the Cold War. Nine of the crew, including the Marine, were Naval Security Group cryptologic technicians (CTs) and linguists in Russian and Korean.

The United States responded by hastily activating Task Force 71 for possible contingency response to the unprovoked North Korean attack and to protect reconnaissance flights over international waters in the future. While various contingency plans were considered, the new administration of President Richard Nixon and National Security Advisor Henry Kissinger failed to retaliate. Kissinger was ashamed of the outcome of the event, revealing, "Our conduct in the EC-121 crisis [was] weak, indecisive and

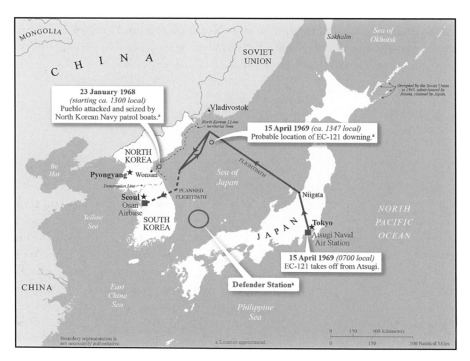

Incident map showing North Korean attacks on the USS *Pueblo* and EC-121, 1968 and 1969. *Map by Richard A. Mobley.*

North Korean attack and shootdown of VQ-1 EC-121M reconnaissance aircraft in international waters on April 15, 1969. *U.S. Navy.*

disorganized....We made no demands North Korea could either accept or reject. We assembled no force that could pose a creditable threat until so long after the event that it became almost irrelevant."[115]

THE TRAGIC YEAR 1968

The events of few years in our Cold War history had more impact on our country than those of 1968. In January, North Korea captured USS *Pueblo*. One week later, on January 30, the North Vietnamese and Viet Cong launched the massive Tet Offensive, designed to bring the war to urban centers of South Vietnam to demonstrate to the world that America was not winning the war. During that year, 14,584 Americans died in Vietnam. On April 4, civil rights leader Martin Luther King Jr. was assassinated. Two months later, on June 5, Senator Robert F. Kennedy was assassinated. In August, Chicago police attacked activists outside the Democratic Convention, while Warsaw Pact troops invaded Czechoslovakia to crush the Prague Spring movement. A sad year, indeed.

LUNAR ORBIT CHRISTMAS EVE APOLLO 8'S CHRISTMAS READING, SAVING 1968

To the astronaut crew of Apollo 8, the first manned mission to the Moon, late in 1968 was their chance to close out that tragic year on a positive cord—successfully entering lunar orbit on Christmas Eve. That evening, astronauts Commander Frank Borman, Command Module Pilot Jim Lovell and Lunar Module Pilot William Anders performed a live television broadcast to raise American spirits from lunar orbit, while they showed photos of the Earth and Moon as seen from Apollo 8. Lovell said, "The vast loneliness is awe-inspiring and it makes you realize just what you have back there on Earth." The crew ended the broadcast taking turns reading from the book of Genesis.

William Anders said, "For all the people on Earth the crew of Apollo 8 has a message we would like to send you....In the beginning God created the heaven and the earth." Jim Lovell added, "And God called the light Day, and the darkness he called Night. And the evening and the morning

Iconic image taken by Apollo 8 crewmember Bill Anders on December 24, 1968, while in orbit around the Moon, showing Earth rising above the lunar horizon. It was signed by Frank Borman. *Author's collection.*

were the first day." Frank Borman continued, "And God said, Let the waters under the heavens be gathered together unto one place, and let the dry land appear: and it was so. And God called the dry land Earth; and the gathering together of the waters called the Seas: and God saw that it was good." Borman then added, "And from the crew of Apollo 8, we close with good night, good luck, a Merry Christmas, and God bless all of you—all of you on the good Earth."

Colonel Frank Borman, Apollo 8 commander, spoke of his experiences in space to the 120th Operations Group at MANG's Dining Out dinner. *From the* Great Falls Tribune, *January 12, 2010.*

Colonel Borman Reflects

In 2018, fifty years after the pathbreaking orbit of the moon by Apollo 8, Colonel Frank Borman was interviewed at his Billings home by a *Gazette* journalist. Their phone conversation ranged from the remarkable mission to Colonel Borman's motivation and faith and his concern for divisiveness in American society.

Frank Augustin Borman was born in Gary, Indiana, and raised in Arizona, and he spent a challenging career in the air force moving from test pilot into the second group of NASA astronauts. Retiring in 1988, Colonel Borman became president and later chairman of the board of American Airlines. One decade later, he bought a cattle ranch in Big Horn County, Montana, living in nearby Billings.[116]

GENE MARIANETTI AND THE APOLLO 17 TOUR

To Colonel Frank Borman, and likely all astronauts, major events in space were battles in the Cold War. One Montanan prominent in these battles was Gene Marianetti, a leader in the important NASA Public Affairs team. Marianetti and his team played the key role in coordinating a highly successful campaign to sell the space program to the American public and around the globe.

Marianetti was born in 1935, the only child of Italian immigrant parents who settled in ethnically rich Black Eagle, a town across the Missouri River from Great Falls and adjacent to the Anaconda copper and zinc refineries. Educated in journalism and broadcasting, Marianetti joined NASA as a protocol officer in August 1967. His job soon expanded to hosting high-level visitors to Apollo launches and showcasing astronaut public appearances around the country. During his twenty-seven-year career as head of NASA's Public Appearances Branch, he was involved with most of the historic events and personalities during those Golden Years of the space program. His outstanding service was rewarded with three NASA Exceptional Service Medals, presented in 1973, 1981 and 1990.

Marianetti's primary job was to get astronauts at NASA's Manned Space Craft Center in Houston out of their space suits and around the country as salesman to promote the program through public appearances. He was in Great Falls on March 28–29, 1973, accompanying Apollo 17 moon explorers Mission Commander Eugene Cernan, Captain Ronald E. Evans and geologist Dr. Harrison H. Schmitt during their stopover while on a nationwide tour. Apollo 17 was the last Apollo mission, and Cernan was the last man to walk on the moon. The crew was in Great Falls thanks to Marianetti, who, on short notice, arranged the stop between a midday visit to Billings and an appearance in Seattle the next day.

When the goodwill tour arrived in Great Falls, the astronauts attended a dinner at the Meadow Lark Country Club, while their wives went to the Marianetti family home for his mom's homemade Italian dinner.

Captain Cernan called Marianetti to the microphone and introduced him by saying that this is a man who has been "a vital part of the crew on our national tour." Marianetti in turn told his hometown crowd, "Getting to the moon is not an easy thing. It was a great period in American history. I hope we never forget it, and I was proud to be part of the moon landing."

Geologist Harrison H. Schmitt reminisced about prior visits to Montana, saying that old-time explorers never had it so good as in the space missions.

Walking on the moon with the friendly voices of the mission control team in their ears was much like working in the Beartooth Mountains of Montana, where he and Cernan trained for the moon walk.[117]

From a Childhood Ranch to Outer Space: Montana Astronaut Loren Acton

Loren Wilber Acton was born in 1936 on a ranch in central Montana near Lewistown, yet he became a highly respected solar physicist and astronaut. Graduating like a rocket from Billings High School, Montana State University (MSU) and the University of Colorado with a PhD in astro-geophysics, Dr. Acton joined Lockheed and became senior staff scientist with the Space Sciences Laboratory, Lockheed Palo Alto Research Laboratory, California.

As a research scientist, he conducted scientific studies of the Sun and other celestial objects using advanced instruments and served as co-investigator on one of the Spacelab 2 solar experiments, Solar Optical Universal Polarimeter (SOUP). In Dr. Acton's words, "Being an experimentalist, not a theorist, I sent in proposals to NASA to build and fly instruments into space to study the sun's output at X-ray wavelengths." In 1978, Acton and his Lockheed team won a NASA contract to fly the instrument SOUP on a Spacelab mission to study Sun-Earth relations. Acton leaped at the chance to fly a mission and run the instrument, yet their launch was delayed for years.

STS-51F/Spacelab-2 *Challenger* launched on July 29, 1985, from Kennedy Space Center, Florida. At five minutes and forty-five seconds into ascent, the number one engine shut down prematurely due to a sensor problem and an abort to orbit was declared. Despite this problem, the mission continued successfully, traveling more than 2.8 million miles in 126 Earth orbits, logging more than 190 hours in space and returning to land at Edwards Air Force Base, California, on August 6. STS-51F was the first pallet-only Spacelab mission and the first mission to operate the Spacelab Instrument Pointing System (IPS), which provided excellent pointing accuracy and stability for telescopes, cameras and other scientific instruments attached to it. The mission carried thirteen major experiments in astronomy, astrophysics and life sciences.

Dr. Acton continued his Sun research with Lockheed until 1993, when he accepted a research professorship in the physics department at Montana State University. In addition to teaching, he oversaw the solar physics group at MSU, which carried on an active research program with NASA support. The group was actively involved in projects like the day-to-day operation and scientific utilization of the Japan/U.S./U.K. Yohkoh mission for studies of high-energy solar physics.[118]

OTHER MONTANANS IN THE SPACE RACE

After her retirement from NASA in 2003, JoAnn H. Morgan lived in Bigfork, Montana, and Florida. She was the only woman in the flight room for the famed Apollo 11 mission when Commander Neil Armstrong and lunar module pilot Buzz Aldrin landed the Apollo Lunar Module Eagle on the Moon on July 20, 1969, and took the "one giant leap for mankind." Joining NASA in 1958, the agency's inaugural year, JoAnn Morgan set many firsts, including the first woman to work in the launch control center and as senior executive at Kennedy Space Center. In her last position during her forty-five-year NASA career, she served as director of external relations and business development at the Kennedy Space Center.

Philip J. Weber grew up in Glasgow and graduated from Montana State University before joining NASA at the Kennedy Space Center in 1985. Weber's lightning path to NASA was revealed in an article in the *Great Falls Tribune* by Kristen Inbody:

> *With their parents, six-year-old Phil Weber and his eight siblings gathered around a black-and-white television in their farmhouse south of Glasgow to watch the moon landing.*
>
> *"It was amazing. It almost didn't seem real," he said. "I was all about rockets* [growing up], *figuring out how to use firecrackers to launch soup cans, then building model rockets—trying for bigger and better."*
>
> *…Weber went to Montana State University to study mechanical engineering. His senior year he took a fateful spring break trip to Cocoa Beach, Florida for some fun in the sun in 1985.*
>
> *"It was beyond a fantasy when I was a freshman in Bozeman to work at NASA on the launch pad," he said. "Most of my classmates got jobs with Boeing or oil companies."*
>
> *Weber saw an ad in the newspaper that a NASA contractor needed 300 engineers. He interviewed in the jeans he'd brought with him on vacation. By the end of the day, he had five job offers. That's how hungry*

The Cold War extended to the Olympics, exemplified by Lones W. Wigger, of Carter and Fort Benton, who earned All-American honors at Montana State University Bozeman. Army Lieutenant Colonel Wigger became a four-time Olympian, defeating Soviet and Warsaw Pact small-bore shooters to earn two gold medals and one silver, as well as an induction into the Olympic Hall of Fame. *From the* New York Times, *December 18, 2017.*

they were for engineers—even those who had to go back to Montana for one last quarter of college.

"Two weeks after graduation, I walked into the vehicle assembly building and started my job" he said. "It was a dream but so impossible."

This is Weber's 32nd year with NASA (after two years with the contractor). He's the senior technical integration manager for the Exploration Ground Systems Program at NASA's Kennedy Space Center in Florida.[119]

Montanans continue to be drawn to the Space Program since the end of the Cold War, as exemplified by Bryan von Lossberg and Christina Koch. Von Lossberg helped the Pathfinder land the first rover on Mars before moving to Missoula and serving as city council president. Christina Hammock Koch left her home in Livingston to move to Houston when she was selected as astronaut in 2015, and since then, she has served nearly eleven months in orbit on the International Space Station.[120]

CHAPTER 5

PROXY WAR VIETNAM

PROTESTS AND POWs

Our Second Proxy War: Vietnam

Not since the Civil War had the United States endured so divisive a war both at home and abroad as the Vietnam War. Yet, the nation fought the war in Vietnam because of the geopolitics of the Cold War and forfeited the war because of the need to preserve domestic political support for the Cold War.[121]

Despite the advice of General Douglas MacArthur in April 1961 to President John F. Kennedy to avoid a land war in Asia, the United States entered the quagmire of Vietnam. From its shrouded beginnings in the 1950s, American soldiers fought to stop the spread of Communism throughout Southeast Asia—driven on the one hand by the "domino theory" that if one country fell all of Southeast Asia would follow, and on the other by concern that both enemies and allies around the globe might interpret American retreat as a sign of weakness in military capacity and lack of political resolve. The Cold War reputation of the United States for power and determination, the basis of its rank in the regional and global hierarchy, was at stake.[122]

Over the decade that followed from the Gulf of Tonkin incident in August 1964 to the Tet Offensive of 1968 to the long drawdown of U.S. forces from 1969 throughout the effort to "Vietnamize" the war, culminating in the final withdrawal of U.S. forces in 1973, the Vietnam War proved a disaster. The final sad chapter came in April 30, 1975, when the combined People's Republic of Vietnam (North Vietnam) and Viet Cong forces overwhelmed the army of the Republic of Vietnam (South Vietnam) to capture Saigon, renaming it Ho Chi Minh City.

More than 58,000 U.S. deaths (41,000 killed in action) and almost 304,000 wounded—with 267 Montana deaths, about 1,400 wounded and 22 prisoners of war (POW)/Missing in Action (MIA) among the 36,000 Montanans serving—were toll enough, but tragic also was the loss of public support that brought American service men and women to return to their homeland shunned for their service and bravery.[123]

Vietnam: A Time for War, a Time for Peace

Vietnam gained independence from France in 1954 and was divided into two countries: the Communist North and the non-Communist South. The U.S. government supported South Vietnam, believing in the "domino theory" that if Vietnam fell to the Communists, nearby countries would follow. During the 1960s, the United States first covertly supported anti-Communist forces in Laos and Cambodia and then escalated with massive troop deployments in South Vietnam. The result was an undeclared and unpopular war.

The Tet Offensive in 1968 shocked many Americans. Mounting casualties and growing opposition at home brought on the beginning of peace talks as President Lyndon B. Johnson began negotiations with the North Vietnamese in Paris. His successor, President Richard M. Nixon, pledged to reduce American troop presence by "Vietnamizing" the war, and eventually a peace agreement was signed. In early 1973, the last American troops were withdrawn, and American POWs returned during Operation Homecoming. On April 29–30, 1975, helicopters ferried evacuees from rooftops as North Vietnamese tanks slammed into Saigon. Laos and Cambodia soon fell to Communist forces, and Cambodia became a "killing field." The Southeast Asia war ended—the dominoes had fallen, yet the U.S. military actions in Korea and Vietnam, and in protecting Formosa, maintained U.S. Cold War military creditability.

In the aftermath, more than 50,000 anti-Communist Hmong tribesmen fled Laos, with hundreds finding sanctuary in the Bitterroot Valley in western Montana. More than 120,000 Vietnamese fled South Vietnam, most by small boats picked up in the Philippine Sea by the U.S. Navy. More than 2 million Cambodians were murdered by the Communist Khmer Rouge.[124]

Key Events of the Vietnam War

1959   President Dwight D. Eisenhower begins program to maintain South Vietnam as an independent Republic of Vietnam.

1960   CIA begins covert support for anti-Communist Hmong tribesmen and Royal Laotian government in Laos.

1961   General Maxwell Taylor advises President John F. Kennedy that prompt U.S. action can lead to victory.

1962   Covert U.S. Special Forces are inserted in South Vietnam and Laos.

1963   Buddhists stage demonstrations against Catholic-led Saigon government—a coup deposes President Ngo Dinh Diem.

1964   USS *Maddox* reports attack by North Vietnamese patrol boats in Gulf of Tonkin; U.S. Congress Gulf of Tonkin resolution gives Johnson broad authority for war.

1965   First American overt combat troops land in Vietnam; students for a Democratic Society sponsor antiwar rally in Washington; antiwar protests are held in about forty cities.

1967   "March on the Pentagon" antiwar demonstration is conducted; U.S. public opinion shifts to increased opposition to the war.

1968   Coordinated, massive Communist attacks during Tet holiday occur in major cities throughout Vietnam, before attackers are repulsed with heavy casualties; Tet shocks the United States, increasing antiwar sentiment; President Johnson announces that he will not run for reelection. Peace talks begin in Paris; riots occur at Democratic National Convention in Chicago. Richard M. Nixon is elected president.

1969   Nixon withdraws twenty-five thousand troops. National antiwar demonstrations across the nation take place.

1970   U.S. Air Force bombs Cambodia; National Guardsmen kill four students at an antiwar rally at Kent State University.

1972   President Nixon is reelected; North Vietnam's Easter invasion of South Vietnam takes place; Paris talks are deadlock. The United States escalates bombing of North Vietnam late in the year to increase pressure.

1973   President Nixon halts offensive actions; Paris Peace Agreement is signed; last American troops leave; 591 American POWs are released from North Vietnam during Operation Homecoming, together with 69 from South Vietnam and 3 from the People's Republic of China.

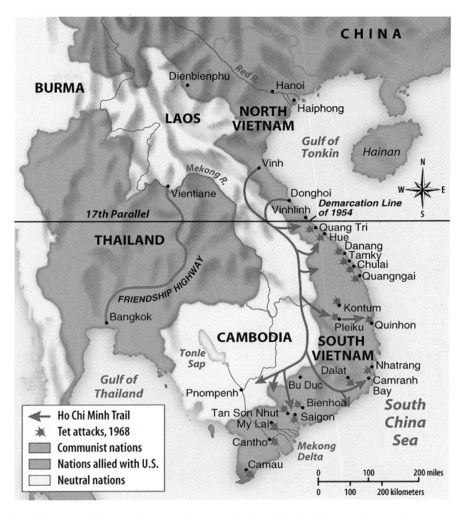

This Southeast Asia map depicts combatants North and South Vietnam, Laos and Cambodia, the Ho Chi Minh Trail used by the North to supply the Viet Cong in the South and cities in the South attacked during the Tet Offensive of 1968. *Author's collection.*

1974   Congress cuts aid to South Vietnam; President Gerald R. Ford offers clemency to draft evaders.

1975   Saigon falls to Communist North; Vietnam War ends on April 30, 1975.[125]

From 1965, for a decade, my navy assignments involved the war in Vietnam. From 1965 to 1968, at the Naval Reconnaissance and Technical Support Center in Suitland, Maryland, I managed the operation of a testbed for an innovative new shipboard intelligence system, the Integrated Operational Intelligence Center (IOIC), using then state-of-the-art computer and microform image systems. My testbed supported the shipboard installation of IOICs on navy attack carriers (CVAs) conducting naval air strike operations in Vietnam. The CVA IOICs were integrated with the navy's new multi-sensor reconnaissance system, the RA-5C Vigilante aircraft. After an RA-5C recce mission, the imagery and electronic intelligence it acquired was processed, exploited and fused with other intelligence in the IOIC in an early form of the future navy operational intelligence system.

In 1968, I flew to the Western Pacific (WESTPAC) to join the staff of CTF-77 directing navy strike operations in Southeast Asia. TF-77 and 7th Air Force aircraft struck authorized targets in North Vietnam during Operations Rolling Thunder and Linebacker. TF-77 aircraft supported the 7th Air Force in providing close air support and Ho Chi Minh Trail interdiction operations in South Vietnam and Laos. CTF-77 was at sea 90 percent of the time, cross-decking from carrier to carrier, operating on Yankee Station off the southern coast of North Vietnam and sometimes farther south on Dixie Station off northern South Vietnam, in a very high-paced, demanding environment with 'round-the-clock strike and recce operations.

This RA-5C Vigilante tactical reconnaissance aircraft launching from the USS *Ranger* during Vietnam operations. *U.S. Navy*.

A Long-Overdue Welcome Home

At long last, the 2011 Montana legislature declared March 30 "Welcome Home Vietnam Veterans Day in Montana," to be commemorated until 2025. Journalist Phil Drake covered the 2016 event honoring Montana's Vietnam veterans:

> *Vietnam Veterans Told "Welcome home"*
> *Helena—Vietnam veterans were not only the guests of honor at an observance at the state Capitol on Wednesday, they also got to shake hands with the governor and state's adjutant general and received a personal "welcome home."*
>
> *"You returned to a nation that could not separate the warrior from the war," Maj. Gen. Matthew Quinn said to more than 200 people who attended the first Welcome Vietnam Veterans Day observance in Helena. "Thank you for looking out for each other when the nation should have been looking out for you."*
>
> *He then asked all the Vietnam War veterans to line up on the sidewalk by the state Capitol so that he and Gov. Steve Bullock could give them a "long overdue" handshake and to be told "welcome home."*
>
> *…"We must never forget the sacrifices made by our Vietnam veterans, as well as those made by all servicemen and women from Montana," Bullock said, adding the country owed them a debt of gratitude that it could never repay.*[126]

First American POW in Vietnam: George Fryett Jr.

George Fryett Jr., born in 1935 in Helena, enlisted in the army in October 1956 and trained as a clerk, serving one year with the artillery in South Korea. He studied Russian at the Army Language School before serving with the Military Assistance and Advisory Group (MAAG) in the Republic of Vietnam from July 1961. In his off-duty hours, he taught English; on Christmas Eve 1961, he was on his way to visit one of his students when he was ambushed by Viet Cong guerrillas and taken prisoner. Fryett later described his capture:

> *On Christmas Eve 1961, he set out mid-morning in hopes of finding a swimming pool he'd heard was just a few miles outside of Saigon. A few*

Following that one-year unaccompanied tour, my family rejoined me in the early fall of 1969 in Hawaii, serving on the Staff of Commander, U.S. Pacific Fleet. As the reconnaissance and special projects officer, my focus was in support of 7th Fleet in WESTPAC, including Commander, 7th Fleet, with special reconnaissance missions, as well as Reconnaissance Squadron VQ-1, CTF-77 and the Pacific Fleet Intelligence Center Facility at Naval Air Station Cubi Point in the Philippines.

In early 1972, I flew to WESTPAC to join USS *Constellation* (CVA-64) on Yankee Station as the senior intelligence officer in *Connie*'s IOIC. Just weeks after I took charge, the North Vietnamese launched their massive Easter invasion of South Vietnam. *Connie* and other carriers responded by launching air strikes on North Vietnam around the clock. In a single memorable day, May 10, our Air Wing-9 conducted major Alpha Strikes on targets in the vital North Vietnamese port of Haiphong. During those strikes, our fighter aircraft shot down eight enemy aircraft—this included a trio of MiGs downed by Lieutenants Randy Cunningham and Willie Driscoll, making them the first "aces" (five MiGs) during the Vietnam War. In turn, our new aces themselves were shot down over the coast and recovered in the Tonkin Gulf by a search and rescue helicopter.

Throughout the strikes, our RA-5C Vigilantes flew reconnaissance missions for pre- and post-strike bomb damage assessment (BDA) and to identify North Vietnamese air defense threats (surface-to-air missiles and anti-aircraft artillery). With constant briefings and debriefings, after-action flash reports were flooding the communications airwaves. We selected several post-strike BDA images to load on a waiting F-4 aircraft to fly to Tan Son Nhut to transmit over the 7th Air Force new Compass Link imagery transmission system. That post-strike imagery was briefed to the Joint Chiefs of Staff the next morning at the Pentagon. USS *Constellation* and our Air Wing were awarded the Presidential Unit Commendation for our performance in helping stem the North Vietnamese tide.

In a very quick turnaround, six months later *Connie* sailed from North Island, San Diego, in the fall of 1972 to return to WESTPAC. This was a time of major antiwar protests at home, and the navy received some of the fallout with a racial incident onboard USS *Kitty Hawk*. While the navy had long had racially integrated crews, many

USS *Constellation* (CVA-64) was a "warrior" during the Vietnam War, receiving the Presidential Unit Commendation for its exceptional performance with Carrier Air Wing-9 during a decisive stage in the war. *U.S. Navy.*

specialty rates were not open to African American sailors. I had recruited three young Black undesignated seamen to join my IOIC to become the first Black photo interpreters in the navy. As *Connie* prepared to sail for WESTPAC, several dozen Black sailors formed a peaceful protest. This led one of my new seaman to join the protest group, and the result was the group was permitted to go ashore and leave the navy. *Connie* immediately sailed for WESTPAC.

My tour on *Connie* continued into that next deployment, and as the Paris Peace Agreement was reached in early 1973, I was activated to participate in Operation Homecoming during the return of our POWs from Hanoi. After two years on *Connie*, my family and I moved to Washington, D.C., for Defense Attaché School and Swedish language training in preparation to serve as assistant naval attaché at the U.S. embassy in Stockholm.

*days earlier, Fryett had written home to let his father know that things didn't
seem quite right.*

*"I told him things were going to get worse there before they'd get better,"
Fryett remembers.*

"Little did I know just how bad things were going to get."

*With a pair of camera straps crisscrossing his shoulders, Fryett pedaled
out into the countryside dressed in a light shirt, Bermuda shorts and sandals.
He'd passed a few isolated huts, but saw relatively few people out in the fields.*

*Sometime toward early afternoon, he passed a pair of bikers about 500
yards off. He didn't pay much attention to them until he heard their shouts
from behind.*

*"They were screaming at me in Vietnamese and French," Fryett said.
"One of them passed me and rammed his bicycle into mine. I fought back,
but then one pulled out a grenade."*

*The next thing Fryett remembers was waking up with blood dripping
down the side of his face from a large gash in the back of his head.
His hands were tied behind him. A stick across his back forced his arms
painfully pinioned back.*[127]

Fryett was held in captivity until released by the Viet Cong on June 24,
1962. He was the first American taken prisoner during the Vietnam War.[128]

First Montanan Killed in the Southeast Asia War

On March 23, 1961, Staff Sergeant Leslie Verne Sampson was killed in
Laos, the first Montanan to die in the Southeast Asia war. Born in 1936
in Richey, Dawson County, after graduating from Richey High School,
Sampson joined the air force and served several years at Malmstrom AFB
and Biloxi, Mississippi.

By 1961, Staff Sergeant Sampson had become a member of 314th Air
Division, Osan Air Base, Korea. Squadrons rotated to bases in Thailand,
and on March 23, 1961, he was radio operator on a C-47 Skytrain aircraft
flying a reconnaissance mission from Vientiane, Laos, to Saigon. En route,
the pilot turned north toward Xieng Khouangville, northeastern Laos, to
gather intelligence. Pathet Lao anti-aircraft shot the aircraft down, and just
one of the eight crewmen survived. Staff Sergeant Sampson was reported
missing in action.

Staff Sergeant Sampson left his wife, Deanna, and two young daughters, Suzanne, age three, and Sondra, age one. In December 1990, Malmstrom AFB named Dormitory 764 Staff Sergeant Sampson Hall in his honor.[129]

On July 11, 1991, through a Laotian government and U.S. cooperative effort, Staff Sergeant Sampson's remains were recovered at the crash site in the jungle and identified on November 29, 1991. His name is inscribed on the Courts of the Missing at Honolulu Memorial, and his remains were shipped for burial at Dawson Memorial Cemetery, Glendive, Montana.[130]

FIRST MONTANAN KILLED IN ACTION IN SOUTH VIETNAM

Manford Lloyd Kleiv, born in Whitefish, Flathead County, in 1924, joined the army in 1943 and saw action in the Ardennes and Rhineland during World War II. He became a ranger and served with the 82nd Airborne Second Ranger Battalion. In June 1964, Chief Warrant Officer (CWO) Kleiv transferred to Vietnam as a helicopter pilot with the 7th Aviation Platoon. He described some combat action: "A Special Forces camp was being overrun and they couldn't get the Viet Nam air force to come out. We were Johnny-on-the-spot. We made several runs back and forth, dumped about 16,000 rounds of 4.72 machine gun rounds, and 64 rockets around the area. That was enough for the Viet Cong and they made a fast retreat."[131]

On October 9, 1964, CWO Kleiv was piloting a UH-1B Huey on a support mission in Quang Nam province when hostile small-arms fire caused a loss of engine oil pressure. He made a successful autorotation landing. According to James Williams in *A History of Army Aviation*, CWO Kleiv, in working "to send a distress call for his downed crew, he repeatedly braved enemy fire to return to the aircraft and was mortally wounded. His actions let [*sic*] the rest of his crew to be rescued." He was awarded the Silver Star for his bravery. CWO Manford L. Kleiv became the first Montanan killed in action in South Vietnam. Today, he rests at Whitefish Cemetery.[132]

MORATORIUM DAY 1969
AT THE UNIVERSITY OF MONTANA

While protests against the war began as early as 1965, they remained small-scale until the late 1960s. The Moratorium to End the War in Vietnam involved massive demonstrations and teach-ins across the nation against U.S. involvement in the war. The Moratorium occurred on October 15, 1969, with Montana's largest events in Missoula. The university student newspaper, the *Montana Kaimin*, filled its front page the morning after with Moratorium Day coverage and headlines: "2,000 Join in Moratorium March"; "UM Students Debate Ways to End War"; "Montana Joins War Protest"; and "Mayor's Speech Climaxes Young Republicans' March."

About two thousand students, faculty members, clergymen and Missoula residents, some carrying antiwar signs and wearing black armbands, chanted and sang in a long column through downtown Missoula to protest the war

Moratorium Day featured a large march through the streets of Missoula on October 15, 1969. Demonstrators against the war in Vietnam lay down in front of the Missoula Post Office to symbolize 120 Montanans lost in the war. *Photo by Harley Hettick, from the* Missoulian, *October 16, 1969.*

in Vietnam. American flags were carried at the head of the march next to a banner reading "Blessed are the peace makers." A nearby sign read "American's strength—the ability of the people to change the system."

The one-hour march began at 3:00 p.m. on the Oval, went west on University Avenue, turned north on Higgins and then east on Broadway to the Federal Post Office. There, Gary Curtis, a Vietnam War veteran and junior in education, read a list of 120 Montanans killed in action. As each name was read, a marcher lay down on the sidewalk, marked by a moment of silence to honor the dead.

One marcher, Associated Students of UM President Ben Briscoe, said that he was there representing no one but himself. Earlier, on a local radio talk show, Briscoe revealed that he would be willing to participate in both the Moratorium Day parade and a march sponsored by the UM Young Republicans (YR) planned for the evening before. He failed to show at the YR march, which drew about 125 persons, highlighted by a speech given by Missoula Mayor Richard Shoup, who told the crowd that he was thankful President Nixon supported the Constitution and would not submit to mob rule.[133]

And Around Montana

Compared with Missoula, only modest events occurred elsewhere in Montana—just a few small marches and groups gathered for prayer, matched by patriotic demonstrations. Montana State University–Bozeman held a flagpole rally with white crosses planted around a flagpole for Montana's war dead. A Campus Peace Committee sold peace symbols, while nearby Young Republicans sold modified peace symbols with B-52 images and captions "Peace through Victory."

A parade in downtown Helena drew about 170, mostly Carroll College and high school students. A memorial mass at parochial College of Great Falls Chapel drew 100 students. At Northern Montana College in Havre, a morning "Care for Peace" service honored all Vietnam servicemen. In Billings, some black armbands were worn on both Rocky Mountain College and Eastern Montana College, although few turned out for gatherings. At Billings High School, some students wore black armbands until they were warned that school policy prohibited non-school insignia, and the armbands were removed.[134]

A Modest Strike

By May 1970, UM campus was besieged with demonstrations, embargoes of classes and sit-ins at the ROTC building to protest America's continuing presence in Vietnam. The *Missoulian* summarized these Vietnam War campus protests:

> *Missoula was generally on edge during the critical times protests about Vietnam were flourishing. On other campuses across the nation, violence had broken out in some instances and Missoula feared the same.*
>
> *The Missoula protests reached their zenith in May of 1970, after National Guard troops fired on students at Kent State and four youngsters died. The reaction on UM was prompt. Soon 2,000 striking students gathered in the University Oval. [University President Robert] Pantzer, highly visible during earlier times of crisis was there again to tell students he felt their frustration and to caution them that destroying the campus would only harm the university and keep it from being part of social change. Despite a sit-in in the ROTC building, a few false bomb scares and much marching, chanting and student speeches, the campus and Missoula were spared the violent disruptions which had caused grief to others around the nation.*[135]

In the aftermath of the 1970 protests, a referendum was held among both students and faculty members over the fate of the Army and Air Force ROTC programs. Both students and faculty voted more than two to one to retain ROTC in what likely came as backlash to the strike and protests.[136]

Original Dove in Congress: Jeannette Rankin

Pathbreaking legislator Jeannette Rankin wished to be remembered "as the only woman who ever voted [in Congress] to give women the right to vote." Yet U.S. Representative Rankin became even better known as "the original dove in Congress"—after all, she voted against our entry in both world wars.

In January 1968, at age eighty-seven, she considered running once again for Congress, on a Vietnam War peace platform. Instead, she determined to return to Washington, D.C., this time to lead a march of women against the Vietnam War. Her passion for peace knew no bounds. She said, "I worked for suffrage for years, and got it. I've worked for peace for 55 years and haven't come close."[137]

The *Chicago Tribune* reported that day, January 15, 1968, when Rankin led the peace march:

> *Former congresswoman* [Rankin] *today stole the spotlight from United States senators and representatives assembled to launch the second session of the 90th Congress.*
>
> *It was Jeannette Rankin day on Capitol hill and the former Republican congresswoman from Montana made the most of it as she led a peace march of 4,000 women…*
>
> *As the head of the "Jeannette Rankin brigade," she conferred first with House Speaker John McCormack* [D., Mass.] *and then with Sen. Mike Mansfield* [D., Mont.], *the Senate majority leader.*
>
> *Tho she didn't know it at the time, she was responsible for virtually the only development in the Senate today. This was a wrangle spearheaded by two doves who sought to read her petition asking, in part, that Congress end the war in Viet Nam and immediately arrange the withdrawal of all American troops there.*
>
> *Mansfield, backed by Vice President Humphrey who was presiding over the Senate, dashed efforts by Senators Ernest Gruening* [D., Alaska] *and Wayne Morse* [D., Ore.] *to read her peace petition.*
>
> *…*[Mansfield] *insisted that by tradition no business is conducted until after the President's state of the Union address.*
>
> *…Tho Miss Rankin, wearing the black all marchers were requested to don, described the meeting with McCormack as a "very delightful visit," others among the 15 march leaders who also met with the speaker were more critical.*
>
> *"He said we were like those who didn't feel Hitler should be stopped," said* [a woman from Illinois, whose husband is a rabbi].[138]

The Rankin Brigade represented a broad spectrum: Mrs. Martin Luther King was in the front line of marchers, as was Sister Marguerite Hafner of the School Sisters of St. Francis; members of the Black Congress and Black Panther Party; Chicago Abeta Hebrew Center; Chicago Peace Council; trade unions; Latin Defense Organization; Women's International League for Peace and Freedom; and many others.[139]

In March 1972, Rankin spoke to the Montana Constitutional Convention about peace, telling the delegates that the military created the enemy in

Vietnam. "That's why we haven't decided who the next enemy is going to be." One year later, on May 18, 1973, just before her ninety-third birthday, the dove from Montana died in her sleep at Carmel, California.[140]

Today, the Jeannette Rankin Peace Center in Missoula "exists to connect and empower people to build a socially just, non-violent and sustainable community and world."[141]

ENDING VIETNAM: OPERATION HOMECOMING POWS HOME AT LAST

On January 27, 1973, National Security Advisor Henry Kissinger agreed to a ceasefire with officials of North Vietnam, providing for the withdrawal of American military forces from South Vietnam. The agreement arranged the release of POWs held by North Vietnam and its allies within sixty days of the withdrawal of U.S. troops.[142]

Operation Homecoming brought the return of American POWs. The operation unfolded in three phases: 69 POWs held by the Viet Cong; 591 POWs interred in North Vietnam were released at Hanoi; and 3 POWs held by the People's Republic of China were freed in Hong Kong. The POWs were flown to Clark Air Base, Philippines, where debriefer/escort officers from their own military service met them, and they received physical examinations and initial debriefings. In the final phase, the POWs with escorts flew to military hospitals closest to their homes for necessary medical treatment and detailed debriefings.

On February 12, 1973, three USAF C-141A transports flew to Hanoi, and one C-9A aircraft was sent to Saigon to board released POWs. From February 12 to April 4, fifty-four C-141 missions flew out of Hanoi, bringing former POWs home. Early flights brought POWs in order of longest length in prison—the first group having spent six to eight years in captivity. Of this total, 325 served in the air force, 138 navy, 26 Marine Corps and 77 army, with 25 civilians from government agencies.[143]

MONTANA'S VIETNAM POWS

Lincoln's Birthday, Monday, February 12, 1973, was a day long yearned and prayed for by American POWs held in captivity in North Vietnam. On this day to remember, their release began, and the first group of POWs boarded

As Operation Homecoming was executed, I was serving as the senior intelligence officer in the IOIC on board USS *Constellation*, operating in the Gulf of Tonkin off the coast of North Vietnam. With Operation Linebacker II combat flight operations suspended with the Paris Peace Agreement, I boarded a C-2 COD to arrive at Clark Air Base before the POWs. On February 12, I met Captain James Bond Stockdale, the senior navy POW, and with U.S. Air Force Colonel Robinson Reisner, the "leader" of all the POWs, as he limped slowly off the C-141. My assignment as his escort and debriefer was the honor of a lifetime as we spent the next two months together, first for medical processing and initial debriefings at Clark and then after the long flight across the Pacific back to the United States, more medical at North Island Naval Air Station Hospital and, finally, for six more weeks on the back patio of the Stockdale home in nearby Coronado for a very detailed debriefing. The exceptional story of courage and bravery that Captain Stockdale related to me each morning, and which I transcribed each afternoon to send back to the Pentagon, was so powerful in documenting his extraordinary bravery and leadership that it led to his award of the Medal of Honor.

Rear Admiral James Bond Stockdale received the Medal of Honor from President Gerald Ford for his "valiant leadership and extraordinary courage in a hostile environment" while a POW in Vietnam. At great personal cost, then Captain Stockdale led American POW resistance to interrogation and propaganda exploitation. *Author's collection.*

three US C-141s for the two-and-a-half-hour flight to Clark Air Base. Arriving that first day at Clark, to be greeted by Operation Homecoming, was Captain James Bond Stockdale, senior U.S. Navy POW and legendary hardline military leader of all POWs, as well as Montana's two credited Vietnam POWs: U.S. Navy Lieutenant Rodney Knutson of Billings and U.S. Air Force Captain Lynn Guenther, of Glasgow. A fourth POW, Major Fred Vann Cherry, also released that fateful day, was the first and highest-ranking Black officer among the POWs. Major Cherry had close Montana ties, having served at Great Falls/Malmstrom AFB from 1953 to 1957, and while stationed there had married a Great Falls woman.

Montana's POWs

Lieutenant Rodney A. Knutson:
First POW to Endure Extreme Torture

October 17, 1965, was a chaotic and tragic day for the naval aviators from USS *Independence*, launching strikes from Yankee Station in the Gulf of Tonkin on targets in North Vietnam. On that fateful day, Air Wing-7 lost three F-4B Phantoms during day strike missions on the Thai Nguyen bridge northeast of Hanoi, just below the Chinese border.

Six naval aviators were shot down over North Vietnam, with four surviving to become POWs and see their eventual release during Operation Homecoming: Lieutenant Junior Grade David Wheat, Lieutenant Junior Grade Porter A. Halyburton, Lieutenant Junior Grade Ralph Gaither and Lieutenant Junior Grade Rodney A. Knutson. Lieutenant Commander Stanley E. Olmstead died in the crash of his F-4B, while Lieutenant Roderick L. Mayer died of severe wounds.

Lieutenant Junior Grade Rodney Knutson was born in 1938, graduated from Billings High School and enlisted in the U.S. Marine Corps. Discharged, he graduated from Eastern Montana College, attended the Naval Aviation School of Preflight, was commissioned ensign in the navy and went on to earn his wings. Assigned to Fighter Squadron VF-84, the Jolly Rogers, he was shot down during his seventy-seventh combat mission over North Vietnam.

Lieutenant Knutson's Phantom was traveling more than five hundred miles per hour when white-hot shells began to fill the sky and hit his jet. Both

Knutson and his pilot, Lieutenant Junior Grade Gaither, ejected before their Phantom crashed. Lieutenant Knutson later described the action:

> *Due to my low altitude ejection at over 500 kts, I suffered a fractured neck and back. During my capture I was fired upon by enemy soldiers and to protect myself I killed two of them before I was knocked unconscious by the muzzle blast of a rifle being fired at point blank range. I had a laceration over my right eye and an abrasion down my face along my nose, powder burns on my face and a swollen knee.*
>
> *While in captivity I suffered some other injuries due to maltreatment by the Vietnamese. I was the first POW to be tortured by the North Vietnamese. I was tortured many times—with ropes on my arms, leg irons, hand cuffs, manacles and beatings. I was suspended by ropes, and also suffered a broken nose, broken wrist, broken teeth, and multiple other minor injuries. One thing they could never take away from me, though, was my character which included my pride, personal self-respect, love for my family and country and my devotion to these things.* [144]

When Lieutenant Knutson regained consciousness, his arms and legs were bound and he was facedown in the bed of a military truck. Taken to Hoa Lo prison, known as "Hanoi Hilton," he joined about thirty-five other POWs.

Crowd at Yellowstone County Fairground welcoming POW Lieutenant Commander Rodney Knutson (USN), freed during Operation Homecoming. On Lieutenant Commander Knutson's left is his mother, Mrs. Arvin Knutson, while Billings Mayor Joseph E. Leone speaks. *From the* Billings Gazette, *March 8, 1973.*

While all early POWs were mistreated, beginning in late 1965, just as Knutson arrived, the application of torture against U.S. prisoners became especially severe. Knutson believed he was the first American prisoner to be severely tortured with the new "rope torture" process, and he likely was.

Lieutenant Commander Knutson was released after seven and a half years of captivity. He remembered that event with these words: "I was a prisoner just under 2800 days and when released on the first C-141 out of Hanoi I was a man who was so happy I couldn't even speak."

At Naval Hospital Oak Knoll, he reunited with his parents, Mr. and Mrs. Arvin M. Knutson. His mother, Persis Bowman Knutson, had long served as Montana coordinator for the League of Families of POW-MIA, very active in promoting the plight of prisoners. She toured embassies in Europe and attended the International Red Cross Conference in France, seeking support.

Rodney Knutson remained on active duty, regaining flight status, this time as a pilot, and retired as a highly decorated navy captain in 1993.[145]

A Montana POW Returns to Malmstrom AFB

Born in Glasgow, Captain Lynn E. Guenther, USAF, was shot down in December 1971 while flying an OV-10 Bronco observation plane on forward air controller duty near the border of Laos and North Vietnam. Captain Guenther related his ordeal:

> In August of 1971 I departed the States for my year's duty in Vietnam. My stops enroute were Da Nang, Pleiku (for two months) and finally NKP [Nakhon Phanom Air Base] Thailand.
>
> On December 26, 1971, after flying about three months over Laos, I was shot down by Anti-Aircraft-Artillery. I sustained two injuries—one to my left eye and the other to my left shoulder. While in captivity I underwent two operations, one for each injury. As far as my thoughts and feelings go I feel I have learned a great deal about myself, my fellow Americans and all of mankind. I now know the real meaning of tolerance and love—tolerance for those around us and love for the country and world we live in.[146]

Held captive by the North Vietnamese for fourteen months, Captain Guenther faced criticism after his return. Arriving at Travis AFB, California, in a press conference, he discussed antiwar statements he made over Hanoi radio and his friendship with some North Vietnamese guards. He admitted

Glasgow-born Captain Lynn Guenther, *far right*, is joined by two other released POWs, Captain Terry Geloneck and Lieutenant William Arcuri, at a Travis Air Force Base news conference. Captain Guenther faced questions regarding his antiwar statements and friendship with North Vietnamese guards. *From the* Albany (OR) Democrat Herald, *February 28, 1973.*

that he was "scared" during the B-52 bombing raids in December 1972, noting that these raids hit close to his prison camp in Hanoi, and said, "I had mixed feelings about it. I was scared, let's put it that way. There was a great amount of action around Hanoi and I was quite concerned."

Captain Guenther was asked about statements he allegedly made over Hanoi radio urging Congress to end the war, and he replied, "You know as well as I do we allow free speech in this country. At no time did any of these statements degrade the United States in any way or the way of life in our country." Of his relations with Communist guards, he said, "We made friends with some of the guards. If you live around an individual for an extended period of time you are going to generate some type of friendship; we were on a friendly basis with them. They met our needs, so a friendship developed."

Guenther had missed the extreme torture regime that earlier shootdowns had to endure prior to 1969. His words of empathy toward their captors were not shared by those who had.[147] He remained on active duty, and fifteen years later, on September 16, 1988, Lieutenant Colonel Lynn Guenther, assistant deputy commander of 301ˢᵗ Air Refueling Wing at Malmstrom AFB, spoke to a crowd of four hundred, including one hundred former POWs from throughout Montana, gathered on National POW-MIA Recognition Day to receive a new POW Medal at a ceremony at Malmstrom. Colonel Guenther told the former POWs, families and friends about rats crawling on his body, the screams of other prisoners in the night, the bitter cold and incessant nightmares. He ended his talk with these words:

> *For some, this closes the final chapter of an ordeal that most Americans and other people only read about or are taught in a history book. Yet for most of us, the final chapter will never be closed….POW-MIA Recognition Day should be a day to remember those not lucky enough to return from the foxholes, gun turrets and rice paddies. It should also be a day of rededication to efforts to find out what happened to those classified as missing in action.*[148]

Colonel Guenther retired from the U.S. Air Force in 1996.

Colonel Fred V. Cherry: African American POW

Colonel Fred V. Cherry, the first and highest-ranking Black officer among POWs during the Vietnam War, served at Great Falls Air Force Base during the mid-1950s.

Cherry was born on March 24, 1928, in Suffolk, Hampton Roads, Virginia, to John Cherry, an impoverished farmer, and Leolia Cherry, into a family of eight children. Young Cherry was fascinated by military aircraft flying low over his home and performing aerial maneuvers. He attended segregated public schools, including Virginia Union University in Richmond.

Determined to become a pilot after graduation, in 1951 he tried to enlist in Naval Aviation, without success. Finally, after confronting an air force recruiting officer, Cherry was allowed to take the test for flight school at Langley AFB—he passed with the highest score. Fred Cherry was on his way to become one of the earliest Black pilots in the integrated air force.

Cherry completed the Aviation Cadet Training Program, was commissioned second lieutenant and awarded his pilot wings in October 1952. He immediately deployed to Korea, and from January 1953 until the end of the war, he flew F-84s on fifty combat missions with the 310ᵗʰ Fighter-Bomber Squadron.

Leaving Korea after war's end, Captain Cherry reported for duty at Great Falls AFB, where he flew F-84s with the 515th Strategic Fighter Squadron, 407th Strategic Fighter Wing. Captain Cherry soon met Shirley Ann Brown, a hostess in a nightclub. Shirley, daughter of William R. and Pearl Lindsay Brown, was twenty-two, with ten siblings, and was looking for a ticket out of Great Falls. Her mother was the daughter of a long-serving Buffalo Soldier, and young Shirley likely had heard family stories of military life. Fred Cherry was a dashing, handsome jet fighter pilot, breaking racial barriers in the air force. The couple were married in July 1954, and their first son was born a year later.

Captain Cherry and his family remained in Great Falls for three years. His wing commander, Colonel Murray Bywater, flew himself to bases around the country, accompanied by a second aircraft. Colonel Bywater always chose Captain Cherry for this plum job.[149]

Between 1957 and 1961, the Cherrys were transferred frequently, until he was assigned to the 35th Tactical Fighter Squadron at Itazuke Air Base, Japan, flying F-100 Super Sabres. During this tour, he performed weeklong deployments to South Korea on "nuclear alert." While there, on orders, he could launch in under four minutes en route to an assigned target to drop his nuclear weapon. In 1963, Captain Cherry was due to return to the United States but requested an extension so that he could transition and fly the air force's newest tactical aircraft, the F-105 Thunderchief, at Yokota Air Base, Japan. The Cherry family, Shirley and four children, wanted to continue living in Japan, where the racial environment was somewhat better than in the United States. Shirley enjoyed her life and status as the wife of a highly respected air force officer.

In 1964, Captain Cherry and the 35th TFS deployed to Korat Royal Thai AFB, Thailand, as one of the first air force units to fight in Southeast Asia. The squadron later relocated to Takhli AFB. Captain Cherry served as a flight leader, exercising major control over the mission—all this in an era when many believed that Black service members were unfit to lead Whites into battle. Yet White officers coveted selection to fly in Captain Cherry's flight. His nickname "Chief" connoted respect, and a senior evaluating officer in 1964 praised him, writing, "I consider Captain Cherry one of the most effective officers of his rank that I have worked with during my entire Air Force career."[150]

While the navy launched aircraft from carriers in the Gulf of Tonkin, the air force operated, initially, from crude bases in Thailand. Fred Cherry was promoted to major, flying F-105 tactical bombers with targets along the Ho

Colonel Fred V. Cherry, first and highest-ranking Black officer among POWs, bravely withstood all attempts by his captors to make "race" in the United States a propaganda issue. Colonel Cherry's legacy includes this larger-than-life painting by artist Harrison Benton, *Portrait of a Fighter Pilot*, which hangs in the Pentagon "POW Alcove of Honor." *U.S. Department of Defense photo.*

Chi Minh Trail to disrupt the flow of supplies from the North to the Viet Cong in the South. In February 1965, after Viet Cong attacks on an American compound and helicopter base in South Vietnam, bombing targets opened up in North Vietnam. One month later, the massive Rolling Thunder campaign brought thousands of sorties by both air force and navy aircraft over North Vietnam. In response, with aid from the Russians and Chinese, North Vietnam rapidly developed a sophisticated air defense system.

By October 1965, Major Cherry had executed forty-six combat missions in Vietnam during three tours at Takhli. Due to rotate back to the United States in mid-October, Major Cherry argued persuasively for one last tour at Takhli. On one fateful day, October 22, 1965, while leading his squadron on a low-altitude mission to attack a radar in North Vietnam, his F-105 was hit by anti-aircraft fire. Major Cherry later wrote about his ordeal: "The plane exploded and I ejected at about 400 feet at over 600 miles an hour. In the process of ejection, I broke my left ankle, my left wrist, and crushed my left shoulder. I was captured immediately upon landing by Vietnamese militia and civilians. I remember thinking, 'Damn, I'll be here a long time.'"

Major Cherry was the forty-third American captured by North Vietnam and the first Black airman.[151] He was imprisoned in Hoa Lo Prison, the "Hanoi Hilton," but shortly after taken to Cu Loc Prison, "the Zoo," where his captors assigned young Navy Ensign Porter A. Halyburton, a White southerner, to Cherry's cell in an effort to foster racial strife. For eight months, they would live together. Cherry, a virtual invalid at the time, would have died without Halyburton changing the dressings on his infected wounds, feeding him, bathing him and watching over him. In turn, caring for Cherry rescued Halyburton from his own despair. Together, they were not men of conflicting races, but fellow Americans helping each other survive the brutal regime of their captors. The bond they made in that dark and dirty prison cell led to a lifelong friendship.

On the night of July 6, 1966, Halyburton, with about sixty other POWs, was forced to march through the streets of Hanoi, barely surviving the vilification and physical abuse of Vietnamese mobs. Meanwhile, that same night, Cherry endured excruciating pain while undergoing a third operation on his severely infected shoulder without anesthetic. Five days later, the Vietnamese captors realized at last that their racial ploy had failed completely, and Halyburton was moved to another cell. As they parted, the Black American and the White American hugged, cried and said heartfelt goodbyes. Cherry wrote later, "That was the most lonesome night I ever spent in my life." Halyburton considered their parting as "one of the saddest days of my life," adding, "I was in awe of him, and I had learned to love him."[152]

Major Cherry was captured just as the North Vietnamese cracked down on their American prisoners—imposing what the prisoners called the "Exploitation Era." Senior Navy POW Commander James Bond Stockdale was shot down a month before this change of policy and bravely assumed leadership of all the prisoners. He later observed, "By carrying out a new policy action [of extreme torture], North Vietnam had crossed a boundary. Henceforth, Americans were to be allowed to stay within the bounds of name, rank, serial number, and date of birth only at North Vietnamese sufferance."

This change imposed the Exploitation Era. The North Vietnamese knew the critical importance of public opinion. Torture, the captors believed, would be the tool to extract prisoner confessions and statements that could be used to sway American and world opinion.[153]

Throughout his captivity, Cherry consistently and bravely resisted pressure from his captors to publicly comment on racism in the United States, for which he was repeatedly tortured and placed in solitary confinement over the next seven years. "I spent 702 days in solitary confinement," he added, with the longest period lasting fifty-three weeks. "At one time I was either tortured or in punishment for 93 straight days."[154]

After spending 2,671 days in captivity, on February 12, 1973, newly promoted Colonel Fred Perry boarded the first flight from Hanoi to Clark Air Force Base to join Operation Homecoming. There Cherry and Halyburton would reunite once more.

After processing, Colonel Cherry returned to the United States, as noted in the *Great Falls Tribune*:

> FORMER FALLS MAN FREED IN VIETNAM
> *Lt. Col. Fred V. Cherry, who formerly was stationed at Malmstrom Air Force Base, was declared legally dead seven years after his plane was shot down in Vietnam.*
>
> *Monday, he was among those who were released from prison camps and started home. His family previously had been notified that he was among the POWs. His wife is the former Shirley Brown of Great Falls. She and their four children now are living in Virginia.*
>
> *Her brother, Ray Brown, 319 9th Ave. S., said Monday he "wouldn't be surprised if they came back to Great Falls to live."*[155]

Yet Colonel Cherry came home to a tumultuous environment. His wife, Shirley, had betrayed him during his captivity, considering him dead even after the air force confirmed that he was a prisoner. She deserted him, convinced their children that he was dead, had a child by another man and spent Cherry's life savings of $121,998. He later sued the air force and, after protracted legal action, recovered $50,000.

Remaining on active duty, Cherry attended the National War College in Washington, D.C., and then served in the Defense Intelligence Agency until retiring in 1981. His medals included the Air Force Cross, awarded, according to the citation, for "extraordinary heroism in military operations against an opposing armed force as a POW…extremely strong personal fortitude and maximum persistence in the face of severe enemy harassment and torture, suffering critical injuries and wounds."

Living in Silver Springs, Maryland, Cherry continued to work as a technical consultant and manager for several businesses, while dedicating time as a member of Tuskegee Airmen Inc. to urge Black youth to study subjects leading to a career in aviation. President Ronald Reagan named him to serve on the Korean War Veterans Memorial Advisory Board.

Colonel Cherry and Commander Porter Halyburton remained in close contact over the years, and together they gave many joint talks at military institutions and colleges. In 2004, they toured to promote a book about their story, *Two Souls Indivisible: The Friendship that Saved Two POWs in Vietnam*, by James S. Hirsch. Colonel Cherry also was featured in a public television documentary narrated by Tom Hanks, *Return with Honor*, about Vietnam fighter pilots held as POWs.

On February 16, 2016, Fred Vann Cherry died in Washington, D.C., of heart failure at the age of eighty-seven, and he was buried with full military honors at Arlington National Cemetery. Colonel Cherry's legacy is continued by a college scholarship fund and the Colonel Fred Cherry Middle School in his hometown, Suffolk, Virginia. His larger-than-life likeness in oil by artist Harrison Benton, *Portrait of a Fighter Pilot*, hangs in the "POW Alcove of Honor" in the Pentagon.[156]

Malmstrom Officer Tells of Experiences as POW

Other Vietnam POWs served at Malmstrom AFB. Lieutenant Colonel Norbert A. Gotner came to Great Falls in 1975, commanded the 564th Strategic Missile Squadron and served until 1978, when he retired from the air force. He was a popular speaker for clubs in the area with stories of his shootdown in Laos on his 109th F-4C mission with the 8th Tactical Fighter Wing and his experiences as a POW for more than two years. The critical elements for survival, according to Colonel Gotner, were "rights, responsibility, organization and discipline."

Shot down, he evaded for two days before being captured on February 3, 1971. He reached the lowest point of his life after his capture, when he spent two consecutive nights while very ill during which he gave up hope of coming home alive and wanted to die. Another American, who had been held for six and a half years, two-thirds of them spent in solitary confinement, saved him. Captain Gotner learned that to survive, he would have to have faith that the American people would not forget him, that President Nixon would not let Americans forget him, in his wife and in himself, that he could beat the enemy.

Captain Gotner spent six months in solitary confinement in a jungle camp containing four cells, each measuring eight feet square. Later, he was moved to a camp called the "pig pen," where he became expert at raising pigs. He was bothered most by several American turncoats who worked for the North

Vietnamese and anti-military speeches given at home that called American military Nazi war criminals and reported Americans in Vietnam as killing only civilians, children and the elderly.[157]

"WELCOME HOME, DAUGHTERS OF AMERICA": THE VIETNAM WOMEN'S MEMORIAL

These words came from Montana Vietnam veteran army nurse Diane Carlson Evans, who conceived the idea and fought for ten years to bring into reality the first women's military monument in our nation's capital. Before an estimated crowd of twenty-five thousand, including many Vietnam vets dressed in jungle fatigues on Veterans Day, November 11, 1993, a parade led to the site, just south of the hallowed grounds of the Vietnam Veterans Wall. There, the Vietnam Women's Memorial was dedicated. Admiral William J. Crowe Jr., USN (Ret.), opened his remarks as he choked back tears brought on by memories of his service in Vietnam. Recalling visions of nurses as they jumped from a landing helicopter to take charge of wounded soldiers, he spoke, "I have just seen an angel of the Lord."

Of the 250,000 women in the U.S. military during the Vietnam War, barred from combat, some 11,000 served in-country, most as nurses but others as physicians, air traffic controllers, intelligence officers, clerks and other positions. Many civilian women also served in Vietnam as news correspondents and workers for Red Cross, USO and other humanitarian organizations.

Lieutenant Diane Carlson (later Carlson Evans) served as an army nurse in-country during 1968–69, beginning at Vung Tau Evacuation Hospital about eighty miles east of Saigon and then in the 71st Evacuation Hospital at Pleiku near the Central Highlands, at a time of heavy fighting and mass casualties and where night belonged to the Viet Cong in the spring of 1969. She returned with other Vietnam veterans to a divided nation that failed to honor the men and women it had sent into combat in distant Southeast Asia.

Lieutenant Carlson Evans conceived of a memorial to remind Americans of the importance of women in the Vietnam War. She became the founder and chair of the Vietnam Women's Memorial Foundation, the first woman in American history to spearhead a campaign to place a national monument in Washington, D.C.

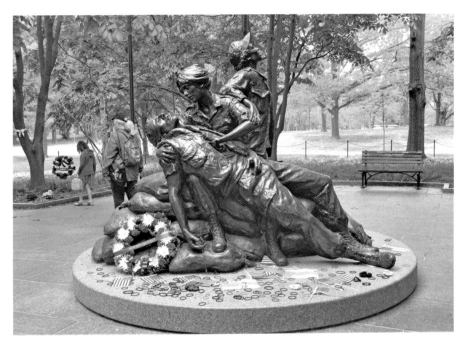

Lieutenant Diane Carlson Evans, an army combat nurse in Vietnam, led a successful effort to build the Vietnam Women's Memorial in Washington, D.C., designed by Glenna Goodacre and dedicated on November 11, 1993. *Wikimedia Commons.*

The memorial depicts three uniformed women nurses, one of whom is caring for a wounded soldier. Surrounding the memorial site are eight yellowwood trees, planted to symbolize the eight women whose names are on The Wall—one killed in action and the other seven who died of disease or accidents. The grove provides a flowered canopy in the spring and a subtle yellow color in the autumn. The multi-figure bronze monument, designed by New Mexico sculptor Glenna Goodacre, is a sculpture in the round.

Today, Diane Carlson Evans, proud Vietnam veteran, founder and president of the Vietnam Veteran's Memorial Foundation, and her family live in Helena, where she remains an active advocate nationally for women in the military.[158]

THE SECRET WAR IN LAOS

In early 1961, Louise Daniels received a short letter from her husband, Jerry, who broke through the veil of secrecy around his trip to Southeast Asia. His Central Intelligence Agency (CIA) employers had finally given him permission to let his wife know what he was doing. Jerry Daniels wrote that he was "dropping cargo which mainly consists of rice, gasoline and some medical supplies to the Meo [Hmong] tribe refugees. The dropping is being done in Laos." From this beginning, the heart and soul of this nineteen-year-old smokejumper from Missoula would remain in the wild mountains of civil war–riven Laos. Jerry "Hog" Daniels rose through the ranks to become CIA liaison officer and closest advisor to the legendary, fiercely anti-Communist and charismatic leader of the Hmong, General Vang Pao, in their life-and-death struggle against Laotian Communists and their powerful North Vietnamese masters.

Jerrold B. "Jerry" Daniels was born in California in 1941 and moved with his family to an old mining town, Helmsville, Powell County, Montana, when he was ten. Jerry began smokejumping with the U.S. Forest Service to fight fires in Montana and the West before graduating from Missoula High School. Jerry was just the type of young man the CIA was recruiting to join its Air America covert operation in Laos—he had "the physical stamina, can-do spirit, knowledge of parachutes, and the survival skills of a good woodsman" to be selected as a smokejumper and, therefore, a perfect cargo handler "kicker" for the CIA.[159]

During the 1960s, CIA recruited almost one hundred western smokejumpers for its covert operations in Laos, Tibet and other secret battlefields in the war on Communism. Many, including Jerry Daniels, came to the agency from Missoula. Throughout the "Secret War" in Laos, these brave men worked closely with the Hmong in their desperate struggle against Communist domination. The powerful role played by Daniels, known by his CIA call sign "Hog," raised his profile with General Vang Pao and the Hmong to legendary proportions. As the only strongly anti-Communist force in Laos, the Hmong were under constant pressure and assault by both Laotian Communists and invading North Vietnamese troops. From their bastion in northern Laos at Long Cheng in the Plain of Jars, General Vang Pao and his Hmong fighters held out with the support of the CIA. Hog Daniels named his American headquarters there the "Sky compound," for his Big Sky Country home in Montana.

With the collapse of the Republic of Vietnam in 1975, the Hmong position in Laos became untenable. The CIA had long promised assistance to the Hmong in such a situation, and Jerry Daniels orchestrated a daring fourteen-day airlift evacuation of 2,500 Hmong fighters and their families to temporary sanctuary in Thailand. With the assistance of Hog Daniels, Vang Pao bought a house in Missoula and a large ranch in the Bitterroot Valley, south of Missoula, where about 750 Hmong were resettled. For years, Vang Pao and his family lived among his people in Missoula and the Bitterroot, before they and many of their people began relocating elsewhere.

From 1975 to 1982, Jerry Daniels, from his base in Thailand, continued to work with some fifty thousand more Hmong tribesmen who continued to flee to refugee camps in Thailand. These American allies, also, were resettled in the United States and other countries. Daniels continued to serve the people he loved, the Hmong, as a State Department Ethnic Affairs officer at the American embassy in Bangkok. On April 29, 1982, he died accidently in his apartment in Bangkok of asphyxiation caused by a leaking propane water heater. His body was sent home to Missoula in a sealed coffin with strongly worded orders that it not be opened—all in suspicious circumstances. The

Montanans, including hundreds of Hmong tribesmen, gathered for a traditional three-day Hmong funeral at Missoula Cemetery for their beloved adviser Jerry Daniels. *Daniels family photo, from the* Missoulian, *November 25, 2017.*

Hmong assembled at the Missoula cemetery to honor their hero with a full, formal, three-day traditional Hmong funeral celebration—the first ever such tribute for any non-Hmong. In the words of one of Daniels's Sky Compound Hmong employees, "Jerry died in Bangkok, but he was buried in Montana. At his funeral his mother said, 'Well, Vang Pao, this is your son, and you can do whatever you want. You can do his funeral by the Hmong custom.' So, that's what we did. With drums [*nruas*] and *qeej* [reed pipe], we did it the Hmong way for Jerry."[160]

In the words of Missoula historian Kim Briggeman, "Daniels was as fascinating, provocative, mysterious, ribald and heroic a figure as Missoula…ever produced."[161] For many years, Hmong around the world reported seeing Hog Daniels, with some believing that he secretly had gone underground and was still working for them. The mystery shrouding his death fueled speculation until thirty-five years later, on October 25, 2017, his body was exhumed under the auspices of Montana's chief medical examiner, Dr. Robert Kurtzman, and Missoula County's chief deputy coroner, Lieutenant Jace Dicken, and in the presence of Daniel's son Dan and Hmong witnesses. In the opinion of Daniels biographer Gayle L. Morrison, the exhumation answered key questions: "The grave had not been disturbed, she's '99 percent sure that it's Jerry in there,' and it appears he didn't suffer some 'grisly trauma.'"[162]

With the exhumation and analysis proving that the body in the casket was that of their beloved Hog Daniels, the Hmong accepted the reality that he had entered the spirit world. More than half a century after the young smokejumper from Missoula left in secrecy for a good, although dangerous job, to serve his country in Southeast Asia, the folk hero to tens of thousands of Hmong Americans rests under the mountain trees at Missoula Cemetery, not far from where hundreds of Hmong Americans live in their new country.

CHAPTER 6

THE WALL FALLS

AN END TO THE COLD WAR

PROTECTING STRATEGIC MISSILES

From the beginning of the ICBM programs, concern about these strategically vital missiles led to planning for their protection through Anti-Ballistic Missile (ABM) programs. The Sentinel Program, begun by the Johnson administration in response to Soviet efforts to build ABMs, was a U.S. Army system designed to provide a light layer of protection for cities as well as the Minuteman ICBMs.

When President Richard Nixon took office, public opinion was growing against ABM deployment to protect cities. After review, in March 1969, the president ordered cancelation of the Sentinel Program and pressed on with a Safeguard Program, designed to protect only the ICBM fields. At the time, anti-military opinion was growing, fueled by the protests against the Vietnam War. In addition, the air force favored building more ICBMs rather than investing in the army's ABM program. Overlaying the Safeguard Program were strategic arms talks with the Soviet Union.

Regardless, President Nixon pressed on with the new Safeguard Program. In late 1968, the Department of Defense added Malmstrom AFB to the list of locations to receive the Safeguard ABM. With President Nixon's reorientation of the BMD to protect U.S. strategic forces, suddenly the proposed Safeguard sites at Malmstrom and Grand Forks, North Dakota, rose to the top construction priority.

An Army Air Defense Command Antiballistic Missile Safeguard Site is shown in this artist's concept, including Missile Site Radar (*center-right foreground*) and missile cells for Spartan and Sprint (*on left*). *Author's collection.*

The plan unfolded at a meeting at Malmstrom AFB providing for six ABM sites in the $5 billion program within Montana's north-central Golden Triangle: Dutton, Conrad, Valier, Shelby, Devon and Galata. Announcing that four of the six locations likely would be chosen, the Army Corps of Engineers began surveys and rights of entry to each property. Each installation required two unique radars for both short-range (Sprint) and long-range (Spartan) missiles, as well as supporting solid-state electronic data processing equipment. Up to 250 acres of land were required for each Spartan-Sprint site. The long-range Spartan missile was designed to intercept an approaching hostile missile in outer space, outside Earth's atmosphere, while the shorter-range, faster-traveling Sprint would strike down an approaching missile nearer the ground.

Each center required a long-range perimeter acquisition radar (PAR) system on a three-hundred-acre tract apart from the missile area. Every project involved spending about $100 million, with 80 percent earmarked for construction. When operational, each installation would require four hundred to seven hundred persons, half civilians. The estimated total annual payroll for each center would be $2 million to $3.5 million.

The construction phase would last two years, after twelve months' design work. The system would be operatonal in the early 1970s, with five hundred to eight hundred skilled workers required for construction drawn from local labor. Western Electric Company was the prime contractor, and the Army Air Defense Command would operate the Safeguard system.[163]

The attraction of big construction money and potential operations manpower brought supporters, yet many opposed the project both in Montana and in the Senate. Senate Majority Leader Mike Mansfield opposed the program, yet by narrow majorities, the Senate continued to support Safeguard. The debate within Montana ranged from a symposium on ABMs held in Great Falls, where the *Tribune* reported, "There are those who are fer 'em, and there are those who are agin 'em, and a thousand shades and intensities of feeling in between."

This massive Perimeter Acquisition Radar Building is the only remnant of the ABM Safeguard site in Montana. A victim of U.S.-Soviet ABM Treaty, construction of this site located east of Conrad consumed twenty-five thousand cubic yards of concrete and more than 6 million pounds of steel reinforcing bar. *Author's photo.*

Through Congressional debates and votes during the summer of 1969, little construction occurred in Montana. Yet once funding appeared assured, the army announced the pending deployment of a Safeguard ABM system to sites near Shelby and Conrad. The PAR radar would be located east of Conrad, with the missile site radar (MSR) located nearby.[164]

During 1970, construction began near Conrad to be operational by 1974. By August, Strategic Arms Limitation Treaty (SALT) talks were underway, with the United States offering to abandon its ABM System if the Soviet Union would limit its missile defenses. Yet the Safeguard project was in full swing, with massive construction taking place, most centered near Conrad. By late May 1972, the project was 10 percent complete, and the contractor was mobilizing resources to launch full-scale construction.

However, on May 26, 1972, President Nixon and Russian General Secretary Leonid Brezhnev signed the ABM Treaty, limiting each nation to one ABM site to protect strategic forces and one site to protect its national command authority. The Grand Forks, North Dakota Safeguard complex was nearly 85 percent complete, so construction was suspended at the Malmstrom complex, to the relief of many Montanans. Its certain fate came in October, when the U.S. Senate ratified the SALT I and ABM Treaties. Terminating the large ABM project was complex, with many contracts to close out and compensation claims to be settled. Remnants of the Montana PAR site are still located east of Conrad, while the Missile Site Radar was dismantled and buried.[165]

STOROZHEVOY: A WARNING SHOT

By the mid-1970s, cracks were beginnig to show in the Soviet monolith. Signs were coming to the surface of the stagnation in the Soviet economy and corruption that permeated the empire. Suddenly, on the night of November 8, 1975, a warning shot was fired from within the same Baltic Naval Fleet that had led the Bolshevik Revolution of 1917. The Soviet navy Krivak-class frigate *Storozhevoy* was in the port of Riga to celebrate of the fifty-eighth anniversary of the Russian Revolution. Normal daytime tours were conducted for local citizens, and half the crew enjoyed shore leave to join in the festivities.

On the evening of November 8, the *Storozhevoy's* political commissar, Captain Third Rank Valery Sablin, with the support of many officers and most of the crew, seized control of the ship, led a mutiny and set sail out of the Bay of Riga into the Baltic Sea. Captain Sablin's goal of his "revolution"

Shortly before the *Storozhevoy* mutiny, I arrived with my family in Stockholm, Sweden, to serve as assistant U.S. naval attaché, responsible for reporting on Soviet military and naval activity and events. The *Storozhevoy* incident provided a stunning start to this fascinating tour of duty. During the first half of my three-year tour, we were blessed with American Ambassador Robert Strausz-Hupé, a prophet of the Cold War. Embassy staff meetings led by Ambassador Strausz-Hupé were conducted like a graduate seminar in international relations. In the opinion of his friend Harvey Sicheman, "The history of the Cold War is the unfolding of a protracted conflict eventually won by the West in a way strikingly similar to [Strausz-Hupé's] ideas."*

_____

* Sicherman, "Robert Strausz-Hupé: His Life and Times."

was to conduct a nationwide broadcast protesting against the rampant corruption of the Leonid Brezhnev era. In his address, he intended publicly to proclaim that socialism and the Russian motherland were in danger; that the rulers were corrupt demagogues, fueled by graft; that Communism had been abandoned; and to plead for a return to Leninist principles of justice. This broadcast was made but never heard—it was transmitted inadvertantly encrypted in code.

Discovering the mutiny, the Kremlin feared that Captain Sablin would defect to Sweden and ordered Baltic Fleet aircraft and ships to locate and regain control of *Storozhevoy*. As the mutiny ship neared twenty miles of Swedish territorial waters, Soviet aircraft strafed it, disabling its steering controls and stopping *Storozyhevoy* dead in the water. Sablin, who had suffered a minor wound to his leg, apparently ordered his men not to return fire. In turn, the Soviet navy was ordered to stop the *Storozhevoy* with the least damage necessary. In the "fog of war," one pursuing Krivak frigate was mistakenly attacked by naval aircraft and suffered serious damage. Defenseless, the mutiny ship was boarded by naval commandos.

Secrecy shrouded this entire episode. Despite Soviet attempts to hide this sign of weakness, reporting from Sweden enabled the story to emerge. Captain Sablin was tried, convicted of high treason and executed in August 1976. The fate of his men remains less clear.[166]

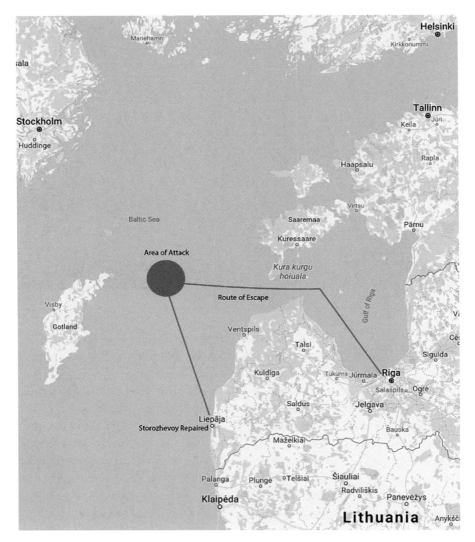

Above: Baltic Sea map revealing *Storozhevoy*'s escape route from Riga, the area of attack by Soviet air and naval forces, and Liepāja, where *Storozhevoy* underwent secretive repair. *Author's collection.*

Opposite: An aerial starboard bow view of a Soviet anti-submarine Krivak I Class guided missile frigate at anchor—the same Burevestnik-class frigate as the *Storozhevoy*, the Soviet mutiny ship. *Author's collection.*

A Stunning Defection:
Lieutenant Belenko and His Foxbat

On September 6, 1976, Lieutenant Viktor Belenko of the Soviet air force, disillusioned with the Soviet military and decaying society, made a daring flight across the Sea of Japan and with just seconds of fuel landed his super-secret fighter MiG-25 Foxbat in Hokkaido, Japan. His amazing defection stunned the Soviet Union and provided a gold mine of information for the CIA and the U.S. military. Protected by the CIA, Belenko moved often while giving insightful talks to many military groups around the country. He spent many years in Montana over several decades, reportedly attracted by the mountains of southern Montana, which resemble the Urals in Russia. During one visit to the Montana Air Guard at Gore Hill, Belenko provided insight into the MiG-25 and Soviet fighter tactics. The 120th acted on one tip that Belenko gave, that the cockpit in the Foxbat was tinted light blue to reduce reflection and ease pilot vision. The F-106 cockpits of the 120th soon bore the same shade of blue as Belenko's MiG-25.[167]

Lieutenant Viktor Belenko shocked the Soviet Union in September 1976 when he defected by flying his super-secret, high-altitude MiG-25P Foxbat to Japan. This Cold War epic provided a gold mine of information about his aircraft and the Soviet military. *Author's collection.*

THE IRANIAN HOSTAGE RESCUE
OPERATION EAGLE CLAW

An intense low-level dust storm, a "haboob," occurred in the Dasht-e Lut (Lut Desert) of southeastern Iran in April 1980. This haboob led to the catastrophic failure of a daring secret attempt by the U.S. military to rescue hostages from the American embassy in Tehran. The rescue attempt failed, and eight servicemen died in a helicopter/fixed-wing aircraft collision caused by low visibility in the Iranian desert.[168]

The stage was set by the fall of the Shah of Iran, the rise of Ayatollah Khomeini and his radical Islamist followers—this was the Iranian Islamic Revolution. On November 4, 1979, militant Iranian students stormed the U.S. embassy in Tehran, seizing sixty-three American hostages. Over time, the hostage count was reduced to fifty-three, while President Jimmy Carter searched widely for either a diplomatic solution or, as a last resort, a covert rescue. Diplomatic efforts failed, so the president authorized planning for a rescue attempt.

A CRITICAL FINAL WEATHER BRIEFING

After we had been at sea for months on Gonzo Staton in the Indian Ocean, at long last the order came to execute Operation Eagle Claw. I was serving as the CTF-70/CTF-77 intelligence officer, under Rear Admiral Robert E. Kirksey, onboard the *Nimitz*. At 6:00 p.m. on the evening of April 24, 1980, I was asked to go to my intelligence office, where I admitted our CTF-70 staff meteorologist and the intelligence officer for the Marine Helicopter Detachment. In this final weather briefing, our meteorologist used the latest satellite weather to brief in detail the conditions the helicopter pilots would encounter as they lifted from USS *Nimitz*, proceeded to the Iranian coast and on into the desert destination. He emphasized that intense low-level sand storms were active at that time and would create major problems with visibility. The Marine officer responded that dust storms would not be a problem because the helos were equipped with GPS. The meteorologist again clearly emphasized that these were exceptionally strong, low-level sand storms. The Marine acknowledged but again stated that they would have no problem.

One hour later, we watched the thrilling sight of all eight Sea Stallions lifting off the deck of the *Nimitz*—the first time in the four months they had been aboard that all eight were able to fly at the same time because of frequent maintenance problems.

Complicated by extreme secrecy and an absence of trained Special Forces for this complex operation, planning and preparation continued with four branches of the military involved. The final plan called for Marine pilots with eight RH-53 Sea Stallion helicopters deployed in secrecy to USS *Nimitz* in January 1980. Strike Force 7th Fleet/CTF-70 commanded U.S. naval forces in the Indian Ocean, while the Marine helicopter detachment operated under a Joint Task Force Command.

The plan called for an operation whereby helicopters from the *Nimitz* and C-130s from a covert land base, following different routes, would rendezvous on a salt flat (codenamed Desert One) two hundred miles southeast of

Tehran. Here the helicopters would refuel from the C-130s and embark combat troops who had flown in on the C-130s. The helicopters would then transport the troops to a mountain location (Desert Two) closer to Tehran, from which the actual rescue raid would be launched into the city the following night. The operation was supported by an in-country CIA team. Upon completion of the raid, the American hostages were to be driven to a captured Tehran airport to be flown to Egypt.

While complex, the daring plan was judged feasible, yet weeks turned to months while the operation prepared and President Carter dithered, trying to decide whether to execute—meanwhile, the hours of darkness shrunk and the onset of extreme low-level haboob sand dust storms began as summer approached. Adding to the complexity was the tough problem of maintaining eight RH-53 helicopters.

Finally, nearing the last possible week that the plan could be conducted, orders came to execute at 7:00 p.m. on October 24.[169]

A Long Evening as Operation Eagle Claw Unravels

The helos were underway for hundreds of miles of low-altitude night flight to the refueling site, Desert One. The C-130 element with the rescue force executed on a different route and time schedule to Desert One. About two hours after takeoff, the crew of Helicopter #6 received cockpit indications of an impending rotor blade failure, forcing them to land, verify the problem (an automatic abort situation) and abandon their aircraft. The crew was picked up by another helicopter, which then continued the mission.

An hour later, the helicopter formation encountered the haboob just as the CTF-70 meteorologist had warned. The helicopters broke out of the first area of haboob but, within an hour, entered a second, larger and denser storm. While navigating through this second storm with severely degraded visibility, a second helicopter experienced a failure of several critical navigation and flight instruments. With the situation deteriorating, the pilot aborted the mission, reversed course and recovered on *Nimitz*. Eventually, six of the original eight helicopters arrived at the refueling site fifty to eighty-five minutes behind schedule—endangered by the amount of darkness remaining.

A third helicopter experienced a partial hydraulic failure en route, but the pilot elected to continue to Desert One, believing that repairs could be made there. Upon landing, however, the crew and the helicopter detachment

Throughout the early morning hours of April 25, in our CTF-70 Command Center on the *Nimitz*, we watched the return of the crippled RH-53 and then endured the flow of news of the disaster at Desert One. Throughout the operation, Carrier Air Wing-8 aircraft from *Nimitz* and Carrier Air Wing-14 from USS *Coral Sea* provided defense combat air patrol cover for Task Force-70 ships and the helicopters.

Much reporting in the aftermath of the failed rescue attempt emphasized that the operation failed largely because preflight weather briefings to the crews failed to warn of the haboob storms. I was present and know that the Marine Detachment intelligence officer was specifically warned that the haboobs were intensely strong and would be in their path. Despite his confidence that their navigation aids would enable them to successfully fly through the desert areas, sadly this was not the case and the mission failed.

commander determined that a hydraulic pump had failed due to a fluid leak, and no replacement pump was available.

With just five helicopters available to proceed on to Desert Two, the on-scene commander recommended up the chain of command to President Carter that they abort the mission. The president concurred, and preparations began to withdraw the five operational helicopters and the C-130s with the rescue force. During refueling, the sad situation became tragic when one RH-53 collided with one of the refueling C-130s. Both aircraft went up in flames, and eight crewmen were killed and five others injured. In the fog of this disaster, the decision was made to abandon all helos and fly the crews out by C-130s. Adding insult to disaster, the force failed to remove classified mission material and blow up the abandoned helicopters.[170]

The aftermath of the Operation Eagle Claw afforded Ayatollah Khomeini a propaganda coup of major proportions. The Imam proclaimed, "Who crushed Mr. Carter's helicopters? We did! The sands did! They were God's agents. Wind is God's agent....These sands are agents of God. They can try again!"[171]

RH-53 Chinook helicopters on the elevator of the USS *Nimitz*, waiting to lift off on their way to attempt to rescue American embassy hostages in Tehran. *U.S. Navy.*

To preclude a second rescue attempt, the American hostages were scattered across Iran, and they would not be released until January 20, 1981, just minutes after Ronald Reagan took the oath of office after defeating President Carter.

A THEATER OF ILLUSIONS AND REALITY

Cold War historian John Lewis Gaddis has written that as the decade of the 1980s approached, big changes in the Cold War were coming: "All at once a single individual, through a series of dramatic performances, was changing the course of history. That was in a way appropriate, because the Cold War itself was a kind of theater in which distinctions between illusions and reality were not always obvious."[172]

The cast for this grand Cold War theater began to assemble in 1978 with the ascendance of actor Karol Wojtyla as Pope John Paul II. Shortly after, this Polish pope visited his homeland, bringing a powerful theme: "Be not afraid." That spiritual awakening trip through Poland answered Josef Stalin's earlier scoffing question about the pope, "How many divisions

President Reagan meeting Pope John Paul II during his visit to the Papal Library, Vatican Pontifical Palace, Italy, June 7, 1982. *Ronald Reagan Presidential Library, C8407-14.*

has *he* got?" Stunning the Soviet leadership, the pope brought out massive crowds in the millions. John Paul II kissed the earth upon arrival at Warsaw airport on June 2, 1979, and "began the process by which communism in Poland—and ultimately in Europe—would come to an end."[173]

The Iron Lady:
Prime Minister Margaret Thatcher

Next on the stage was Margaret Thatcher, who became prime minister of the United Kingdom one memorable day in May 1979. Three years earlier, she had delivered a "Britain Awake" speech lambasting the Soviet Union for being "bent on world dominance." In response, the Soviet army journal *Red Star* critically responded to her speech with the headline "Iron Lady Raises Fears." She immediately embraced her cognomen, saying, "I stand before you tonight in my *Red Star* chiffon evening gown, my face softly made up and my fair hair gently waved, the Iron Lady of the Western world."[174]

President Reagan and Prime Minister Margaret Thatcher standing before a painting of Winston Churchill during the president's visit to 10 Downing Street, London, June 8, 1982. *Ronald Reagan Presidential Library, C8572-5.*

Prime Minister Thatcher became the first woman and the longest-serving British prime minister of the twentieth century. The Iron Lady ruled with an uncompromising political and leadership style.

A PRESIDENTIAL ACTOR TAKES THE STAGE: RONALD REAGAN

The November election of 1980 brought an essential player to the scene when Ronald Reagan became the fortieth president of the United States. The former governor of California and actor, Reagan swept to victory in 1980, defeating incumbent President Jimmy Carter on a platform to ignite the spirit of the American people, reduce their reliance on the government and build up national defense. Montana, one of the forty-four states Reagan carried, voted overwhelmingly for him. President Reagan formed close ideological bonds with Pope John Paul II and Prime Minister Thatcher, and the stage was set for dramatic change throughout this last decade of the Cold War.[175]

A Rip-Roaring Visit to Billings

The year after he took office, President Reagan visited Billings on August 11, 1982, and packed MetraPark with an overflow crowd of ten thousand. He rode into the arena atop a horse-drawn Wells Fargo stagecoach. As the coach entered the arena, the crowd cheered, whistled and applauded at deafening decibels. Dropping confetti spooked the horses pulling the stage, causing it to bounce wildly as the driver struggled to regain control. Laughing, Reagan waved his Montana-size cowboy hat to more cheers from the crowd as their lovefest was underway.

In his speech, the president praised Montana: "You still admire independence, resourcefulness and determination. You have a legacy of those ideals and you have a history so colorful, even your sunsets can't match it." The president vowed to help make the world safe for everyone, including the young twin sons of a Billings-area woman who wrote to him expressing concern about their future because of the buildup of nuclear arms. President Reagan spoke to her and millions concerned about the nuclear arms race:

Rip-roarin' Montana welcome greets presidential road show

President Reagan receives a rip-roarin' Montana greeting as he rides into the Billings Metra aboard a replica 1873 Wells Fargo coach, driven by owner B.J. Lawrence. *From the* Billings Gazette, *August 12, 1982.*

I want her to know I will work hard and unceasingly to protect her sons from nuclear war or any war just as surely as I will work to ensure that her sons will grow up in freedom. Peace and freedom are our goals. At this very minute we are proceeding in a number of areas to reduce nuclear risks…

I don't need to tell the common-sense citizens of Montana about the importance of a prepared military. Just let me say that with the help of the Congress, we are making solid headway in strengthening America's defenses…

I'm told that Montana was known to the Indians as the Land of Shining Mountains. Well, let us keep the mountains of Montana shining in hope and optimism…

For if we can make the values of our people shine again, their glow will light America's path for generation after generation to come. And we can be a shining city on a hill. Thank you and God bless you all.[176]

Meanwhile, a sparse group of about one hundred protesters chanted and waved placards outside MetraPark. Most belonged to the Clergy and Laity Concerned (CALC) or the Yellowstone Valley Chapter of the National Organization for Women, with signs including, "Bread, not bombs."[177]

CHALLENGING THE "EVIL EMPIRE"

President Ronald Reagan did not agree with two principles that had been accepted by both the United States and the USSR: Mutual Assured

Destruction and the Brezhnev Doctrine. Secretary of Defense Robert S. McNamara, as an outcome of the dangerous Cuban Missile Crisis, advocated a new principle—that each side should target the other's cities to cause the maximum number of casualties from nuclear war. The new strategy, Mutual Assured Destruction, with its appropriate acronym MAD, restated Eisenhower's belief that thermonuclear weapons made war no longer viable as an instrument of statecraft. In the aftermath of the ruthless Soviet invasion of Czechoslovakia in August 1968, Brezhnev claimed the right to violate the sovereignty of any country that attempted to replace Marxism-Leninism with capitalism.[178]

President Reagan challenged both strategies, concluding that "the march of freedom and democracy…will leave Marxism-Leninism on the ash-heap of history." In a speech before the National Association of Evangelicals on March 8, 1983, Reagan suggested to these religious leaders:

> *I urge you to speak out against those who would place the United States in a position of military and moral inferiority.…I urge you to beware the temptation of pride—the temptation of blithely declaring yourselves above it all and label*[ling] *both sides equally at fault,* [of ignoring] *the facts of history and the aggressive impulses of an evil empire.*[179]

1983 NUCLEAR FALSE ALARMS

The president unveiled the Strategic Defense Initiative (SDI) to replace the outdated MAD and Brezhnev Doctrine, not by freezing nuclear weapons but rather by rendering them "impotent and obsolete." Reagan's rhetoric and intention to implement SDI panicked the aged Soviet leadership. In the autumn of 1983, two highly dangerous "close calls" occurred in succession. On September 26, a nuclear false alarm could have and almost did trigger war. Soviet Lieutenant Colonel Stanislav Petrov, commanding Serpukhov-15, a satellite-based detection systems bunker, near midnight, was faced with panic when an alarm sounded signaling that the United States had launched five ICBMs toward Russia. The warning alarm was false—one of its satellites misinterpreted the glint of sunlight off clouds near Montana as if it were missile launches. But from the Soviet perspective, it appeared that the United States was initiating a nuclear attack. Colonel Petrov's orders were to report any sign of missile launch to Soviet high command. Yet, on snap judgment, he did not; rather, he judged it to be a false alarm and so refused what may have led to a nuclear holocaust. After the Cold War ended, the incident and Petrov's actions emerged from secrecy and led to honors for his exceptional judgment and action.[180]

Able Archer 83

For many years, NATO conducted codename Able Archer exercises each November. Able Archer 83 began on November 7, 1983, to last five days, with NATO forces throughout Western Europe participating. Able Archers were designed to simulate how a conventional attack by Soviet forces through the Fulda Gap in Germany could be met by a U.S. nuclear strike. A new element in 1983 increased realism by the participation of NATO heads of government. This set the stage, coupled with deteriorating relations with the United States and the nearing arrival of Pershing II nuclear missiles in Europe, for members of the Soviet leadership to conclude, briefly, that they were facing a nuclear first strike. The Soviets, in secrecy, responded by raising their alert level in East Germany and Poland and readying their nuclear forces. One hundred nuclear-armed Soviet fighter-bombers were placed on thirty-minute alert, and Warsaw Pact forces were poised for a counterstrike.

Fortunately, U.S. Air Forces Europe intelligence chief Lieutenant General Leonard Perroots correctly interpreted the Warsaw Pact actions and advised against responding to them. This stopped what otherwise might have been a deadly escalation, and Able Archer 83 ended without incident on November 11. Only later, from KGB spy Oleg Gordievsky, did Britain and in turn the United States learn that their realistic simulation of World War III had so very nearly triggered the real thing.[181]

The revelation about Able Archer 83 and a long-standing concern about the danger of nuclear war led President Reagan to temper his rhetoric and press the Soviets to resume arms control negotiations. Complicating the problem was the aged Soviet leadership. Premier Andropov died in February 1984, succeeded by the fatally ill Konstantin Chernenko, who died in March 1985, leading President Reagan to quip, "How am I supposed to get anyplace with the Russians, if they keep dying on me."[182]

MIKHAIL GORBACHEV ENTERS STAGE LEFT

Upon Chernenko's death, fifty-four-year-old Mikhail Gorbachev became premier and general secretary of the Communist Party. Gorbachev brought striking change to Soviet leadership. Remarkably, he was much younger, university-educated, open about his country's shortcomings and candid about admitting the failures of Marxist-Leninist ideology. The final actor entered the stage to find a changed President Reagan, deeply concerned by the Able Archer 83 War Scare and ready for rapprochement with a new Soviet leader who advocated openness (*glasnost*) and change within the Soviet Union (*perestroika*). The elimination of the entire class of intermediate-range nuclear weapons (Pershing IIs, SS-20s and so on) and initiation of the Strategic Arms Reduction Treaty (START I) built mutual trust between Gorbachev and Reagan that became a key element in bringing the peaceful end to the Cold War. Cold War historian Nate Jones concluded, "The 1983 War Scare served as the fulcrum that pivoted U.S.-Soviet relations from the worst days of the Cold War to their best cooperation since World War II."[183]

President Reagan meeting Soviet General Secretary Gorbachev at Hofdi House during the Reykjavik Summit, Iceland, October 11, 1986. *Ronald Reagan Presidential Library, C37406-14.*

During this dangerous phase of the Cold War, from 1980 to 1984, I served as assistant deputy chief of staff for intelligence at the U.S. Navy European Command in downtown London near Grosvenor Square. Over my desk hung the words of Maggie Thatcher: "NATO is the Real peace movement!" While the other European Component Commands focused on the serious threat of a Soviet invasion through the Fulda Gap in Germany, our attention centered on the powerful Soviet Northern Fleet and dangers lurking in the Mediterranean Sea, like the bombing of the Marine Barracks in Lebanon. Terrorism already loomed in the Middle East.

DANCING ON THE WALL

Since East Germany's Communist leaders, encouraged by their Soviet masters, began building the fourteen-foot wall to stem the flow of workers to the West, the Berlin Wall was a visible symbol of the Iron Curtain. When President Ronald Reagan in June 1987 challenged, "Mr. Gorbachev, tear down this wall," he could well have added "and dismantle the Iron Curtain."

For twenty-eight years, the Berlin Wall encased a decaying and stagnant East Berlin from the burgeoning economy of free West Berlin. Yet, winds of change began to blow all across Eastern Europe and even within the Soviet Union thanks to profound events taking place under the leadership of Premier Gorbachev. And change was coming within East Germany, suddenly ignited by a botched reading of a hastily drafted new decree designed to relieve mounting tensions throughout East Germany. The intended new policy relaxing travel was presented as word that East German citizens were free to leave "through any of the border crossings."

The result was stunning, as massive, festive crowds poured across the newly opened border from East Berlin to West on Saturday, November 11, 1989. More than 1 million East Germans tasted freedom for the first time in their lives—certainly not under the Third Reich, Soviet occupation or the puppet German Democratic Republic. Checkpoint Charlie was opened at the Friederichstrasse crossing point, and there, Soviet exile and renowned cellist Mstislav Rostropovich gave an impromptu concert to honor Berliners killed in attempts to flee to the West.

President Reagan delivers his "Mr. Gorbachev, tear down this wall" speech at the Berlin Wall, Brandenburg Gate, Federal Republic of Germany, June 12, 1987. *Ronald Reagan Presidential Library, C41252-6.*

Openings appeared in the Berlin Wall, cut by East Berlin workers. In an extraordinary sight near the Brandenburg Gate on the border, scores of young West and East Germans climbed to the top of the wall to greet one another, sitting, standing and dancing in celebration. Even East German border guards, who one day earlier would have fired to kill, stood shoulder to shoulder atop the wall on Saturday, watching the sea of celebrants.[184]

Over the next days, the Wall crumbled, and that deadly symbol of the Iron Curtain was no more. In the words of John Lewis Gaddis, "With the wall breached, everything was possible." And so it was.[185]

All Montana joined the nation and the Western world in cheering the fall of the Berlin Wall. That Wall symbolized Soviet dominance and iron-fisted rule over Eastern Europe for almost three decades. Yet few Montanans had as much incentive to cry for joy as did Winfried "Wynn" Hubich, Missoula's postmaster, when that barrier to freedom fell. After all, as a boy, he, led by his father, fled from East Germany to the West.[186]

THE COLLAPSE OF THE SOVIET UNION

The USSR was the largest country in the world on January 1, 1991, yet by the end of the year the Soviet Union had dissolved. Its one hundred distinct nationalities had fragmented as its constituent republics separated. The Communist Party was banned from all activity. What caused this stunning, sudden collapse of the Soviet Union? The factors were many and complex, but the key was Mikhail Gorbachev. From his assumption of power on March 11, 1985, he struggled to ignite the moribund Soviet economy and streamline the cumbersome corrupt government bureaucracy—the very targets of the *Storozvehoy* mutiny and Lieutenant Belenko's defection. When he instituted the policies of *glasnost* and *perestroika*, the result was a flood of criticism of the Soviet system. Economic and military factors, the defeat in the war in Afghanistan and the Chernobyl nuclear disaster of April 1986 all poured fuel on a growing powder keg.

Gorbachev wanted to save socialism, but he was not willing to use force to do that. Historian John Lewis Gaddis concluded, "In the end, [Gorbachev] gave up an ideology, an empire and his own country, in preference to using force....It made little sense in traditional geopolitical terms. But it did make him the most deserving recipient ever of the Nobel Peace Prize."[187]

THE END OF THE COLD WAR

On December 25, 1991, in a bold Christmas gift to the world, President Mikhail Gorbachev resigned from his extinct office and transferred power, including control of the still-potent nuclear launch codes, to Boris Yeltsin, president of the new Russian Federation. That evening, the Soviet flag was lowered at the Kremlin for the last time. The next day, the Soviet of the Republics, the Supreme Soviet's upper chamber, recognized the independence of the former Soviet republics, formally dissolving the Soviet Union. The combination of the fall of the Berlin Wall, the revolutions in Eastern European countries that followed and this dissolution of the Soviet Union marked the end of the Cold War. At the end of this masterful play, the stunning cast—Pope John Paul II, Maggie Thatcher, Ronald Reagan (succeeded by George H.R. Bush), Mikhail Gorbachev and others—deserved the hearty cheers of all Montana and the world. We all breathed a great sigh of relief and rested more easily in the days that followed.

The fall of the Soviet Union depicted in a political cartoon by Gary Brookins, showing the Communist Party dejectedly leaving the Kremlin after hanging an "Out of Business" sign on the locked door of the "Evil Empire." *From the* Great Falls Tribune, *January 1, 1992.*

The Aftermath

Eleven years after the dissolution of the Soviet Union, Great Falls dismantled five relics of the Cold War—yellow air raid sirens that stood thirty feet high in five city parks. The yellow sirens were installed at the height of the Cold War. According to Mayor Randy Gray, the sirens were erected at a time during the Cold War when Great Falls was high on the Soviet target list because of the missile silos surrounding Malmstrom Air Force Base. At that time, more than 130 fallout shelters dotted Cascade County, and twenty-two air raid sirens were scattered around Great Falls and outlying communities.

"The history of that time is right here in Great Falls," said Mayor Gray. "Talk to anybody in the 50s age group, and they'll remember practicing air raid drills and getting under their desks." Each siren had a pivoting head and blared once each week during civil defense drills. The red alert consisted of three-minute-long blasts and signaled residents to move immediately to a public fallout shelter or their own bunker and wait for further radio or TV instructions.

"This is the best representation of the end of the Cold War," Mayor Gray said.[188] And so it was.

NOTES

Introduction

1. Kennedy, "Remarks at High School Stadium, Great Falls, Montana."
2. Good Reads, "If You Know the Enemy and Know Yourself."

Chapter 1

3. *Great Falls Tribune*, February 7, 1943.
4. *Great Falls Tribune*, November 22, 1942.
5. Hays, *Alaska-Siberia Connection*, 135; Geust, "Lend-Lease History and People"; Hardesty, *Red Phoenix*, 220.
6. Jordan, *Major Jordan's Diaries*, 66; Rhodes, *Dark Sun*, 96–99.
7. *Great Falls Tribune*, May 30, 1999.
8. *Great Falls Tribune*, August 20, 1944; Stuwe, *East Base*, 56–59.
9. *Great Falls Tribune*, August 20, October 5, 1942; November 11, 1943.
10. *Great Falls Tribune*, July 25, November 29, 1944; January 28, 1945; Wikipedia, "Robert MacArthur Crawford."
11. *Great Falls Tribune*, November 24, 25, December 2, 1944; *Billings Gazette*, May 11, 2003.
12. Gott, *Hazel Ah Ying Lee*, 35–36.
13. Montana Military Museum, "First Special Service Force"; United States House of Representatives, "Joint U.S.-Canadian Group Receives Congressional Gold Medal."

14. *Great Falls Tribune*, May 30, 1999; Black Art Depot Today, "Forgotten Facts"; Wikipedia, "Alaska Highway."

15. Since Montana State University changed to the University of Montana and Montana State College became Montana State University, the names have been simplified herein to University of Montana for the Missoula campus and Montana State University for the Bozeman campus.

16. Urey, "ATOMIC ENERGY."

Chapter 2

17. Gaddis, *Cold War*, 10–11.

18. Churchill, "Sinews of Peace," 7,285–293.

19. *Billings Gazette*, March 6, 1946.

20. Ibid.

21. Kelly, "Study of the Defeat of Senator Burton K. Wheeler."

22. Michaelis, *Eleanor*, 449–50.

23. *Fort Benton River Press*, October 13, 1948.

24. *Fort Benton River Press*, February 8, 1950.

25. *Fort Benton River Press*, March 5, 1952.

26. Arolsen Archives.

27. *Great Falls Tribune*, August 12, 1946.

28. Ibid.

29. *Great Falls Tribune*, August 8, 9, 1946; May 30, 1999.

30. *Great Falls Tribune*, August 9, 1946.

31. *Great Falls Tribune*, August 10, 1946.

32. Ibid.

33. Ibid.

34. *Army Air Force, Report of Major Accident, August 9, 1946, 2:05 p.m.*

35. *Public Papers of President of the United States: Harry S. Truman, 1947*, 178–79.

36. Kennedy, "Halvor O. Ekern."

37. *Washington Times*, April 13, 2006; *Missoulian*, August 13, 1955; Find a Grave, "Halvor Ekern."

38. Miller, *To Save a City*, 2.

39. Ibid.

40. History, "Berlin Airlift History."

41. Haulman, "Operation Vittles."

42. *Great Falls Tribune*, July 25, 1999.

43. *Billings Gazette*, August 5, 1949; *Reno (NV) Gazette Journal*, October 23, 1948.

44. Other crewmen on board the PB-4Y were LTJG Robert D. Reynolds, Dansville, New York; ENS Tommy L. Burgess, Osawatomie, Kansas; AN Joseph N. Rinner, Philadelphia, Pennsylvania; AL3 Joseph J. Bourassa, Linwood, Michigan; AD1 Jack W. Thomas, Stillwater, New Jersey; AT1 Frank L. Beckham, Newport, Kentucky; Cryptologic Technician 3 Edward J. Purcell, Southwestville, New Jersey; *Great Falls Tribune*, October 28, November 1, 1975; *Daily Inter Lake*, April 21, 1951.

45. *Great Falls Tribune*, April 21, 1955; October 28, 1975; November 1, 1975; *Billings Gazette*, April 22, 1955.

46. Caswell, "Remembering Crew Members."

Chapter 3

47. *Great Falls Tribune*, May 21, 1950.

48. Gaddis, *Cold War*, 40–42.

49. Ibid, 43.

50. Garrett, *Task Force Smith-Korea*.

51. *Missoulian*, August 13, 1946.

52. Hall of Valor: The Military Medals Database, "Lovless, Jay. B."; Garrett, *Task Force Smith-Korea*.

53. *Missoulian*, December 5, 1952; October 26, 1962; *Fort Benton River Press*, June 21, 1989.

54. Defense POW/MIA Accounting Agency, Korea Report for Montana.

55. *Montana Standard*, November 9, 2002.

56. Camp 5 was the first permanent Chinese POW camp on the south bank of the Yalu River; *Great Falls Tribune*, September 8, 1953.

57. *Montana Standard*, November 9, 2002.

58. *Great Falls Tribune*, December 21, 1951.

59. *Great Falls Tribune*, February 3, 1958.

60. Montana State Korean War Memorials, "Butte, MT—United States," and "Missoula, MT—United States."

61. *Missoulian*, October 26, 1962.

62. *Missoulian*, October 5, 6, 1952.

63. *Billings Gazette*, July 25, 1950; *Independent-Record*, June 17, 1956.

64. *Billings Gazette*, April 1, 1953.

65. *Great Falls Tribune*, August 23, 1946.

66. *Great Falls Tribune*, August 5, 2012.
67. *Great Falls Tribune*, March 15, 1958; March 28, 1972; October 22, 1987; August 5, 2012; *Splendid Service*, 478–83; *Montana Air National Guard: The First 59 Years*.
68. *Missoulian*, October 15, 1952.
69. *Billings Gazette*, October 18, 1970; May 21, 1983.
70. *Montana Standard*, May 12, 23, 1951.
71. *Missoulian*, October 6, 1974.
72. *Great Falls Tribune*, December 30, 1961; *Missoulian*, March 21, 1962.
73. *Missoulian*, October 6, 1974; *Montana Standard*, October 1, 1989.
74. Captured were Wing Commander Colonel John K. Arnold Jr., Silver Spring, Maryland; Major William H. Baumer, instructor pilot, Lewisburg, Pennsylvania; Lieutenant John Woodrow Buck, aircraft observer, Armathwaite, Tennessee; Captain Elmer Llewellyn, navigator, Missoula, Montana; Airman Second Class Daniel Schmidt, aircraft observer, Coeur d'Alene, Idaho: Airman First Class Steve Kiba, Akron, Ohoi; Captain Eugene Vaada, aircraft commander, Clayton, New York; Lieutenant Wallace L. Brown, pilot, Banks, Alabama; Airman Second Class Harry Benjamin Jr., aircraft observer, Worthington, Minnesota; Tech Sergeant Howard Brown, flight engineer, St. Paul, Minnesota; and Airman John W. Thompson III, aircraft observer, Orange, Virginia. First Lieutenant Henry Weese, radar operator, San Bernadino, California, and First Lieutenant Paul Van Voohris, radar operator, Ozone Park, New York, were captured and, apparently, murdered. Airman First Class Alvin Hart Jr., tail gunner, Saginaw, Michigan, was apparently killed in action during the MiG attack. *Missoulian*, December 26, 1954; Kiba, *The Flag*.
75. *Missoulian*, May 25, 2009; *Sioux City Journal*, September 14, 1998; *Spokesman-Review*, July 3, 2004.
76. *Missoulian*, December 15, 1955; January 7, 1956.
77. *Missoulian*, May 3, 1981; *Great Falls Tribune*, November 24, 1954.
78. American Presidency Project, "Ground Observer Corps Operation Skywatch."
79. *Laurel Outlook*, July 15, 1953; *Great Falls Tribune*, March 21, 1951.
80. Axline, "Operattion Skywatch," 34, 37; Mills, *Cold War in a Cold Land*, 145.
81. *Billings Gazette*, July 13, 1957.
82. Axline, "Operation Skywatch," 40–42.
83. *Great Falls Tribune*, November 22, 1958.
84. *Billings Gazette*, February 4, 1959.

85. *Great Falls Tribune*, March 10, 1955; "91st Strategic Reconnaissance Squadron, Chapter 5, Post Korea."
86. *Great Falls Tribune*, October 5, 6, 11, 1950; *Daily Inter Lake*, September 4, 1956; Wikipedia, "Mariana UFO Incident"; Wall, "UFOs Are Real."
87. *Great Falls Tribune*, August 22, 1954.
88. *Chicago (IL) Tribune*, April 17, 1983.
89. *Great Falls Tribune*, March 17, August 22, 1954.
90. *Great Falls Tribune*, September 4, 1954.
91. *Great Falls Tribune*, June 16, 1956.
92. *Helena Independent-Record*, June 18, 1956.
93. *Missoulian*, June 17, 2013; Axline, *Taming Big Sky.*
94. *Missoulian*, October 23, 1966; Gaddis, *Cold War*, 108–9; *Great Falls Tribune*, November 24, 1956; *Helena Independent-Record*, January 21, 1957.
95. *Missoulian*, November 8, 1956.
96. *Missoulian*, October 23, 1966.
97. *Great Falls Tribune*, March 1, 1959; *Montana Kaimin*, April 20, 1959.

Chapter 4

98. Gaddis, *Cold War*, 74–76.
99. More than $48 billion in wealth in copper, gold, silver and other minerals have been taken from Butte's "richest hill on earth." Western Mining History Butte, "Butte's Richest Hill on Earth"; *Great Falls Tribune*, September 22, 1960.
100. Kennedy, "Remarks at High School Stadium, Great Falls, Montana." While Kennedy used the term "ace in the hole" on occasion in his speeches, he is not known to have used this term during the Cuban Missile Crisis.
101. Little, "JFK Was Completely Unprepared."
102. Kennedy, "Radio and Television Report."
103. Ibid.
104. Mills, *Cold War in a Cold Land*, 164–65.
105. Hallsell, "Building Malmstrom's Minuteman Missile Fields," 13–14.
106. Andrews, "5 Cold War Close Calls."
107. Ibid.; Sherwin, *Gambling with Armageddon*, 5–16.
108. Hallsell, "Building Malmstrom's Minuteman Missile Fields," 13.
109. *Great Falls Tribune*, April 17, 1966.
110. *Billings Gazette*, September 26, 1963.
111. Kennedy, "Remarks at High School Stadium, Great Falls, Montana."

112. *Great Falls Tribune*, November 23, 1963.
113. Glasrud and Wintz, *Black Americans*, 89–90.
114. Mobley, *Flash Point*, 64.
115. Ibid., 140.
116. *Billings Gazette*, December 24, 2018; *Great Falls Tribune*, January 17, 2010.
117. *Great Falls Tribune*, March 30, 1973.
118. NASA, "Biography: Loren W. Acton"; DeRose, "Montana Astronaut Loren Acton."
119. *Great Falls Tribune*, July 19, 2019.
120. Ibid., and February 6, 2020.

Chapter 5

121. Lind, *Necessary War*.
122. Sempa, "New Take on MacArthur's Warning."
123. *Great Falls Tribune*, March 30, 2016.
124. *Great Falls Tribune*, April 30, 2000.
125. Ibid.
126. *Great Falls Tribune*, March 30, 2016.
127. *Missoulian*, December 24, 2016.
128. Vietnam Tributes, "George F. Fryett, Jr."
129. *Great Falls Tribune*, December 16, 1990.
130. *Billings Gazette*, June 15, 1992.
131. *Missoulian*, January 17, 1965.
132. *Great Falls Tribune*, May 30, 2014; *Missoulian*, October 18, 1964; Vietnam Helicopter Pilots Association, "Kleiv Manford Lloyd."
133. *Kaimin*, October 16 1969.
134. Ibid.
135. *Missoulian*, July 2, 1976.
136. *Missoulian*, May 14, 1970.
137. *Missoulian*, July 2, 1976; Homestead National Monument of America, "Jeannette Rankin"; O'Brien, *Jeannette Rankin*.
138. *Chicago Tribune*, January 16, 1968.
139. Ibid.
140. *Missoulian*, July 2, 1976.
141. Jeannette Rankin Peace Center.
142. Kutler, *Encyclopedia of the Vietnam War*, 442.
143. Wikipedia, "Operation Homecoming."

144. Wyatt and Powers Wyatt, *We Came Home*; *Missoulian*, July 4, 2008.
145. Wyatt and Powers Wyatt, *We Came Home*.
146. Ibid.
147. *Albany Democrat-Herald*, February 28, 1973.
148. In 1988, some 266 former POWs from all wars resided in Montana; *Great Falls Tribune*, September 14, 17, 1988.
149. Hirsch, *Two Souls Indivisible*, 14–15.
150. *Great Falls Tribune*, July 30, 1954; July 12 1955; May 27, 1956; Hirsch, *Two Souls Indivisible*, 21–29.
151. Hirsch, *Two Souls Indivisible*, 134–44.
152. Ibid.
153. Ibid., 36–37; Stockdale, *In Love and War*.
154. Hirsch, *Two Souls Indivisible*, 154–62.
155. *Great Falls Tribune*, February 13, 1973.
156. Hirsch, *Two Souls Indivisible*, 154–62; *New York Times*, April 28, 1925; *Washington Post*, February 20, 2016; *Billings Gazette*, July 2, 1981.
157. *Great Falls Tribune*, February 20, 1875.
158. *Missoulian*, November 12, 1993; Evans and Welch, *Healing Wounds*; Vietnam Women's Memorial.
159. Morrison, *Hog's Exit*, 3; Wikipedia, "Jerry Daniels."
160. Morrison, *Sky Is Falling*.
161. *Missoulian*, July 28, 2013.
162. *Missoulian*, November 25, 2017.

Chapter 6

163. *Great Falls Tribune*, November 20, 1968.
164. *Great Falls Tribune*, May 11, 1969.
165. *Great Falls Tribune*, August 17, 1970; Wikipedia, "Sentinel Program; Safeguard Program."
166. Young, "Mutiny on *Storozhevoy*"; Young and Braden, *Last Sentry*; Wikipedia, "Soviet Frigate *Storozhevoy*."
167. Barron, *MiG Pilot*; photo, Benjamin Donnelly, March 25, 2021.
168. Henderson, "Dust Storms and the 1980 Iran Hostage Rescue Attempt."
169. Holloway, "Holloway Report"; Wikipedia, "Operation Eagle Claw."
170. Holloway, "Holloway Report"; Wikipedia, "Operation Eagle Claw"; Ryan, *Iranian Rescue Mission*, 69–94.
171. Wikipedia, "Operation Eagle Claw."

172. Gaddis, *Cold War*, 195.
173. Ibid., 192–94.
174. Speech at Kensington Town Hall ("Britain Awake"), Margaret Thatcher Foundation.
175. White House, "Ronald Reagan."
176. *Billings Gazette*, August 12, 1982.
177. Ibid.
178. Gaddis, *Cold War*, 80–81, 150.
179. Ibid., 224–25.
180. Ibid., 226; Andrews, "5 Cold War Close Calls."
181. Gaddis, *Cold War*, 227–28; Jones, *Able Archer 83*; *Times of London*, February 20, 2021; Kaplan, " World Came Much Closer to Nuclear War."
182. Gaddis, *Cold War*, 228.
183. Ibid., 229; Jones, *Able Archer 83*, 57–58.
184. Gaddis, *Cold War*, 245–46; *Billings Gazette*, November 12, 1989.
185. Gaddis, *Cold War*, 246.
186. *Missoulian*, November 10, 1989.
187. Gaddis, *Cold War*, 252–57.
188. *Great Falls Tribune*, November 17, 2002.

BIBLIOGRAPHY

Newspapers and Journals

Note: Montana newspapers unless otherwise noted.

Albany (OR) Democrat-Herald.
Billings Gazette.
Chicago Tribune (IL).
Conrad Independent.
Daily Inter Lake (Kalispell, MT).
Dillon Examiner.
Fort Benton River Press.
Great Falls Tribune.
Helena Independent-Record.
Laurel Outlook.
Missoulian (Missoula).
Montana Kaimin (University of Montana).
Montana Standard (Butte).
Reno (NV) Gazette Journal.
Sioux City (IA) Journal.
Spokesman-Review (Spokane, WA).
Washington Times (Washington, D.C.).

Books and Articles

Army Air Force, Report of Major Accident, August 9, 1946, 2:05 p.m. Report released by the Air Force Historical Research Agency, Maxwell Air Force Base, Alabama.

Ashby, Norma Beatty. *Movie Stars & Rattlesnakes: The Heyday of Montana Live Television.* Helena, MT: Farcountry Press, 2004.

Axline, Jon. "Operation Skywatch: The Montana Ground Observer Corps, 1952–1959." *Montana, Magazine of Western History* 67 (Summer 2017).

———. *Taming Big Sky County: The History of Montana Transportation from Trails to Interstates.* Charleston, SC: The History Press, 2015.

Barron, John. *MiG Pilot: The Final Escape of Lieutenant Belenko.* New York: McGraw-Hill Book Company, 1980.

Bath, David W. *Assured Destruction: Building the Ballistic Missile Culture of the U.S. Air Force.* Annapolis, MD: Naval Institute Press, 2020.

Bird, Joan. *Montana UFOs and Extraterrestrials.* Helena, MT: Riverbend Publishing, 2013.

Borman, Frank. *Countdown: An Autobiography.* New York: William Morrow, 1988.

Bows, Ray. *Vietnam Military Lore: Legends, Shadows and Heroes.* Hanover, MA: Bows & Sons Publishing, 1997.

Brinkley, Douglas. *American Moonshot: John F. Kennedy and the Great Space Race.* New York: Harper Perennial, 2020.

Churchill, Winston. "The Sinews of Peace." In *Winston S. Churchill: His Complete Speeches, 1897–1963.* Vol. 7, *1943–1949.* Edited by Robert Rhodes James. New York: Chelsea House Publishers, 1974.

Dolitsky, Alexander B. *Allies in Wartime: The Alaska-Siberia Airway during World War II.* Juneau: Alaska-Siberia Research Center, 2007.

Downing, Taylor. *1983: Reagan, Andropov and a World on the Brink.* New York: De Capo Press, 2018.

Ethell, Jeffrey, and Alfred Price. *One Day in a Long War: May 10, 1972, North Vietnam.* New York: Random House, 1989.

Evans, Diane Carlson, with Bob Welch. *Healing Wounds: A Vietnam War Combat Nurse's 10-Year Fight to Win Women a Place of Honor in Washington, D.C.* New York: Permuted Press, 2020.

Gaddis, John Lewis. *The Cold War: A New History.* New York: Penguin Press, 2005.

Garrettt, Major J. *Task Force Smith-Korea: The Lesson Never Learned.* Fort Leavenworth, KS: U.S. Army Command and General Staff College, 1999.

Glasrud, Bruce A., and Gary A. Wintz. *Black Americans and the Civil Rights Movement in the West*. Norman: University of Oklahoma Press, 2019.

Gott, Kay. *Hazel Ah Ying Lee, Women Air Force Service Pilot, World War II: A Portrait*. N.p.: self-published, 1996.

Hagberg, David, and Boris Gindin. *Mutiny: The True Events that Inspired the Hunt for Red October*. New York: Tom Doherty Associates Book, 2008.

Hallsell, Troy A. "Building Malmstrom's Minuteman Missile Fields in Central Montana, 1960–1963." *Air Power History* 68 (Spring 2021): 5–16.

Hardesty, Von. *Red Phoenix: The Rise of Soviet Air Power, 1941–1945*. Washington, D.C.: Smithsonian Institution Press, 1982.

Hays, Otis, Jr. *The Alaska-Siberia Connection*. College State: Texas A&M University Press, 1996.

Hirsch, James S. *Two Souls Indivisible: The Friendship that Saved Two POWs in Vietnam*. New York: Houghton Mifflin Harcourt Publishing Company, 2005.

Jones, Nate, ed. *Able Archer 83: The Secret History of the NATO Exercise that Almost Triggered Nuclear War*. New York: New Press, 2016.

Jordan, George Racey. *From Major Jordan's Diaries*. New York: Harcourt, Brace and Company, 1952.

Kaplan, Fred. "The World Came Much Closer to Nuclear War than We Ever Realized." *Slate Magazine* (February 18, 2021).

Kiba, Steve. *The Flag: My Story: Kidnapped by Red China*. Bloomington, IN: Authorhouse, 2002.

Kidston, Martin J. *Poplar to Papua: Montana's 163rd Infantry Regiment in World War II*. Helena, MT: Farcountry Press, 2004.

Kutler, Stanley I. *Encyclopedia of the Vietnam War*. New York: Charles Scribner's Sons, 1996.

Larson, Lieutenant Colonel George A. *Malmstrom Air Force Base*. Images of Aviation series. Charleston, SC: Arcadia Publishing, 2020.

Lind, Michael. *The Necessary War: A Reinterpretation of America's Most Disastrous Military Conflict*. New York: Free Press, 1999.

Michaelis, David. *Eleanor*. New York: Simon & Schuster, 2020.

Michel, Marshall L., III. *Operation Linebacker I 1972: The First High-Tech Air War*. Oxford, UK: Osprey Publishing, 2019.

Miller, Roger G. *To Save a City: The Berlin Airlift*. College Station: Texas A&M University Press, 2008.

Mills, David W. *Cold War in a Cold Land: Fighting Communism on the Northern Plains*. Norman: University of Oklahoma Press, 2015.

Mobley, Richard A. *Flash Point North Korea: The Pueblo and EC-121*. Annapolis, MD: Naval Institute Press, 2003.

Montana Air National Guard: The First 59 Years (120ᵗʰ Fighter Wing—Montana National Guard, 1947–1997). N.p.

Morrison, Gayle L. *Hog's Exit: Jerry Daniels, the Hmong, and the CIA*. Lubbock: Texas Tech University Press, 2013.

———. *Sky Is Falling: An Oral History of the CIA's Evacuation of the Hmong from Laos*. Jefferson, NC: McFarland & Company, 1999.

Mowbray, C. Margo. *Havoc Red: Surviving the Alaska-Siberia Route, 1943*. Polson, MT: Clarity Communications, 2015.

Newman, Rick, and Don Shepperd. *Bury Us Upside Down: The Misty Pilots and the Secret Battle for the Ho Chi Minh Trail*. New York: Ballentine Books, 2006.

"91ˢᵗ Strategic Reconnaissance Squadron, Chapter 5, Post Korea: A Time of Change and Adaptation and Looking for a Tactical Solution." Copy held by author.

O'Brien, Mary Barmeyer. *Jeannette Rankin, 1880–1973: Bright Star in the Big Sky*. Helena, MT: Falcon Press, 1995.

Page, Joseph T., III. *Malmstrom Air Force Base through Time*. N.p.: Fonthill Media, 2021.

Pedersen, Dan. *Top Gun: An American Story*. New York: Hachette Books, 2020.

Pedlow, Gregory W., and Donald E. Welzenbach. *The Central Intelligence Agency and Overhead Reconnaissance: The U-2 and OXCART Programs, 1954–1974*. New York: Skyhorse Publishing, 2016.

Perlstein, Rick. *Reaganland: America's Right Turn, 1976–1980*. New York: Simon & Schuster, 2020.

Powers, Francis Gary, Jr., and Keith Dunnavant. *Spy Pilot: Francis Gary Powers, the U-2 Incident, and a Controversial Cold War Legacy*. New York: Prometheus Books, 2020.

Public Papers of President of the United States: Harry S. Truman, 1947. Washington, D.C.: Government Printing Officer, 1963.

Rhodes, Richard. *Arsenals of Folly: The Making of the Nuclear Arms Race*. New York: Alfred A. Knopf, 2007.

———. *Dark Sun: The Making of the Hydrogen Bomb*. New York: Touchstone Book, 1995.

Robison, Ken. *Cascade County and Great Falls*. Charleston, SC: Arcadia Publishing, 2011.

Rochester, Stuart, and Frederick Kiley. *Honor Bound: American Prisoners of War in Southeast Asia, 1961–1973*. Annapolis, MD: Naval Institute Press, 2007.

Rose, Lisle A. *The Cold War Comes to Main Street*. Lawrence: University Press of Kansas, 1999.

Ryan, Paul B. *The Iranian Rescue Mission: Why It Failed*. Annapolis, MD: Naval Institute Press, 1985.

Samuel, Wolfgang W.E. *Silent Warriors, Incredible Courage: The Declassified Stories of Cold War Reconnaissance Flights and the Men Who Flew Them*. Jackson: University Press of Mississippi, 2019.

Schaffel, Kenneth. *The Emerging Shield: The Air Force and the Evolution of Continental Air Defense, 1945–1960*. Washington, D.C.: Office of Air Force History, 1991.

Sharp, U.S. Grant. *Strategy for Defeat: Vietnam in Retrospect*. San Rafael, CA: Presidio Press, 1978.

Sherwin, Martin J. *Gambling with Armageddon: Nuclear Roulette from Hiroshima to the Cuban Missile Crisis*. New York, Alfred J. Knopf, 2019.

Sicherman, Harvey. "Robert Strausz-Hupé: His Life and Times." *Orbis* 55, no. 3 (2011): 416–37.

Smith, Blake W. *Warplanes to Alaska*. Blaine, WA: Hancock Publishing House, 1998.

Spires, David N. *On Alert: An Operational History of the United States Air Force Intercontinental Ballistic Missile Program, 1945–2011*. Colorado Springs, CO: Air Force Space Command, 2012.

Strausz-Hupé, Robert. *In My Time*. New York: W.W. Norton & Company, 1965.

Stuwe, Jane Willits. *East Base*. N.p., n.d.

Svingen, Orlan J. *Splendid Service: The Montana National Guard, 1867–2006*. Pullman: Washington State University, 2010.

Urey, Dr. Harold C. "ATOMIC ENERGY: Master or Servant?" Pamphlet, Montana State University, February 18, 1946. Overholser Historical Research Center, Fort Benton, Montana.

Virtue, John. *The Black Soldiers Who Built the Alaska Highway: A History of Four U.S. Army Regiments in the North, 1942–1943*. Jefferson, NC: McFarland and Company, 2013.

Westad, Odd Arne. *The Cold War: A World History*. New York: Basic Books, 2017.

Wyatt, Frederic A., Captain (USNR, Ret.), and Barbara Powers Wyatt. *We Came Home*. Toluca Lake, CA: P.O.W. Publications, 1977.

Young, Gregory D., and Nate Braden. *The Last Sentry: The True Story that Inspired The Hunt for Red October*. Annapolis, MD: Naval Institute Press, 2005.

Web Sources

The American Presidency Project. "Ground Observer Corps Operation Skywatch." https://www.presidency.ucsb.edu/documents/statement-the-president-the-ground-observer-corps-operation-skywatch.

Andrews, Evan. "5 Cold War Close Calls." History. https://www.history.com/news/5-cold-war-close-calls.

Arolsen Archives. https://collections.arolsen-archives.org/en/archive/817 45179/?p=1&s=Vanasek&doc_id=81745179.

Black Art Depot Today. "Forgotten Facts About the Blacks Who Built the Alaska-Canada Highway." https://blackartblog.blackartdepot.com/black-history/forgotten-facts-about-the-blacks-who-built-the-canada-highway.html.

Caswell, Jim, Lieutenant Colonel. "Remembering Crew Members of U.S. Navy PB4Y-2 Shoot Down, April 8, 1950—And Shocking Cold War Case Study." Station HYPO. https://stationhypo.com/2018/04/08/remembering-the-crew-members-of-u-s-navy-pb4y-2-shootdown-by-the-soviets-april-8-1950.

Defense POW/MIA Accounting Agency. Korea Report for Montana. https://www.dpaa.mil/portals/85/KoreaAccounting/pmkor_una_MONTANA_20210115.pdf.

DeRose, Chris. "Montana Astronaut Loren Acton: How He Got from a Lewistown Ranch to Outer Space." KRTB, January 7, 2021. https://www.ktvq.com/news/local-news/montana-astronaut-loren-acton-how-he-got-from-a-lewistown-ranch-to-outer-space.

Find a Grave. "Colonel Halvor Olaf Ekern." https://www.findagrave.com/memorial/23025645/halvor-olaf-ekern.

Geust, Carl Fredrik. "Lend-Lease History and People." Lend-Lease. https://lend-lease.net/articles-en/aircraft-deliveries-to-the-soviet-union.

Good Reads. "If You Know the Enemy and Know Yourself." www.goodreads.com/quotes/316251-if-you-know-the-enemy-and-know-yourself-your-victory.

Hall of Valor: The Military Medals Database. "Lovless, Jay. B." https://valor.militarytimes.com/hero/31844.

Haulman, Daniel L. "Operation Vittles." Air Mobility Command Museum. https://amcmuseum.org/history/operation-vittles-berlin-airlift.

Henderson, J.P. "Dust Storms and the 1980 Iran Hostage Rescue Attempt." Google Scholar. https://scholar.google.com/scholar_lookup?title=Dust%20storms%20and%20the%201980%20Iran%20hostage%20rescue%20attempt&publication_year=2014&author=J.P.%20Henderson.

History. "Berlin Airlift History." https://www.history.com/topics/cold-war/berlin-airlift#section_3.

Holloway, Admiral James L., III. "The Holloway Report." The National Security Archive—The George Washington University. https://nsarchive2.gwu.edu//NSAEBB/NSAEBB63/doc8.pdf.

Homestead National Monument of America. "Jeannette Rankin, First Woman Elected to Congress, Peace Advocate, Daughter of Homesteaders, 1880–1973, Missoula, Montana." 2019. https://www.nps.gov/home/learn/historyculture/upload/MW,pdf,RankinBio,b.pdf.

Jeannette Rankin Peace Center. https://jrpc.org.

Kelly, Joseph P. "Study of the Defeat of Senator Burton K. Wheeler in the 1946 Democratic Primary Election." 1959. Graduate Student Theses, Dissertations & Professional Papers, ScholarWorks, University of Montana. https://scholarworks.umt.edu/etd/374.

Kennedy, Charles Stuart. "Halvor O. Ekern." Association for Diplomatic Studies and Training. www.adst.org/OH%20TOCs/Ekern,%20Halvor.toc.pdf.

Kennedy, John F. "Radio and Television Report to the American People on the Soviet Arms Buildup in Cuba, 22 Oct 1962." The American Presidency Project. https://www.presidency.ucsb.edu/documents/radio-and-television-report-the-american-people-the-soviet-arms-buildup-cuba.

———. "Remarks at High School Stadium, Great Falls, Montana, 26 September, 1963." John F. Kennedy Presidential Library and Museum Archives. https://www.jfklibrary.org/asset-viewer/archives/JFKPOF/047/JFKPOF-047- 001.

Little, Becky. "JFK Was Completely Unprepared for His Summit with Khrushchev." History. https://www.history.com/news/kennedy-krushchev-vienna-summit-meeting-1961.

Margaret Thatcher Foundation. Speech at Kensington Town Hall ("Britain Awake") (The Iron Lady). https://www.margaretthatcher.org/document/102939.

Montana Military Museum. "The First Special Service Force." http://www.montanamilitarymuseum.org/?page_id=3258.

Montana State Korean War Memorials. "Butte, MT—United States," https://koreanwarmemorials.com/memorial/butte-mt-united-states.

———. "Missoula, MT—United States," https://koreanwarmemorials.com/memorial/missoula-mt-united-states.

NASA. "Biography: Acton, Loren W." https://www.nasa.gov/sites/default/files/atoms/files/acton-lw.pdf.

Sempa, Francis P. "A New Take on General MacArthur's Warning to JFK to Avoid a Land War in Asia." The Diplomat, October 5, 2018.

https://thediplomat.com/2018/10/a-new-take-on-general-macarthurs-warning-to-jfk-to-avoid-a-land-war-in-asia.

Sicherman, Harvey. "Robert Strausz-Hupé: His Life and Times." Foreign Policy Research Institute. https://www.fpri.org/article/2003/05/robert-strausz-hupe-life-times-2.

United States House of Representatives. "Joint U.S.-Canadian Group Receives Congressional Gold Medal." https://www.house.gov/feature-stories/2015-2-6-1st-special-service-force-honored.

Vietnam Helicopter Pilots Association. "Kleiv Manford Lloyd." https://www.vhpa.org/KIA/incident/64100909KIA.HTM.

Vietnam Tributes. "George F. Fryett, Jr." http://www.veterantributes.org/TributeDetail.php?recordID=109.

Vietnam Women's Memorial. https://www.nps.gov/thingstodo/vietnam-womens-memorial.htm.

Wall, Mike. "UFOs Are Real, but Don't Assume They're Alien Spaceships." Space.com. https://www.space.com/ufos-real-but-not-alien-spaceships.html.

Western Mining History Butte. "Butte's Richest Hill on Earth." https://westernmininghistory.com/towns/montana/butte.

The White House. "Ronald Reagan." https://www.whitehouse.gov/about-the-white-house/presidents/ronald-reagan.

Wikipedia. "Alaska Highway." https://en.wikipedia.org/wiki/Alaska_Highway.

———. "Jerry Daniels." https://en.wikipedia.org/wiki/Jerry_Daniels.

———. "Mariana UFO Incident." https://en.wikipedia.org/wiki/Mariana_UFO_incident.

———. "Operation Eagle Claw." https://en.wikipedia.org/wiki/Operation_Eagle_Claw.

———. "Operation Homecoming." https://en.wikipedia.org/wiki/Operation_Homecoming.

———. "Robert MacArthur Crawford." https://en.wikipedia.org/wiki/Robert_MacArthur_Crawford.

———. "Safeguard Program." https://en.wikipedia.org/wiki/Safeguard_Program.

———. "Sentinel Program." https://en.wikipedia.org/wiki/Sentinel_program.

William, James W. *A History of Army Aviation: From Its Beginnings to the War on Terror*. New York: IUniverse Inc., 2005.

Young, Gregory D. "Mutiny on *Storozhevoy*—A Case Study of Dissent in the Soviet Navy." All World Wars. https://allworldwars.com/Mutiny-on-Storozhevoy.html.

INDEX

A

Able Archer 83 9, 190, 191
"Ace in the Hole" 9, 112, 115, 118,
    122, 124
Acheson, Dean 80, 117
Acton, Loren 139
African Americans 31, 56, 61, 129,
    131, 149, 155, 158, 162, 163, 164,
    165, 166
aircraft (U.S.)
  A-20 17, 21, 22
  A-26 42, 44, 75
  B-17 16, 23, 24, 28, 97
  B-24 53, 97
  B-25 17, 19
  B-29 83, 84
  B-36 93, 94
  B-52 90, 153, 161
  C-9A 156
  C-47 17, 22, 28, 49, 77, 83, 150
  C-54 48, 49, 50, 51
  C-130 181, 182, 183
  C-141 156, 157, 158, 160
  F-4 148, 158, 167
  F-16 78, 79

  F-47 27
  F-51D 75, 76
  F-84 93, 162, 163
  F-86A 76
  F-89 76, 77
  F-94 95, 96
  F-100 163
  F-101B 90
  F-102 77, 116
  F-105 163, 164
  F-106 77, 78, 179
  Fw-190 98
  KB-29 89
  OV-10 160
  P-39 17, 22
  P-47 97
  P-51 27, 75, 76
  P-63 17, 27
  P-80 41
  RF-84K 93, 94
  T-6 19, 22
  T-33 76, 99
  U-2 94, 108, 113, 116
Alaska 8, 16, 17, 18, 19, 22, 30, 31, 41,
    57, 88, 92, 116, 155

Alaska Highway 30, 31
Alaska-Siberia Route (ALSIB) 17, 18,
    19, 26
Anaconda Copper Mining Company
    40, 91, 138
Anaconda, MT 67, 90, 91
Anders, William 135, 136
Andrus, Burton C., Jr. 114
Antiballistic Missile Systems (ABM)
    Safeguard Program 173, 174, 175
    Sentinel Program 173
    Soviet ABM Program 173, 176
Antiballistic Missile Treaty 175, 176
Arkhipov, Vasily 117
Arlington National Cemetery 167
Arnold, H.H. (Hap) 15
Aronson, J. Hugo 72, 74, 101
atomic bomb 20, 33, 86, 87
atomic research 22
Ayres, Harold 61, 62

B

Babcock, Tim 113
Baltic Sea 53, 54, 55, 176, 178
Baltic States 35
Bartol, J. Wante 93
Bary, Art 82
Beartooth Mountains, MT 139
Belenko, Viktor 10, 179, 180, 194
Berlin
    Berlin Airlift 9, 48, 49, 51, 52, 53
    Berlin Blockade 47, 48, 49, 51, 86,
        113
    East, Soviet Sector 48, 49, 192
    Templehof Airport 50, 52
    Wall 10, 76, 113, 123, 192, 193, 194
    West, Allied Sectors 48, 49
Billings, MT
    Billings Airport 114
    Billings High School 124, 139, 153, 158
    Filter Center 92
    Rocky Mountain College Vietnam
        War protests 153

Black Eagle, MT 91, 138
Blackfeet Reservation 76, 89
Blair, Gary 79
Boehner, John 30
Boeing Airplane Company 16, 23,
    111, 140
Borman, Frank 135, 136, 137, 138
Bozeman, MT 38, 41, 72, 74, 140,
    141, 153
Brezhnev Doctrine 189
Brezhnev, Leonid 176, 177
Briggeman, Kim 12, 172
Briscoe, Ben 153
Brockes, John T. 65, 68, 69
Bullock, Steve 147
Burrows, Emma Jane Windham 28
Butcher, Lloyd 132
Butte, MT 65, 66, 67, 72, 81, 88, 91,
    109
    fallout shelters 114
    Korean War Memorial 10, 69
Bywater, Murray 163

C

California 50, 76, 83, 139, 156, 170,
    187
    Edwards Air Force Base 139
    George Air Force Base 74, 76
    Hamilton Field 88
    Travis Air Force Base 85, 160
Cambodia 143, 144, 145
Carter, Jimmy 180, 182, 183, 184, 187
Cernan, Eugene 138, 139
Cherry, Fred 158, 162, 163, 164, 165,
    166, 167
Cherry, Shirley Ann Brown 163, 166
China, People's Republic of 27, 40, 53,
    55, 58, 60, 64, 65, 80, 83, 85, 86,
    144, 156
China, Republic of 27, 40, 58
Chinese Americans 27
Civil Defense Act of 1950 87
civil rights 31, 129, 135

Act of 1964 129, 130, 131
Executive Order 9981 56, 57
Clark Air Base, Philippines 156, 157, 158, 166
Clark, Carl 95, 96
Clark, Mark 46, 47
Clowes, Arthur W. 81, 82
Colvin, Milton 102, 103
Communist Party, U.S.A. 79, 80, 81, 82
Communists 38, 40, 68, 79, 80, 81, 86, 103, 170
Congressional Gold Medal 30
Conrad, MT 174, 175, 176
containment policy 45
Crawford, Robert M. 26, 27
Crowe, William J., Jr. 168
Cuban Missile Crisis 9, 112, 113, 114, 115, 116, 117, 118, 123, 124, 189
Cunningham, Randy 148
Curtis, Gary 153
Cut Bank, MT 53, 80, 91
Air Force Base 16, 24
Czechoslovakia 37, 39, 61
Prague Spring 135, 189

D

Danens, Joseph H. 53
Daniels, Jerrold B. "Jerry" 170, 171, 172
Daniels, Louise 170
Dean, William F. 60, 61, 62
De Arce, Leroy Ponton 16
Devil's Brigade. *See* Special Service Force 28, 29, 30
Dick, Ronald 78, 79
displaced person (DP) 38, 39, 105
domino theory 142, 143
Donnelly, Benjamin 20, 94
Dostal, Elmer 39
Drake, Phil 147
Driscoll, Willie 148
Dulles, John Foster 106

E

Eastern Europe 7, 8, 35, 37, 40, 102, 103, 105, 192, 193, 194
Ecton, Zales N. 38, 72, 79, 80
Eisenhower, Dwight D. 63, 72, 89, 101, 102, 105, 106, 108, 144, 189
Ekern, Halvor Olaf 46, 47
Erickson, Leif 38
Evans, Diane Carlson 168, 169

F

Fairbanks, Alaska 30
Ladd Army Airfield 8, 16, 17, 19
Federal Bureau of Investigation (FBI) 81
Finland 35
First Special Service Force (FSSF) 28, 29
Fort Benton, MT 39, 63, 64, 91, 141
Fort Peck Dam, MT 90, 91
Fryett, George, Jr. 147, 150

G

Gaddis, John Lewis 184, 193, 194
Gaither, Ralph 158, 159
Gannon, Jack 114
Geddes, Paul 95
Georgia
Moody Air Force Base 74, 76
German aircraft
Focke-Wulf Fw-190 98
Messerschmitt Bf-109 98
Germany 8, 9, 37, 38, 40, 45, 46, 63, 102
East, Soviet Sector, German Democratic Republic 48, 190, 192, 193
Stalag Luft 1 97
West, Allied Sectors, Federal Republic of Germany 47, 48, 49, 50, 53, 193
Glasgow, MT 74, 91, 140, 158, 160, 161

Air Force Base 9, 24, 90, 129, 154
Army Air Base 16, 24
Goldhahn, Elizabeth 89
Goldhahn, Harold 89
Goldsworthy, Harry 109
Goldwater, Barry 124
Goodacre, Glenna 169
Gorbachev, Mikhail 10, 191, 192, 193, 194
Gordievsky, Oleg 190
Gotner, Norbert A. 167
Grand Forks, ND 173, 176
Gray, Randy 195, 196
Great Falls, MT 8, 9, 15, 20, 30, 41, 43, 44, 45, 56, 65, 68, 69, 77, 89, 90, 94, 95, 112, 118, 123, 124, 128, 131, 138, 166, 175
Air Force Base. *See* Malmstrom Air Force Base
air raid sirens 195
Army Air Base. *See* Malmstrom 8, 11, 12, 15, 16, 19, 22, 23, 24, 25, 27, 28, 41, 48, 50, 51, 53, 57, 75
Chamber of Commerce 15, 75, 99
Civic Center 16
Gore Field 8, 15, 16, 21, 22, 26, 51, 75, 76, 77, 99, 179
Green Mills Dance Hall 22
Legion Baseball Park 94, 96
Lewis and Clark Portage 11, 22
Malmstrom Air Force Base 9, 10, 57, 67, 83, 87, 91, 93, 94, 96, 99, 100, 101, 106, 111, 123, 124, 129, 150, 151, 158, 162, 166, 167, 195
North Montana State Fairgrounds 16, 41, 43
Public Library 98, 99, 129
Greece
civil war 45
Greiner, Paul E. 87, 88
Ground Observer Corps (GOC) 9, 86, 87, 88, 89, 91, 92, 93, 95

Guenther, Lynn E. 158, 160, 162
antiwar statements 160, 161
friendship with guards 160, 161

H

haboob (dust storm) 180, 181, 182, 183
Hallsell, Troy A. 12, 113, 114
Halyburton, Porter A. 158, 165, 166, 167
Havre 74, 91
Northern Montana College 153
Helena, MT 74, 75, 76, 147, 153, 169
Carroll College Vietnam War protests 153
Filter Center 89, 95
Fort William Henry Harrison 10, 29, 74
Hellman, John Cyril 81, 82
Hirsch, James S. 167
Hiss, Alger 22, 79, 80
History Museum, The (Great Falls) 12
Hmong tribesmen 143, 144, 170, 171, 172
airlift evacuation 171
anti-Communism 143, 144, 170
Bitterroot Valley Ranch 143, 171
Hog Daniels's funeral 172
Hopkins, Harry 20
Hubich, Winfried 193
Huigen, Doug 118
Hungary 40
Hungarian Revolution 10, 102, 103, 104, 105
refugees 38, 102
Soviet invasion, 1956 102, 105
hydrogen bomb test 87, 91, 101, 122

I

Inbody, Kristen 12, 140
International Atomic Energy Agency 47
International Space Station 141

Interstate Highway System 101
Iran
   American hostages 180, 182, 184
   Iranian Islamic Revolution 180
   U.S. embassy seizure 180
Iron Curtain 7, 10, 36, 37, 38, 40, 126,
   192, 193

J

Jacobs, Alma 98, 99, 129, 131
Jacobson, Lyle 65, 66, 67
Japan 7, 8, 27, 31, 60, 61, 62, 68, 179,
   180
   Itazuke Air Base 163
   navy 30
   World War II surrender 31, 58
   Yokota Air Base 83, 163
Johnson, Lyndon B. 131, 132, 143
Johnstone, Bill 39
Johnston Island 122
Jones, Junious W. 45
Jones, Nate 191
Jones, Tate 10
Jordan, George Racey 8, 20, 21, 22

K

Kalispell, MT 75, 91, 95, 96
Karpat, Kemal 106
Kennan, George F. 45
Kennedy, John F. 9, 108, 112, 113,
   114, 117, 123, 128, 142, 144
   assassination 112, 128
   visit to Billings 123, 124
   visit to Great Falls 9, 112, 124, 125,
      126, 127
Kennedy, Robert F. 135
Khomeini, Ayatollah 180, 183
Khrushchev, Nikita 103, 108, 112,
   113, 117
Kiba, Steve 84, 85, 86
Kissinger, Henry 133, 156
Kleiv, Manford Lloyd 151
Klemme, H.G. 38, 39

Knutson, Persis Bowman 159, 160
Knutson, Rodney 158, 159, 160
Koch, Christina 141
Korea, Democratic Republic of (North
   Korea) 53, 58
Korean War 65, 67, 69, 71, 72, 76,
   101, 105
   38th Parallel 58, 64, 65, 68
   Battle of Pyongtaek 61
   Chinese Communists People's
      Volunteer Army (PVA) 64, 65,
      66, 83
   EC-121 crisis 132, 133, 134
   Invasion 58, 59, 60, 68, 76, 79, 83
   North Korean People's Army (NKPA)
      58, 66, 67, 69
   Pueblo crisis 134, 135
   Pusan Perimeter 59, 60, 62, 63, 64
   Yalu River 65, 66, 83, 84
Korean War Veterans Memorial
   Advisory Board 166
Korea, Republic of (SouthKorea) 58,
   60, 61, 147, 163
Kotikov, Anatoli M. 20, 21
Kuter, Laurence S. 50, 57, 58

L

Laos 9, 124, 127, 133, 143, 144, 145,
   150, 160, 167, 170, 171
   Long Chen, Plain de Jars 170
   Pathet Lao 150
   Royal Laotian government 144
   "Sky Compound" 170, 172
Latvia 53, 54, 55
League of Families of POW/MIAs 160
Lee, Hazel Ying 27, 28
LeMay, Curtis 50
Lend-Lease Program 8, 12, 17, 18, 19,
   20, 21, 22, 25, 27, 28, 53, 79
Liedmann, Gwendolyn 77
Llewellyn, Elmer F. 83, 84, 85, 86
Lockheed Missiles and Space Company
   139

Lovell, James 135
Lovless, Jay B. 60, 61, 62
Lutsky, Alan L. 119, 121

M

MacArthur, Douglas 60, 63, 64, 66, 71, 142
Malmstrom, Einar A. 97, 99, 100
Manhattan Project 22, 31, 32, 33
Mansfield, Michael 9, 72, 79, 80, 123, 124, 125, 126, 128, 130, 131, 155, 175
Mansfield, Patrick 125
Mariana, Nick 94, 95, 96
Marianetti, Gene 138
Marshall, George C. 40, 46
Marshall Plan 45
Marton, Endre 103
Maultsby, Charles 116
Mayer, Roderick L. 158
McCarthy, Joseph R. 79, 80
McCormack, John 155
McNamara, Robert 108, 117, 189
Metcalf, Lee 72, 126, 130, 131
Milburn, Frank W. 62, 63, 64, 70, 71, 72
Military Air Transportation Command (MATS) 50, 53, 57
"missile gap" 108
Missoula, MT 31, 32, 41, 61, 62, 63, 71, 72, 75, 79, 83, 84, 85, 86, 89, 102, 106, 140, 152, 153, 154, 170, 171, 172, 193
  Cemetery 171, 172
  High School 83, 170
  Jeannette Rankin Peace Center 156
  Montana State Korean War Memorial 10, 70, 71
Mitchell, S.H. 74, 75
Moler, Murray M. 109
Molotov, Vyacheslav 19

Montana Air National Guard 12, 14, 77
  120th Fighter Group (Air Defense) 76, 77, 78, 79, 137, 179
  186th Fighter Interceptor Squadron 74, 75, 76, 88
Montana Constitution
  Declaration of Rights 131
Montana House Un-American Activities Committee (HUAC) 80, 81
Montana Kaimin (University of Montana) 152
Montana Military Museum 10
Montana National Guard 10
  163rd Armored Cavalry Regiment 74, 75
Montana State University 41, 140, 141
  Space Program 139, 140
  Vietnam War protests 153
Montana State Veterans Memorial 10
Morgan, JoAnn H. 140
Morocco 129
Morrison, Gayle L. 172
Murray, W.D. 81, 82
Mutual Assured Destruction (MAD) 10, 189

N

Nagy, Ferenc 105
National Aeronautics and Space Administration (NASA)
  Apollo 8 135, 136, 137
  Apollo 11 140
  Apollo 17 138
  Exploration Ground Systems Program 141
  Kennedy Space Center 139, 140, 141
  Manned Space Flight Center 138
  Solar Optical Universal Polarimeter (SOUP) 139
  Spacelab 2 139

National POW-MIA Recognition Day 162
Native Americans 129
Neely, Harold L. 92
Nixon, Richard M. 108, 133, 143, 144, 153, 167, 173, 176
Nobel Prize 31, 194
Norby, Fritz 75
North Atlantic Treaty Organization (NATO) 8, 9, 47, 49, 190, 192
nuclear deterrance 110, 118
Nuclear Test Ban Treaty 1963 123, 127
Nutter, Donald 77

O

Oak Ridge, TN 22
Olmstead, Stanley E. 158
Operation Alert 89, 90
Operation Eagle Claw 180, 181, 182, 183
Operation Homecoming 143, 144, 149, 156, 157, 158, 166
Operation Revise 102
Operation Skywatch 86, 87, 89, 90, 92, 95
Operation Vittles. *See* Berlin Airlift 48
Oregon 24, 27, 75, 86
  Aviation Hall of Honor 28
Overcash, Victor O. 80

P

Pantzer, Robert 154
Parrella, Carmine D., Jr. 119, 121
Pattison, Dick 128
Perroots, Leonard 190
Petrov, Stanislav 189
Poland 35, 184, 190
Poore, Robert A. 81, 82
Pope John Paul II 10, 184, 185, 187, 194
Portland, OR 27, 86
Portrait of a Fighter Pilot 164, 167

Potter, Hugh K. 90
"POW Alcove of Honor" (The Pentagon) 164, 167
Power, Thomas S. 114
Preston, Joseph J. 111
prisoners of war (POWs) 143, 157, 158, 167
  "Hanoi Hilton" Camp (Hoa Lo) 159, 165
  "the Zoo" Camp (Cu Loc) 165
  torture 159, 160, 161, 165, 166
Project Grudge 95
Pyke, Geoffrey 29

Q

Quinn, Matthew 147

R

Rankin, Jeannette 154
  Rankin Brigade 154, 155, 156
Rankin, Walter R. 74
Rankin, Wellington D. 72
Raunig, Virginia 94
Reagan, Ronald 10, 78, 166, 184, 185, 186, 187, 188, 189, 190, 191, 192, 193, 194
  "Evil Empire" speech 188, 189
  "Tear down that wall" speech 192, 193
  visit to Charles M. Russell High School, Great Falls 78
  visit to Metrapark, Billings 187, 188
Reichert, Arlyne 129, 131
Reisner, Robinson 157
Return with Honor 167
Rocky Mountain Museum of Military History 10
Romania 35, 40
Roosevelt, Eleanor 38
Roosevelt, Franklin D. 17, 18, 20, 35, 36, 37, 127
Rostropovich, Mstislav 192

S

Sablin, Valery 176, 177
Sampson, Leslie Verne 150, 151
Savitsky, Valentin 116
Scharff, Hans 98
Schmidt, Daniel C. 84, 86
Schmitt, Harrison H. 138
Sharp, Ulysses S. Grant, Jr. 63, 64
Shields, Ed 15
Shoup, Richard 153
Sicherman, Harvey 177
Smith Act 1940 81, 82
smokejumpers 12, 170, 172
Southeast Asia 133, 142, 145, 146,
    150, 163, 168, 170, 172
Sperry, Willard 75
Spokane, WA 16, 95
Stalin, Josef V. 7, 35, 36, 48
  death 47
  miscalculations 49, 58, 86
Stockdale, James Bond 157, 158, 165
Strategic Arms Limitation Treaty
    (SALT) 176
Strategic Arms Reduction Treaty
    (START 1) 191
Strategic Defense Initiative (SDI) 189
Strausz-Hupé, Robert 177
Suez Canal
  invasion, 1956 102, 105
Sun Tzu 13
Sweden 177
  U.S. embassy, Stockholm 177

T

Taipei, Taiwan 133
Thatcher, Margaret "Maggie" 10, 185,
    186, 187, 192, 194
Truman Doctrine 45
Truman, Harry S 36, 38, 49, 56, 58,
    73, 87, 125
Tunner, William H. 16, 50
Turkey 45, 65, 105, 106, 113, 117
Tuskegee Airmen Inc. 166

*Two Souls Indivisible: The Friendship that
    Saved Two POWs in Vietnam* 167

U

Unidentified Flying Object (UFO) 94,
    95, 96
Union of Soviet Socialist Republics
    (Soviet Union) 35
  Baltic Naval Fleet 53, 54, 55, 176,
      177, 178
  Communist Party 35, 79, 80, 81, 82,
      191, 194
  Eastern Front 17, 19, 21, 26, 27
  espionage 8, 20, 53, 79
  Foxtrot submarine B-59 116, 117
  glasnost ("openness") 191, 194
  Gulag 54, 55
  IL-28 117
  La-11 55
  MiG-21 132
  MiG-25 179
  perestroika ("restructuring") 191, 194
  red star 19, 21, 22, 26
  Sputnik 92, 108
  Storozhevoy 10, 176, 177, 178
United Nations (UN) 38, 58, 105
  Model United Nations 105, 106, 107
United States 9th Court of Appeals 82
United States Air Force/Army Air
    Corps
  7th Air Force 133, 146, 148
  7th (Seventh) Ferrying Group 16, 17,
      26, 50, 75
  8th Tactical Fighter Wing 167
  15th Air Force 99, 101
  22nd Air Division 111
  34th Subdepot 16, 24, 25
  35th Tactical Fighter Squadron 163
  91st Strategic Reconnaissance
      Squadron 83, 93, 94
  301st Air Refueling Wing 162
  310th Fighter-Bomber Squadron 162
  314th Air Division 83, 150

341st Strategic Missile Wing 12, 109,
    113, 117, 118, 121, 124
407th Strategic Fighter Wing 93, 98,
    99, 163
515th Strategic Fighter Squadron 163
517th Air Transport Wing 48
557th Army Air Forces Base Unit,
    Gore Field 75
564th Strategic Missile Squadron 109,
    167
581st Air Resupply and
    Communications Wing 83
4773rd Ground Observer Squadron
    89
7499th Air Command 50
Aircraft Control & Warning (AC&W)
    91
Air Service Command (ASC) 24, 25
air show crash 27, 41, 42, 43, 44
Air Transport Command (ATC) 16,
    25, 27, 50
"Army Air Corps March" 26
Distant Early Warning (DEW) 92
Fighter-Conveyance (FICON) 93, 94
Genie AIR2A Nuclear Missile 76, 77
Hughes Trophy 78
Jupiter Missile (MRBM) 113, 117
Minuteman Missile 9, 12, 108, 109,
    110, 111, 112, 114, 115, 117,
    118, 119, 120, 121, 123, 125,
    126, 173
Semi-Automatic Ground
    Environment (SAGE) 91, 92
Strategic Air Command (SAC) 76,
    92, 101, 111, 114
Women Airforce Service Pilot (WASP)
    19, 27, 28
United States Army
    7th Aviation Platoon 151
    7th Cavalry Regiment 65, 66, 67
    24th Infantry Division 60, 61
    25th Infantry Division 61
    29th Air Division 76, 87, 88, 89, 92
    34th Infantry Regiment 60, 61

69th Tank Battalion 65, 68
163rd Infantry Regiment 74, 75
Air Defense Command 93, 174, 175
Corps of Engineers 30, 31, 111,
    174
I Corps 64, 71
Perimeter Acquisition Radar (PAR)
    175, 176
Rankin's Raiders 74
Task Force Smith 60, 61
UH-1B 151
X Corps 64
United States Navy
    C-2 133, 157
    Commander Task Force (CTF)-
        70/71/77 133, 146, 148, 181,
        182, 183
    Cuban Crisis Naval Quarantine 113,
        116, 117
    EC-121 132, 133, 134
    Fleet Intelligence Center Europe
        (FICEUR) 129, 148
    Fleet Operations Control Center
        (FOCCPAC) 118
    Integrated Operational Intelligence
        Center (IOIC) 146, 148, 149,
        157
    Naval Reconnaissance and Technical
        Support Center (NRTSC) 146
    Naval Security Group 133
    Patrol Squadron 26 (VP-26) 55
    PB4Y-2 53, 54, 55
    RA-5C 146, 148
    racial incident 148
    RH-53 181, 182, 183, 184
    United States Pacific Command 118
    USS *Beale* 116
    USS *Constellation* 148, 149, 157
    USS *Kitty Hawk* 133, 148
    USS *Nimitz* 181, 182, 183, 184
    USS *Pueblo* 131, 132, 134, 135
    USS *Ranger* 133, 146
    VF-84 158
    VQ-1 132, 134, 148

United States Supreme Court 37, 81, 82
University of Montana
  Reserve Officer Training Corps (ROTC) 61, 154
  strike, 1970 154
  Vietnam War protests 142, 144, 148, 152, 154, 155, 173
Urey, Harold C. 31, 32

V

Vanasek, Miloslav 39
Vang Pao 170, 171, 172
Vienna, Austria 37, 46, 112, 113
Vienna Summit, 1961 112
Vietnam, Democratic Republic of (North Vietnam) 142, 144, 146, 148, 156, 157, 158, 160, 164, 165
Vietnam, Republic of (South Vietnam) 143, 144, 145, 146, 148, 150, 151, 156, 164
Vietnam War
  antiwar protests 148
  Easter Invasion 144, 148
  Gulf of Tonkin Incident 1964 142, 144, 157, 158
  Ho Chi Minh Trail 146
  Pleiku 71st Evacuation Hospital 160, 168
  Rolling Thunder 146, 164
  Tet Offensive 142, 143
  Viet Cong 135, 142, 147, 150, 151, 156, 164, 168
  Vung Tao 36th Evacuation Hospital 168
Vietnam Women's Memorial 168
Von Lossberg, Bryan 141
Vyshinsky, Andrei 38

W

Wallace, Henry A. 19
Warsaw Pact 8, 40, 135, 190
Weber, Philip J. 140

Weidman, R.H. 80
Welcome Home Vietnam Veterans Day Montana 147
Welling, Alvin C. 111
Werner, David 105, 107
Western Europe 8, 49
Wheat, David 158
Wheeler, Burton 37
Wigger, Lones W. 141
Williams, James 151
Willkie, Wendell 19
Wojtyla, Karol. *See* Pope John Paul II 184
World War II 7, 8, 10, 12, 16, 27, 28, 31, 37, 41, 42, 46, 50, 53, 56, 60, 64, 68, 72, 74, 75, 87, 97, 99, 102, 118, 119, 151, 154, 191

Z

Zimmerman, Charles 81

ABOUT THE AUTHOR

Ken Robison is a chronicler of neglected western history who lives in Montana. He is a retired U.S. Navy captain after a career in Naval Intelligence spanning the heart of the Cold War from 1960 to 1988. Ken is a Montana native and historian at the Overholser Historical Research Center in Fort Benton, Sun River Valley Historical Society, Great Falls/Cascade County Historic Preservation Commission and Big Sky Country National Heritage Area. The Montana Historical Society has honored Ken as a "Montana Heritage Keeper," and he is on the board of trustees of the society. His books include *Historic Tales of Whoop-Up Country: On the Trail from Montana's Fort Benton to Canada's Fort Macleod*; *Montanans in the Great War: Open Warfare Over There*; *World War I Montana: The Treasure State Prepares*; *Montana Territory and the Civil War: A Frontier Forged on the Battlefield*; *Confederates in Montana Territory: In the Shadow of Price's Army*; and *Yankees and Rebels on the Upper Missouri: Steamboats, Gold and Peace*. He is coauthor of *Black Americans in the Civil Rights Movement in the West*; *Montana, a Cultural Medley: Stories of Our Ethnic Diversity*; *Beyond Schoolmarms and Madams: Montana Women's Stories*; and *The Mullan Road: Carving a Passage through the Frontier Northwest, 1859 to 1862*. Ken edited *Life and Death on the Upper Missouri: The Frontier Sketches of Johnny Healy*. Visit Ken Robison History at https://www.kenrobisonhistory.com.

Lieutenant Commander Ken Robison working in his office at USS *Constellation*'s Integrated Operational Intelligence Center in May 1972. *U.S. Navy.*

Visit us at
www.historypress.com